Sex & marriage in England today

A study of the views and experience of the under-45s

SEX &
MARRIAGE
IN
ENGLAND
TODAY

A study of the views and experience of the under-45s

GEOFFREY
GORER

Nelson

Thomas Nelson and Sons Ltd
36 Park Street London W1Y 4DE
PO Box 18123 Nairobi Kenya

Thomas Nelson (Australia) Ltd
597 Little Collins Street Melbourne 3000

Thomas Nelson and Sons (Canada) Ltd
81 Curlew Drive Don Mills Ontario

Thomas Nelson (Nigeria) Ltd
PO Box 336 Apapa Lagos

Thomas Nelson and Sons (South Africa) (Proprietary) Ltd
51 Commissioner Street Johannesburg

© Geoffrey Gorer and *Times* Newspapers Ltd 1971
First published 1971

ISBN 0 17 138013 4

Printed in Great Britain by
Cox & Wyman Ltd, London, Fakenham and Reading

Foreword

At the end of each chapter (except Chapters Seven and Ten) there are Figures of Distribution, in which the percentages which seem to me significant and which justify the generalizations in the text are extracted from the Tables (given in full in Appendix Three); also several cross-correlations, which are not published in their entirety, are summarized. The difference in type-face should make these summaries easy to find for readers particularly interested in the calculations.

In lieu of an index I am supplying, in the table of contents, a detailed summary of the topics discussed, by chapter and section.

Some of the material in this book appeared, in a different form, in articles in *The Sunday Times* on March 15th, 22nd, 29th, 1970.

All the technical aspects of the survey on which this book is based were handled by Opinion Research Centre. I am deeply grateful to Mr John Hanvey and Mr Humphrey Taylor for their continuous helpfulness.

G.G.

December 1970

Contents

a third tolerant or pitying. Tolerance decreases and hostility increases as one goes down the socio-economic scale. ii. The attitudes of some unmarried men; the small group who acknowledged that they had felt some sort of attraction for a member of their own sex. iii. Correlations between attitudes to homosexuality and to extra-marital heterosexuality and to female orgasm. Suggestion that the attitudes towards sexuality outside marriage are fairly consistent, whatever the sex of the imagined partner. iv. The gamut of attitudes towards sex from the very censorious to the licentious; calculations as to the approximate sizes of the censorious, licentious and unheated groups in the younger English population.

Part two

List of tables in the text

Introduction:
The Research and
the Sample

i

One of the most interesting recent developments in social anthropology has been the re-studying of known societies after a lapse of years to discover what alterations the changes in technology, political organization or raised expectations had produced.* I could not, as I would have wished, do a re-study in the field, partly because of my failing health, and partly because Sikkim had been declared a prohibited area by the Indian government after the frontier clashes with China, so that a return visit to the Lepchas† was not feasible.

The advantages of re-studying a known society were much in my mind in 1968. By having a base from which change could be measured, one can state with far more certainty the direction in which a society is moving than is possible when the only information about the past is based on memory or tradition, either one's own or that of one's informants. The rate and extent of change are frequently misinterpreted by those involved. On the one hand, technological innovations, with their concomitant alterations of social habits, are accepted almost unconsciously, so that it needs an intellectual effort to recollect what our life was like before we had radio, or television, or air-travel, for example (all inventions made in my lifetime); on the other hand, there has been an increasing tendency in this century, and not only in the technologically advanced societies, to state the differences between generations in the

* Margaret Mead's *Growing Up in New Guinea* (1930) and *New Lives for Old* (1956), two studies of the same group of Manus in the Admiralty Islands, were the pioneering works in this field. Since then, there have been several other re-studies.
† *Himalayan Village* (1939) is my original study of these people.

most extreme terms, so that, for the elderly and middle-aged, the young are betraying all the traditions and flouting all the decencies in which they were raised, and, for the young, the middle-aged and old are responsible for all the injustices and inequalities of which they are conscious and the shackling rules which prevent them developing their potentialities.

In England the press, and other media of mass communication, chiefly directed at middle-aged audiences, insisted that there was a major change in the sexual morals of the young; the 'permissive society', 'swinging London' and all the other clichés implied that the young were far more licentious than their elders had ever been and had an ever-diminishing regard for the importance of marriage as an institution. Such casual observations as I had been able to make made me doubt the validity of these observations; I thought the censorious commentators were confusing changes in word-style with changes in life-style; but I knew that my casual observations had no more validity than the generalizations of the Press.

This, it seemed to me, was a situation where a re-study could establish some of the facts about the rate of change and its direction in one institution and topic in our contemporary society. In 1950 I had collected and analysed the views of a very large sample of volunteers on love and sex, on their hopes, fears, and experience of marriage;* if the same questions were to be asked of a sample of young people in 1969, this would surely give an indication as to the changes in attitudes and values over the last twenty years.

From the scientific point of view, the chief drawback of *Exploring English Character* was that it was majorly founded on the replies of volunteers. Although the number was large, there was no guarantee that the sample was representative. True, a number of the same questions had been asked simultaneously of a stratified sample, and the percentages were close enough to give confidence in the representative value of the volunteer sample; but the only questions asked in this checking survey were those with answers which could be ticked, either Yes or

---

* *Exploring English Character* (Cresset Press and Criterion Books, 1955): Chapter VII 'Love', Chapter VIII 'Ideas About Sex', Chapter IX 'Marriage I: Hopes and Fears', Chapter X: 'Marriage II: Experience'; pp. 83–177.

No, or with a limited range of alternatives; and I had found that I got much the most information from 'open-ended' questions, from questions which did not suggest any answers to the respondent. The question from which I had got the most revealing information in 1950 was: 'If you were told that a small child, say between 3 and 8, had done something really bad, what would you think the child had done?'

In the projected re-study, I wanted to combine the relevant open-ended questions with a scientifically valid sample. This was the proposition originally put to Mr Harold Evans, the editor of *The Sunday Times* (I needed a sponsor to pay for the research: I could not afford to pay for it out of my own pocket), by my friend and agent, the late Jean LeRoy. He was sufficiently interested to arrange for me to meet the directors of Opinion Research Centre, Mr T. F. Thompson and Mr H. J. F. Taylor with one of his assistant editors, Mr Ron Hall.

It was at this meeting that the suggestion was first made that, besides repeating the 1950 questions on attitudes towards sex and marriage, we should also ask questions on individual sexual behaviour. This presented a major challenge to the directors of Opinion Research Centre. All previous surveys of sexual behaviour with which I am acquainted had depended on volunteers (as with Kinsey), or on small groups selected from students at a single university or clients of a hospital, birth-control clinic or marriage guidance service. Despite some ingenious statistical manipulation of the raw data, such information had never been collected from the sort of sample which is used to survey all less 'sensitive' attitudes or behaviour; it was widely believed to be impossible.

I agreed that it might be feasible in 1969. Although I doubted whether people's sexual behaviour had changed as much as was frequently alleged, there was no doubt that there had been a major change in the topics which could be discussed openly and seriously, and the language which could be used. I think the turning-point was the acquittal of the paperback edition of *Lady Chatterley's Lover* of obscenity in 1960. By this decision, the old, powerful taboo'd words had been robbed of nearly all their magic, and the objects and actions to which they referred were free for serious discussion. I think the seriousness should be emphasized. The dirty joke and the *double entendre* do not seem to have lost any of their attraction, their ability to titillate and evoke snigger, giggle and guffaw; but exactly the same topics can now be mentioned seriously without undue embarrassment. If the interviewers could ask the questions, I believed the informants would answer them.

The questionnaire was gradually developed over several months' consultation between members of Opinion Research Centre and myself and several different types of pilot survey* were tried out to discover what method would be most likely to get a high proportion of answers to 'sensitive' questions and which forms of words were most easily understood. *The Sunday Times* agreed to undertake the very considerable expense of having the questionnaire administered to an adequate sample and analysed; and the interviews were made in April and May 1969.

ii

Since the validity of this study depends to a great extent on the validity of the sample, this must be discussed in some detail.† Nine hundred and forty-nine men and 1,037 women were interviewed. They were selected from the electoral registers in a hundred parliamentary constituencies (out of 511) in England, stratified by the Registrar General's standard regions, conurbation and size of town, and political complexion. Alternate constituencies were arbitrarily designated as 'male' and 'female'; in the 'male' constituencies men interviewed male informants if they were of the appropriate age; in the 'female' constituencies women interviewed women. In each constituency a random number was generated; every fifth elector thereafter was underlined, until eighty had been designated of the appropriate sex.

Of these 8,000 electors, 65% proved to be ineligible, mostly because they were over 45, but in a few cases because they had moved, or could not be traced, or had died. Two thousand seven hundred and ninety-one interviews were attempted and 1,831 completed, a success rate of 65·6%. One hundred and

* See Appendix One, by Humphrey Taylor.
† Further technical details can be found in Appendix One.

fifty-six young people between the ages of 16 and 21 who were not on the electoral register were also interviewed. Four hundred and sixty-five people were not interviewed because they were out after four calls or, in a few instances, were away on holiday, in hospital or otherwise unavailable; 495 (17·8%) refused to be interviewed. For a random sample these percentages appear satisfactory.

The skilled interviewers from Opinion Research Centre had no freedom of choice as to whom they would interview; their instructions were exactly the same as those in any other survey based on a stratified random sample; and, as far as people aged 21 or over are concerned, this survey would seem to have the same sort of validity as other polls conducted on the same sampling basis.*

In 1969 people under the age of 21 were not on the parliamentary registers. To discover informants between the ages of 16 and 21, interviewers were instructed to ask if there were young men or women (as the case might be) in the households where they were interviewing a parent. In the event of there being more than one of the appropriate age and sex, the interviewers had to attempt to interview the person the initial of whose Christian name was nearest to their own. Even in this situation, the interviewers' preferences were controlled.

Since only young people who were living in their parents' homes were interviewed, they and the unmarried (who are to a large extent the same group) are rather seriously under-represented, in proportion to the figures of the census.† This discrepancy can be rectified in the tables by the appropriate statistical 'weighting' and inspection of the tables will show that this has been done frequently; the difference made by the 'weighting' is usually less than 2%. To minimize the effect of this flaw in the sample as much as may be, the views and

---

* Surveys based on the employment of volunteers run the risk of attracting an undue proportion of exhibitionists; when information is paid for, there is a risk that the informants will say what they think the interviewer wants to hear. Informants traced through a hospital or any counselling service have a tendency to be untypical inasmuch as they hve been led to seek assistance through their disturbed condition.

† There should have been 352 informants aged between 16 and 20; there were in fact only 150. The unmarried should have represented 30% of the sample; they in fact only represented 19%.

experiences of the unmarried are considered exclusively in Part
Two, Chapter Ten; the nine chapters of Part One quote exclusively from the 81 % who were or had been married (though
the unmarried are, inevitably, included in most of the totals).
Sixteen of our informants had been divorced, thirteen had been
widowed, and twenty-four were separated from their spouse.
In absolute figures, interviews were administered to:

age 16–20: 150 people ($7\frac{1}{2}$%)
age 21–24: 321 people ($16\frac{1}{2}$%)
age 25–34: 691 people (35%)
age 35–45: 809 people (41%)

iii

All informants were asked their occupation or, if appropriate,
that of the 'head of the household'; and these were then
grouped according to the categories established by the Registrar
General. The Registrar General has grouped all occupations in a
five-fold list: (I) professional and managerial; (II) inter-
mediate; (III) skilled; (IV) semi-skilled; (V) unskilled. Since
modern technology has produced an absolute majority of
skilled workers, the third category is frequently divided into
'skilled manual' and 'skilled non-manual'. To avoid ambiguity
in writing, the roman numbers are frequently replaced by the
first five letters of the alphabet; and this practice is followed
here, as is the grouping together of the first two classes (AB)
and the bottom two (DE). Skilled non-manual is designated C1
and skilled manual C2.

By these categories our sample were 12% AB, professional
and managerial; 23% C1, skilled non-manual; 44% C2 skilled
manual; 21% DE semi-skilled and unskilled manual. In the
three lower categories men and women are in approximately
equal numbers; but the AB category contains 61% women and
39% men. This disparity between the sexes in the AB category
is relevant where tables are analysed according to the Registrar
General's categories.

There is a similar disparity between the sexes in the claim
to middle-class status in our informants' answers to the question:
'If you were asked to say what social class you were, how would
you describe yourself?' Informants were asked to choose

between: upper class; upper middle class; middle class; lower middle class; skilled working class; upper working class; working class. Twenty-six per cent of the men and 40% of the women (34% of the total) stated that they were middle class. This would suggest that, both subjectively and objectively, women's occupations tend to be graded higher in the social scale than do men's; it is also possible that in meetings with strangers (and the interviewers were, of course, strangers to all the informants) women have a tendency to claim high social status.

Self-classification by social class is clearly congenial to the vast majority of the younger English population. Only 132 individuals (less than 7% of the total) refused to do so; 6% of the men and 4% of the women – and these include informants not born in England – said they could not answer the question, and a further 3% of the men and 1% of the women stated at some length that such classifications were inappropriate today, that they belonged to a repudiated past and so on; they made miniature political speeches rejecting the notion of social hierarchy. The rest of the information in their interviews suggested that it would not be difficult to assign these informants to an appropriate social class; but the rejection of a social class label, like the rejection of a sectarian label,* would seem to be significant indicators of the informants' attitudes to various aspects of sex and marriage; we have therefore included this uncertain or 'rebellious' group under the rubric 'blank' in the analytical tables.

It did not seem worth while including in these tables the eight individuals who called themselves upper class (often with little apparent justification; one had the impression they were teasing the interviewers) or the sixty-seven who called themselves upper middle class. Most of these latter would appear to be objectively justified in their claims through their professions or managerial occupations†; but the number is so small that the figures of distribution appeared to be of little significance. Their attitudes did not appear to differ in any consistent way from

---

* See below, pp. 10–11.
† When I quote informants I am giving their age, their occupation, and, where relevant, their religion; but I am not giving any other information, such as where they live, so as to protect their anonymity.

those of our informants who called themselves middle class without a modifier.

Thirty-one per cent of our sample (32 % of the men and 30 % of the women) described themselves as working class, without a modifier. They, and the 34 % who consider themselves middle class, can be considered the 'core' social classes of contemporary English society.

In many ways the 29 % of the population who place themselves between the two 'core' classes are both the most idiosyncratic and the most consistent in their views and practices. Nine per cent, equally divided between the sexes, call themselves 'lower middle class'; this tends to be the most censorious and most conventional group. Twelve per cent (15 % of the men and 8 % of the women) called themselves 'skilled working class' and 5 % (6 % of the men and 4 % of the women) 'upper working class'.

These two claims to superior position within the working class were included after the pilot surveys, which brought the distinction into prominence. The term 'skilled working class' is much more preferred by those aged over 25 (13 %) than by their juniors (8 % or 9 %), and would seem to be based rather narrowly within the work situation, directly dependent on the length of apprenticeship or other qualifications that the job demands. The term 'upper working class', on the other hand, is much more congenial to the young (9 % of those aged under 20) than to their elders (4 % of those aged between 35 and 45), and would seem to be based on the length of education, earning power, or representative or entertainment activities outside the work situation. In many ways, I would believe the category of 'upper working class' to be a new phenomenon. Twenty years ago, youngsters of working-class origin with outstanding intellectual gifts or talents would have been likely to try to acquire a B.B.C. accent and to be accepted as a newcomer to the middle or upper middle class (an analogue to 'passing' in a multi-racial society); today they feel no need to hide their working-class origins. In many ways, it would seem that the upper working class have replaced the upper middle class as trend-setters for many of their contemporaries.

It will have been noted that 21 % of the men and only 12 % of the women differentiate their positions within the working class; this masculine claim for special working-class status counterbalances to a certain extent the feminine claim to middle-class status.

iv

Twenty-eight per cent of the men and 25 % of the women in our sample finished their education at the age of 14; these are predominantly those aged over 35, whose education was completed before the school-leaving age was raised. A further 39 % of the men and 43 % of the women left school at 15. Two-thirds of our total sample left school at the minimum legal age, with high concentrations among those over 35 and those calling themselves working or skilled working class; even among those calling themselves middle class 59 % left school at the age of 15.

Twenty-four per cent of the men and 26 % of the women finished their education between the ages of 16 and 18. This amount of further education is most general in the lower middle and upper working classes and in those aged under 34. Eight per cent of the men and 6 % of the women continued their education beyond the age of 18, or were still studying when they were interviewed; apart from those still at school or university, this highly educated group is most numerous under the age of 24, and tend to describe themselves as middle class or lower middle class; there are, however, 5 % who call themselves upper working class, but only 1 % who call themselves working class without modification. There is much more further education in the North-East and South-East than there is in the North-West and South-West.

v

Two per cent of the men and 4 % of the women refused to answer the question on approximate income or income of the head of the household; 2 % of the men and no fewer than 17 % of the women said they did not know what their fathers or husbands earned.*

Under 7 % of our sample (7 % of the men and 4 % of the women) were earning less than £13 weekly. This is the group

* See Chapter Four, p. 92, for further discussion of this topic.

which is usually referred to as 'lower paid' workers, but in fact it is composed predominantly of teenagers and apprentices; only 3 % of those aged over 35 had so little money, and in this group were several divorced or separated women, and quite a few immigrants.

Twenty-six per cent had incomes of between £13 and £20 weekly, with a heavy concentration among those aged under 24 and calling themselves working class or skilled working class. Forty-three per cent had incomes between £20 and £35 a week; this figure was achieved by more than half of those calling themselves skilled or upper working class, compared with 35 % of those calling themselves working class without modification, and by half of those in the 25–34 age-group. Incomes above this level are mostly reached after the age of 35 and by people calling themselves middle class or lower middle class; 8 % had incomes between £35 and £50 a week and 4 % incomes of more than £2,600 a year.

vi

In contrast to the 7 % of our sample who refused to place themselves in one of the categories of social class, no less than 23 % refused to place themselves in any religious category. Twenty-five per cent of the men and 21 % of the women said that they had no religion and they are rather heavily concentrated among the younger informants: 35 % of those aged 16–20, 28 % of those aged 21–24, 25 % of those aged 25–34 and 18 % of those aged 35–45. In some ways these figures are echoed by those who claim membership of the Church of England: 37 % of those aged 16–20, 49 % of those aged 21–24, 53 % of those aged 25–34, and 56 % of those aged 35–45. Although I have no evidence to support it, my guess is that there has been little difference in the rate of baptism between 1925 and 1953; but the younger members of our sample did not have the experience of national service, where 'no religion' was not acceptable and so did not grow accustomed to entering 'C. of E.' on the appropriate forms, whatever their private beliefs and practices might be.

Those who reject any religious label are somewhat heavily concentrated in the upper working and working classes and are relatively scarce in the lower middle class; regionally, they make up a quarter of the population in the South-East and North-East and a fifth or less in the North-West and the Midlands.

The rejection of any religious denomination, like the refusal to place oneself in a social class, would appear to have a significant influence on the sexual behaviour and attitudes of these avowed agnostics or atheists, particularly on the age when they start intercourse and the number of their partners before marriage.

Of the three-quarters of the population who claim some religious denomination, 52% said they were members of the Church of England, 10% Roman Catholics, 6% Methodists and 7% members of other groups, predominantly Nonconformist, among whom, I think, the very observant Jehovah's Witnesses can be included; there were also a few Jews, Moslems, Buddhists, Christian Scientists, spiritualists and adherents to other creeds, but none of them reached two figures, and so are not represented in the tables.

Twelve per cent of those who claimed some religious denomination had visited their place of worship in the week previous to the interviews, and the same number say that they worship weekly or more often. This observant group has slightly more women (12%) than men (10%) and is somewhat heavily concentrated in those under the age of 20 (who may have compulsory chapel) and over 35. The observant are somewhat heavily concentrated in the lower middle class and in the North-West, with its high concentration of Roman Catholics.

Thirty-seven per cent of those who accept a religious label either never enter their places of worship at all or only do so for weddings and funerals; they are most numerous in the working classes and the North-East. Six per cent visit their place of worship less than once a week but more than once a month; 9% go once a month or less often and 18% once or twice a year. As will be demonstrated in Chapter Two, there is a close correlation between the active practice of religion and the preservation of virginity until marriage, or at any rate betrothal.

The percentages of religious belief and creed denomination do not differ significantly from those of twenty years ago, apart from a slight diminution of those calling themselves 'C. of E.'

and a slight increase (2 %) of those stating they have no religion. This survey does not suggest that there has been any significant decline in religious belief or practice over the last twenty years; the decline in weekly, or more frequent, church attendance is about 4 %.

vii

Sixty-three per cent of the men and 49 % of the women had grown up in the place where they were interviewed; a further 17 % of the men and 11 % of the women had grown up in the same district; three-quarters of the men and nearly two-thirds of the women (women are slightly more likely to change their residence at marriage) live in their natal district. Less than 20 % of those under twenty were living in a strange area. Those who consider themselves skilled working class or working class are markedly more stable than those who consider themselves middle class or who won't classify themselves; in both these latter groups over a third were living in an area where they did not grow up. I would think that this picture of geographical immobility is unique to England among the highly industrialized countries.

Of the minority who were living outside their natal district, 16 % of the men and 23 % of the women came from another English city and 6 % of both sexes from a village outside the district where they were interviewed. One hundred and eighty-five of our informants (approximately 9 %) were not English. Fifty-six came from other parts of Great Britain – Wales, Scotland and Northern Ireland; 61 came from Eire, 5 from Europe, 17 from the West Indies and 26 from Asia.

In the paragraphs above I have written 'district' or 'area' rather than 'region' to avoid ambiguity. In the coding of the answers to this question, the nine districts designated by the Registrar General were used; figures in parentheses show the proportion of the sample interviewed in each region. North-West (13 %); North (6 %); Yorkshire (11 %); East Midlands (8 %); West Midlands (14 %); East Anglia (4 %); Greater London (17 %); South-East except Greater London (19 %); South-West (8 %). For the purpose of analysis these nine regions were reduced to five, by amalgamating the North and

Yorkshire into the North-East: the East Midlands and West Midlands into the Midlands; and Greater London, the South-East except Greater London and East Anglia into the South-East. By this amalgamation a few interesting distinctions have probably been submerged – Yorkshire and East Anglia both appear to be somewhat idiosyncratic – but this arrangement allows of strict comparability with the figures in *Exploring English Character*.

All the variables described in this chapter proved to be relevant to the interpretation of the differing patterns of sexual behaviour and attitudes of our informants.

Figures of Distribution

The relationship between the Registrar General's categories and self-ascribed social class

Middle class 34% AB 57%; C1 48%; C2 26%; DE 22%.
Lower middle class 9% AB 9%; C1 15%; C2 7%; DE 6%.
Skilled working class 12% AB 2%; C1 6%; C2 19%; DE 17%.
Upper working class 5% AB 1%; C1 5%; C2 6%; DE 5%.
Working class 31% AB 5%; C1 15%; C2 34%; DE 55%.
Blank 5% AB 6%; C1 6%; C2 4%; DE 5%.

Social class and sex

Middle class Male 26%; female 40%.
Lower middle class Male 9%; female 9%.
Skilled working class Male 15%; female 8%.
Upper working class Male 6%; female 4%.
Working class Male 32%; female 30%.
Blank Male 9%; female 5%.

Social class and age

Middle class 16–20 27%; 21–24 31%; 25–34 36%; 35–45 33%.
Lower middle class 16–20 7%; 21–24 9%; 25–34 7%; 35–45 11%.

Skilled working class 16–20 8%; 21–24 9%; 25–34 13%; 35–45 13%.
Upper working class 16–20 9%; 21–24 6%; 25–34 5%; 35–45 4%.
Working class 16–20 35%; 21–24 34%; 25–34 29%; 35–45 30%.
Blank 16–20 9%; 21–24 7%; 25–34 8%; 35–45 6%.

Social class and region

Middle class North-East 27%; Midlands 35%; South-East 36%; South-West 27%; North-West 34%.
Lower middle class North-East 6%; Midlands 7%; South-East 10%; South-West 12%; North-West 8%.
Skilled working class North-East 9%; Midlands 15%; South-East 11%; South-West 7%; North-West 13%.
Upper working class North-East 4%; Midlands 5%; South-East 6%; South-West 3%; North-West 6%.
Working class North-East 32%; Midlands 29%; South-East 26%; South-West 48%; North-West 34%.
Blank North-East 17%; Midlands 3%; South-East 7%; South-West 2%; North-West 1%.

Social class and school-leaving age.

Left school at lowest legal age (14 or 15) Middle 59% lower middle 64%; skilled working 80%; upper working 63% working 81%; blank 66%.
Finished education between 16 and 18 Middle 30%; lower middle 35%; skilled working 16%; upper working 33%; working 15%; blank 27%.
Education beyond the age of 18 and still continuing Middle 10%; lower middle 8%; skilled working 3%; upper working 5%; working 1%; blank 8%.

Social class and income

Under £12 19s 11d a week Middle 5%; lower middle 6%; skilled working 1%; upper working 4%; working 8%; blank 6%.
£13–£19 19s 11d a week Middle 18%; lower middle 23%;

skilled working 30%; upper working 29%; working 36%; blank 28%.
£20–£34 **19s 11d** Middle 35%; lower middle 48%; skilled working 54%; upper working 51%; working 39%; blank 43%.
£35–£49 **19s 11d** Middle 11%; lower middle 8%; skilled working 5%; upper working 4%; working 3%; blank 5%.
Over £2,600 a year Middle 7%; lower middle 3%; skilled working 0%; upper working 1%; working 1%; blank 1%.
Refused and not known Middle 14%; lower middle 13%; skilled working 8%; upper working 12%; working 13%; blank 15%.

Age and income

Under £12 19s 11d a week 16–20 19%; 21–24 7%; 25–34 4%; 35–45 3%.
£13–£19 19s 11d a week 16–20 33%; 21–24 37%; 25–34 24%; 35–45 23%;
£20–£34 19s 11d a week 16–20 15%; 21–24 38%; 25–34 50%; 35–45 45%.
£35–£49 19s 11d a week 16–20 1%; 21–24 3%; 25–34 8%; 35–45 10%.
Over £2,600 a year 16–20 1%; 21–24 1%; 25–34 3%; 35–45 6%.
Refused and not known 16–20 29%; 21–24 14%; 25–34 10%; 35–45 12%.

Social class and religion

Have no religion Middle 20%; lower middle 17%; skilled working 21%; upper working 26%; working 26%; blank 32%.
Church of England Middle 55%; lower middle 56%; skilled working 54%; upper working 47%; working 51%; blank 39%.
Roman Catholic Middle 9%; lower middle 9%; skilled working 12%; upper working 12%; working 11%; blank 11%.
Methodist Middle 6%; lower middle 5%; skilled working 6%; upper working 9%; working 4%; blank 8%.

Region and religion

Have no religion North-East 25%; Midlands 17%; South-East 26%; South-West 22%; North-West 20%.

Church of England North–East 43%; Midlands 57%; South-East 52%; South-West 63%; North-West 49%.
Roman Catholic North-East 9%; Midlands 9%; South-East 10%; South-West 6%; North-West 21%.
Methodist North-East 13%; Midlands 8%; South-East 2%; South-West 4%; North-West 4%.

Age and religion

Have no religion 16–20 35%; 21–24 28%; 25–34 25%; 35–45 18%.
Church of England 16–20 37%; 21–24 49%; 25–34 53%; 35–45 56%.
Roman Catholic 16–20 12%; 21–24 10%; 25–34 10%; 35–45 10%.
Methodist 16–20 8%; 21–24 4%; 25–34 4%; 35–45 7%.

Part One

1 Married people

i

Of our 1,555 married informants 3% had been married for less than a year when they were interviewed; 12% between one and three years; 18% between four and six years, 14% between seven and nine years; 13% between ten and twelve years; 13% between thirteen and fifteen years; 19% between sixteen and twenty years, and 10% over twenty years.

One per cent (only women) were married under the age of 17; 3% (four times as many women as men) between their seventeenth and eighteenth birthdays; 8% (five times as many women as men) between their eighteenth and nineteenth birthdays; 10% (three times as many women as men) between their nineteenth and twentieth birthdays; and 13% (two and a half times as many women as men) between their twentieth and twenty-first birthday. By the time they had reached the then legal age of majority 46% of all the married women and 17% of all the married men were already married. These early marriages seem equally prevalent in all social classes except the lower middle class and those who refuse to classify themselves.

Sixteen per cent got married between their twenty-first and twenty-second birthdays (five women to three men): and 21% between their twenty-second and twenty-third birthdays (when, for the first time, the sexes are equally balanced); 15% between the ages of 24 and 26 (four men to three women); 11% between the ages of 26 and 30 (twice as many men as women) and 5% over the age of 30 (three and a half times as many men as women). On the average, husbands tend to be three or four years older than their wives at marriage.

Fifteen per cent of these marriages were childless at the time of the interview; 21% had one child, 34% two, 16% three, 6%

four and 4% five or more. A few people had adopted children or had step-children, but these made up less than 1% in each case. Most childless marriages were found among those who refused to place themselves in the class-structure. Large families of four or more comprise 11% of working class and skilled working-class parents, 8% of middle-class parents and parents who refused to place themselves in the class-structure, 4% lower middle-class parents and 2% upper working class. These two relatively small social classes seem to be the most prudent and conservation-minded. Naturally, most of the parents of large families are more than 25 years old.

ii

The most usual place for future husbands and wives to meet one another was at a dance; 24% met their spouses there. I have written 'was' rather than 'is' for it is mentioned far less often by those under 25 than by their elders. It is above all those who left school at the minimum age who meet their partners at a dance, and, among those, particularly the skilled working class. Several of our informants specified the exact dance at which they had met; thus a 31-year-old fitter met his future wife at a football social dance; a 36-year-old married woman with her own business met her future husband at a dance in the Empress Ballroom in the Winter Garden at Blackpool; and so on.

The next most likely place to meet a future spouse is at work; 15% of the married people met their future partner there, very evenly divided between all the social classes and age-groups.

Meeting at work is followed by social gatherings, parties and outings where 12% met their future spouses; the same percentage met one another through mutual friends. Parties were mentioned considerably more frequently by those who had left school after 16 and relatively rarely by members of the working class; mutual friends are mentioned much the most frequently by members of the middle class.

Eight per cent, particularly in the upper working and working classes, met their future spouse in a public amusement place. The 36-year-old wife of a builder met her husband at a fun fair; as did the 36-year-old wife of a poultry farmer: 'He

was with some men and I was with some girls'; the 26-year-old
wife of a boat-builder met her husband 'at Wroxham on a bus.
We were all going to a football match and he came and sat by
me on the bus'; a 32-year-old storekeeper met his future wife as
'I was coming out of the cinema'; they courted for over ten
years.

A few people did meet their future spouse in places specially
designed to cater for youth. The 25-year-old wife of a machinist
met her future husband through a friend at a jazz club; they
were engaged for two months. The 23-year-old wife of a builder
met her future husband at a local youth club; they were
engaged for three months. Teen-age coffee bars were mentioned by a couple of informants. Two per cent specifically
mentioned meetings or outings sponsored by their church or
chapel; thus the 37-year-old wife of a tool-maker met her future
husband 'through the Church, he was scoutmaster and I was
helping with the cubs'.

Seven per cent met their future spouse through pick-ups on
the street or in other public places; this chance meeting was
particularly favoured by those who left school at the minimum
age and (rather surprisingly) by the lower middle class. The
23-year-old wife of a police constable met her future husband
at a bus-stop on the way to work; the 32-year-old wife of a
building worker 'in the main road; he rescued me from a
drunk'; the 32-year-old wife of an architect said of her husband:
'He spoke to me when I was a Saturday girl at Woolworth's;
he picked me up really'; a 38-year-old holiday-camp attendant,
widowed and remarried, met his first wife 'in a café – she
was working there' and his second 'in a pub – she worked
there'.

The clientèle of pubs provided spouses for 5 % of our sample,
mostly members of the working class or those who will not place
themselves socially. The 29-year-old wife of a motor mechanic
and her future husband met at a public house: 'We were both
on our own and got talking; he slapped someone annoying me';
and the 27-year-old wife of a skilled worker met her future
husband in a pub 'while courting someone else'.

Only 6 % of our sample married friends or neighbours they
had known since childhood; they are fairly evenly divided,
apart from those calling themselves upper working class who

c

seem almost always to marry recent acquaintances. The 30-year-old wife of a foreman bricklayer said that she and her husband had grown up together and drifted into an engagement; a 41-year-old woman, widowed and remarried, and an ardent Spiritualist, said: 'I grew up with my first husband as friends. He lived near. My second husband also lived near; I think I always knew him.'

School or college provided partners for 4%, not unexpectedly chiefly the highly educated; besides members of both middle classes, a number of social 'rebels' who won't place themselves met their spouses in an academic setting. Two per cent met their spouses on leave or holiday; and a further 3% got in touch with their future spouses in various other ways: on blind dates, by being given a girl's name and address by a mate, in a few cases through a matrimonial agency, starting as pen-pals; a couple of Indian women did not meet their husband before the arranged marriage took place. As far as one can judge from the full questionnaires, the marriages through the matrimonial agencies and the arranged marriages were perfectly satisfactory.

iii

Four per cent of our married respondents had no betrothal; 8% became engaged after an acquaintance of less than six months; 29% between six months and a year after meeting and a further 28% between one and two years; in all 65% became engaged less than two years after meeting their future husband or wife. The skilled working class and upper working class are particularly likely to become engaged after a brief acquaintance, whereas the middle classes tend to wait a relatively long time before committing themselves.* As will be developed in Chapter Two, intercourse begins at betrothal for a sizeable portion of the population.

Eighteen per cent of the men and 30% of the women had seriously considered marrying another woman or man before becoming engaged to the person they did finally marry;† these

---

* Very similar answers were given to the same question in *Exploring English Character*.
† Parallel figures from *Exploring English Character* are 27% of the men and 44% of the women.

people who weigh up alternative mates are heavily concentrated in the middle classes and the Registrar General's AB category; they are most numerous in the North-East and fewest in the North-West. It is as true now as it was twenty years ago that young middle-class women tend to shop around, whereas working-class youths are more likely to settle on the first girl they fall in love with. It is possible, however, that this middle-class consideration of alternative husbands or (more rarely) wives is on the decline; 30% of those aged 35–45 said they had acted in this way, contrasted with 26% of those aged 25–34 and only 18% of those aged 21–24.

iv

One of the most constant products of the English educational system is shyness – the fear that one will be laughed at or rejected by strangers, particularly strangers of the opposite sex. So widespread is this feeling that 57% of our male informants and 61% of the women considered that it is natural for young people to be shy and 47% of the men and 60% of the women thought that they themselves were exceptionally shy. There seems to be some diminution in this disagreeable emotion; 59% of those aged 35–45 thought they themselves were exceptionally shy and 61% of this age-group considered shyness natural; only 47% of those aged 21–24 thought that they themselves had been exceptionally shy, 55% considering it natural for young people.*

Although shyness is considered by so many to be an inevitable affliction of youth, the majority do not consider it desirable; 59% consider it a bad thing, 31% a good thing and 10%, with a rather heavy concentration among young men, are uncertain whether it be good or bad. It is therefore gratifying that three-quarters of our informants considered that they were less shy when they were interviewed than they had been in adolescence; somewhat more women (78%) than men (73%)

* The answers to the same questions in *Exploring English Character* are slightly higher but very similar. Sixty-nine per cent of those aged 35–44 considered shyness natural and 53% thought themselves exceptionally shy; of those aged 18–24 65% thought shyness natural and 53% thought themselves to be have been exceptionally shy.

feel that their shyness has diminished, but otherwise this feeling of relief is spread very evenly throughout the whole sample.*

v

Despite the vagueness of the question's wording, less than 1 % of our sample felt unable to answer 'How old were you when you first started getting really interested in girls/boys?' Objectively, it would be difficult to define what 'really interested' implies, but this difficulty does not seem to have been felt by our informants.

Three per cent of the men and 2 % of the women named some age under 11 and 7 % of the men and 3 % of the women some age after 19; these appear to be somewhat exceptional people. Twelve per cent of the men and 11 % of the women named some age between 11 and 13; 9 % of the men and 10 % of the women between 13 and 14; 18 % of the men and 21 % of the women between 14 and 15; 18 % of the men and 19 % of the women between 15 and 16; 18 % of both sexes between 16 and 17, and 18 % of the men and 17 % of the women between 17 and 19. The median age for the awareness of 'real interest' in the opposite sex is around the sixteenth birthday.

There is, however, a considerable difference between the older and the younger in the age at which they claimed to be 'really interested' in the opposite sex. Seventy-two per cent of those aged between 16 and 20, 69 % of those aged 21 to 24, 61 % of those aged 25–34 and 48 % of those aged 35–45 said this interest had been aroused at or before the age of 16. This change is susceptible of two interpretations: the older people might consider that the feelings they had in their early adolescence was not 'real interest'; or there may have been a real shift in the age of arousal of heterosexual interest in the mass of the popu-

---

* In *Exploring English Character* the repudiation of shyness was somewhat more marked (it should be recalled that the sample included people over the age of 45): 63 % of the men and 68 % of the women thought it a bad thing; 25 % of the men and 20 % of the women approved of it; the remainder were uncertain. Eighty-nine per cent of the men and 79 % of the women thought they were less shy than they used to be.

lation over the last twenty years, concomitant with the reported earlier attainment of physical puberty.*

Early interest in the opposite sex and early puberty do seem to be closely correlated. Of those who stated they were interested in the opposite sex before the age of 12, 73% said they had reached puberty before the age of 15; of those whose interest in the opposite sex was aroused before the age of 14, 81% had reached puberty before they were 15.

vi

Seventy-four per cent of the men and 86% of the women considered they had 'really' been in love; 23% of the men and 11% of the women said they had not; and 3% of both sexes said they were uncertain. This uncertainty is most marked in those under the age of 20; and this age-group also has much the highest percentage – 48% – of those who feel they have never been really in love. Nineteen per cent of those aged 21–24, 10% of those aged 25–34 and 8% of those aged 35–45 said they had never experienced this emotion. This minority is somewhat concentrated in the upper working and working classes.†

Twenty-three per cent of the men and 25% of the women answered affirmatively to the question: 'If you have been ever in love has this happened to you more than once?', with some concentration among those aged 25–34, those who will not place themselves socially and those who consider themselves middle class.

Rather surprisingly, fewer people, by quite a considerable margin, think that 'most people really fall in love', than say they have been in love themselves; 21% of the men and 18% of the women think most people don't really fall in love; and 10% of the men and 8% of the women said they did not know. Those under 20 apart, neither age nor social class make much difference to these views.

* See Chapter Five. In *Exploring English Character* there was less concentration on the mid-teens than in the present survey. Twenty-six per cent of the men and 29% of the women named some age before 15 (21% of both sexes in this survey); and 12% of the men and 6% of the women some age over 19 (7% of the men and 3% of the women in this survey).

† In *Exploring English Character* 13% of the men and 14% of the women said they had never been in love; 7% of both sexes did not answer this question.

Those who think other people 'really fall in love' consider that this is likely to happen to them more than once, in the opinion of 39% of the men and 44% of the women – a considerably higher proportion than the percentages of those who said they had themselves been in love more than once.

Forty per cent of our respondents, very evenly divided by age and sex, thought it possible for a man to be in love with two women simultaneously; 40% of the men and 34% of the women thought that a woman could be in love with two men simultaneously. These views on the possibility of loving more than one person at the same time are held with most emphasis by members of the middle class and are most strongly repudiated by members of the lower middle class.

Figures of distribution

Age at marriage and social class

Married under 20 Middle 18%; Lower middle 15%; skilled working 20%; upper working 16%; working 20%; blank 16%.
Married 20–23.11 Middle 41%; lower middle 39%; skilled working 38%; upper working 33%; working 37%; blank 40%.
Married over age of 24 Middle 26%; lower middle 29%; skilled working 25%; upper working 24%; working 22%; blank 28%.

Number of children and social class*

None Middle 13%; lower middle 10%; skilled working 14%; upper working 8%; working 9%; blank 20%.
One Middle 20%; lower middle 17%; skilled working 16%; upper working 17%; working 15%; blank 19%.
Two Middle 28%; lower middle 34%; skilled working 29%; upper working 29%; working 25%; blank 19%.
Three Middle 13%; lower middle 13%; skilled working 12%; upper working 15%; working 15%; blank 8%.

* These figures are comparable with those in 'Class Fertility Differentials in England and Wales' by Dennis H. Wrong (*Millbank Memorial Fund Quarterly*, Vol. 38, Jan. 1960) and D. V. Glass's 'Fertility Trends in Europe since the Second World War' (*Population Studies*, Vol. 12, No. 1, March 1968).

Four or more Middle 8%; lower middle 4%; skilled working 11%; upper working 2%; working 11%; blank 8%.

Where husband and wife met and social class

(This analysis leaves out the small groups who met through organizations connected with church or chapel; on leave or holiday; and 'other'.)

Dance Middle 18%; lower middle 18%; skilled working 23%; upper working 18%; working 17%; blank 20%.

At work Middle 13%; lower middle 12%; skilled working 11%; upper working 11%; working 12%; blank 10%.

Social gatherings, parties Middle 10%; lower middle 10%; skilled working 12%; upper working 11%; working 8%; blank 8%.

Through mutual friends Middle 11%; lower middle 7%; skilled working 9%; upper working 8%; working 9%; blank 8%.

Pick-up Middle 6%; lower middle 11%; skilled working 6%; upper working 4%; working 6%; blank 5%.

Public amusement place Middle 6%; lower middle 4%; skilled working 5%; upper working 7%; working 8%; blank 5%.

Public house Middle 3%; lower middle 2%; skilled working 3%; upper working 4%; working 6%; blank 7%.

Childhood friends Middle 5%; lower middle 5%; skilled working 6%; upper working 0%; working 4%; blank 7%.

School/college Middle 4%; lower middle 5%; skilled working 1%; upper working 2%; working 2%; blank 7%.

Where husband and wife met and school-leaving age

Left school at 14 Dance 21%; work 15%; social gathering 9%; mutual friends 11%; pick-up 9%; public amusement place 8%; public house 4%; childhood friends 7%; school 3%.

Left school at 15 Dance 20%; work 12%; social gathering 9%; mutual friends 9%; pick-up 5%; public amusement place 7%; public house 6%; childhood friends 5%; school 2%.

Left school at 16 Dance 16%; work 9%; social gathering 10%; mutual friends 10%; pick-up 4%; public amusement place 6%; public house 3%; childhood friends 3%; school/college 3%.

Left school at 17 Dance 16%; work 17%; social gathering 16%; mutual friends 5%; pick-up 5%; public amusement place 2%; public house 3%; childhood friends 4%; school/college 4%.

Left school at 18 and after Dance 16%; work 20%; social gatherings 12%; mutual friends 4%; pick-up 0%; public amusement place 4%; public house 0%; childhood friends 2%; school college 12%.

Length of time between meeting and betrothal and social class

No engagement Middle 2%; lower middle 3%; skilled working 3%; upper working 2%; working 4%; blank 4%.

Under six months Middle 7%; lower middle 3%; skilled working 5%; upper working 6%; working 6%; blank 8%.

Six to twelve months Middle 21%; upper middle 22%; skilled working 28%; upper working 25%; working 22%; blank 18%.

Thirteen months to two years Middle 22%; lower middle 24%; skilled working 22%; upper working 18%; working 20%; blank 23%.

2–5 years Middle 22%; lower middle 18%; skilled working 15%; upper working 22%; working 19%; blank 19%.

Over five years Middle 10%; lower middle 11%; skilled working 9%; upper working 1%; working 7%; blank 12%.

Consideration of marrying someone else and social class

Did consider Middle 25%; lower middle 21%; skilled working 15%; upper working 22%; working 18%; blank 16%.

Shyness and social class

Do you think it is natural for young people to be shy? Yes. Middle 61%; lower middle 60%; skilled working 56%; upper working 63%; working 56%; blank 57%.

Do you think when you left school that you were exceptionally shy? Yes Middle 54%; lower middle 49%; skilled working 50%; upper working 53%; working 58%; blank 52%.

Are you less shy now than you used to be? Yes Middle 76%; lower middle 75%; skilled working 76%; upper working 76%; working 74%; blank 73%.

Do you think shyness is a good thing? Yes Middle 31%; lower middle 28%; skilled working 34%; upper working 27%; working 30%; blank 39%.

Being in love and social class

Would you say that you had ever been really in love? No Middle 15%; lower middle 16%; skilled working 13%; upper working 22%; working 19%; blank 19%. **Don't know** Middle 3%; lower middle 0%; skilled working 1%; upper working 3%; working 2%; blank 2%.

If Yes, has that happened to you more than once? Yes Middle 27%; lower middle 23%; skilled working 27%; upper working 17%; working 22%; blank 30%.

Do you think most people really fall in love? No Middle 20%; lower middle 24%; skilled working 17%; upper working 14%; working 20%; blank 20%. **Don't know** Middle 8%; lower middle 9%; skilled working 10%; upper working 13%; working 9%; blank 14%.

2 *Sexual experience before marriage*

i

Despite the impression given by contemporary mass-communications with all the emphasis on the 'permissive society', 'swinging London', and the like in reporting, and the prevalence of erotic themes in much fiction (not to mention the disappearance of the taboo on printing a few common-speech words), England still appears to be a very chaste society, according to the replies of our informants; and, as a later section of this chapter will demonstrate, their replies are internally consistent. A quarter of our married male informants (26%) and nearly two-thirds of our married women (63%) said they were virgin at marriage; and a further 20% of the men and 25% of the women married the person with whom they first had intercourse. For this latter group intercourse obviously started at betrothal, or was the precipitating cause of betrothal; and if one treats betrothal, rather than the formalization of the marriage, as the relevant point of reference, it would appear that just under half the men (46%) and nearly nine-tenths of the women (88%) reached that stage as technical virgins.

These inexperienced husbands and wives are most numerous in the middle and lower middle classes, the Registrar General's AB category, and are fewest in the skilled working and working classes, the Registrar General's DE category. The regional differences are slight, with a little concentration in the South-West. Nearly two-thirds (64%) of those who left school at the age of 14 (who, it will be remembered, are our older informants) had no sexual experience before betrothal; for their juniors, there appears to be a slight tendency for prolonged education and virginity at betrothal to be correlated.

Of the 52% of the men who did not marry their first partner,

4% had only had one other woman, 8% had had two, 7% three, and 25% more than three; 8% did not answer this question on the number of partners. Three per cent of the 9% of the women who admitted to more than one partner did not say how many they had had; of the remainder 1% said only one other man, 3% two, 1% three and 1% more than three. These experienced people are somewhat heavily concentrated in the working classes (especially the skilled working class) and the Registrar General's DE category; they are fewest in the lower middle and middle classes and in the Registrar General's AB category.

Rather interestingly, those who left school at 14 have the highest percentage of people with numerous partners (16%) as well as the highest percentage of virgins at betrothal; it would seem that in this group the population divided itself between the 'respectable' and the 'wide boys and girls' very early and very markedly. As education continued, there is a slight tendency for promiscuity to be less general.

ii

Immediately after the question: 'How old were you when you first started getting really interested in boys/girls?'* informants were asked: 'How soon after this did you have full sexual intercourse?'† Only 4% of the men and 2% of the women refused to answer this question. Seventeen per cent of the men and 14% of the women said they had never had it, predominantly the young and the unmarried (a couple of the marriages appear not to have been consummated); these virgins were 55% of those aged between 16 and 20, 19% of those aged between 21 and 24, and 4% of those aged between 25 and 45.

Twenty-six per cent of the men and 63% of the women replied 'not until marriage'. It will be recalled that these are

* See Chapter Two, section v, p. 24.
† This form of the question came fairly early in the interview. As a possible test of our informants' accuracy, they were asked quite late in the interview: 'How old were you when you first (if ever) had full intercourse?'; but the discrepancies between the two tables are so insignificant – not more than could be accounted for by coding ambiguities – that it has not seemed worth while reproducing the second table.

the same percentages given in reply to the question about pre-marital partners analysed in the previous section. These virgins were concentrated in the middle and upper working classes and, among our older respondents, those who had left school at 14.

Sixteen per cent of the men and 5% of the women said they had first had intercourse under the age of 17; these were 18% of those aged between 16 and 20, 17% of those aged between 21 and 24, 8% of those aged between 25 and 34, and 6% of those aged between 35 and 45. These early starters are concentrated in the skilled working class (14%) and the working class (13%) in the Registrar General's categories C2 (skilled manual – 11%) and DE (semi-skilled and unskilled – 15%) and in those who left school at the minimum legal age – 7% of those who left at 14, 12% of those who left at 15. An early start to full hetero-sexuality is uncommon in the South-West, with 8%, the other regions all being between 10% and 11%. Nothing suggests that such early entry into sexual life is confined to the biggest cities.

Thirty per cent of the men and 26% of the women first had intercourse after their seventeenth and before their twentieth birthdays, 20% of those aged between 16 and 20, 32% of those aged between 21 and 24, 31% of those aged between 25 and 34, and 25% of those aged between 35 and 45. Between 30% and 31% of the working classes first started intercourse in their late teens, compared with between 25% and 27% of the middle classes. There is again some concentration among early school-leavers: 29% of those who left school at 14, 34% of those who left at 15, and 27% of those who left at 16 or later. The people of the South-West catch up with the rest of the country in their later teens, with 34%, compared with 26% and 27% for the other regions.

Nineteen per cent of the men and 36% of the women first had intercourse after their twentieth and before their twenty-fourth birthday, 23% of those aged between 21 and 24, 37% of those aged between 25 and 34, and 36% of those aged between 35 and 45. This seems to be the preferred age for starting intercourse among the middle classes (37% and 32%) and in the Registrar General's AB (professional and managerial) category with 35%, compared with 26% of the working class and 24% DE (semi-skilled and unskilled). The age of leaving school does not appear to influence this group; regionally they are most numerous in the South-East (30%) and fewest in the two Northern regions (27%).

Finally, 11% of the men and 12% of the women named some age over 24, 10% of those aged between 25 and 34, and 23% of those aged between 35 and 45. A high proportion of the lower middle class (16%) started their heterosexual life so late, compared with 8% of the working class. Twenty-one per cent of those who left school at 14, 7% of those who left at 15, 11% of those who left at 16, and 20% of those who left at 17 are late starters. These figures again suggest that our older informants who left school at 14 divided themselves into the 'rude' and the 'prudish' in a fashion which has little echo among their juniors. Among the younger groups there does seem to have been a marked shift towards earlier intercourse.

Table one

This is a cumulative table; each age-level is a total of all those who said they were married or had first had sexual intercourse at or under that age.

Age	Married (total percentage)	Men (married)	Women (married)	First intercourse (total percentage)	Men (first intercourse)	Women (first intercourse)
17 or under	1	0	1	10	16	5
17–17.11	4	1	5	18	25	11
18–18.11	10	3	14	29	37	21
19–19.11	18	8	26	38	56	31
20–20.11	27	13	39	47	52	42
21–21.11	39	22	54	56	58	54
22–23.11	57	39	72	67	65	67
Over 24	82	71	90	76	76	79
Never and refused	—	—	—	18	21	16

A check on the reliability of our informants' statements about their premarital experience can be obtained by collating the informants' age at marriage (about which they would surely be accurate) and their statements about the age at which they first started intercourse.

This cumulative table shows that at the age of 19 3% of the men were married and 37% having intercourse; by the age of 21 13% are married and 52% having intercourse; at the age of 24 71% are married and 76% having intercourse. These figures are reasonably consistent with the number of premarital partners claimed by men.* As far as women are concerned, there are between 3% and 6% more who have started intercourse than have been married up to the age of 22, with the highest figures in the later teens. Most women over the age of 20 would seem to marry their first partner.

iii

There is a slightly larger percentage of people theoretically in favour of pre-marital experience than of those who admit to any. Sixty-four per cent of the men and 40% of the women answered positively the question: 'Do you think that young men should have some sexual experience before marriage?' Twenty-six per cent of the men and 48% of the women said 'No', and the remainder had not made up their minds. This uncertainty is particularly marked among the young, aged between 16 and 20, nearly a fifth of whom have not made up their minds.

In general, the young are markedly more in favour of pre-marital experience for men than are their elders; 58% of those aged 16 to 20, 65% of those aged 21 to 24, 55% of those aged 25 to 34, and 41% of those aged between 35 and 45 approve of such experience; 25% of those aged between 16 and 24, 36% of those aged between 25 and 34, and 49% of those aged between 35 and 45 disapprove. Twenty years ago there was far less contrast between the views of the different age-groups: those under 18 had 33% in favour and 40% against; those aged 18 to 24 had 36% in favour and 49% against; those aged 25 to 34 had 39% in favour and 48% against; and those aged 35 to 44 had 35% in favour and 51% against.

* See p. 31.

According to these figures, those people who were under 24 in 1950 and between 35 and 45 in 1969 apparently have hardly modified their attitudes on this topic at all in the light of experience; this suggests that people's attitudes towards sexual behaviour (like their political preferences) are determined in late adolescence or very early adulthood and subsequently maintained unquestioned. The figures also suggest that there has been a marked change in the valuation of pre-marital sexual experience for young men in those born since the end of the last war; but even in the most 'permissive' age-groups at least a third consider it undesirable and unnecessary.

The skilled working class (57%) and the working class (56%) are most in favour of a young man having sexual experience, the upper working class (42%) and lower middle class (43%) least, with the middle class in the middle position (50%). Regionally, the South-East and North-East (55%) have the highest percentages in favour of such experience, compared with 51% from the South-West, 50% from the North-West and 47% from the Midlands.

Forty-seven per cent of the men and 24% of the women are in favour of young women having some sexual experience before marriage; 41% of the men and 67% of the women are against, and the remainder are uncertain.* This disparity in the answers of men and women to a question about female sexual behaviour is the first introduction of a theme which will recur in several different settings in this study: the strongly differing views of men and women about the sexual nature of women.

The views of the different age-groups on the desirability of young women having some sexual experience before marriage echo those given in the answer to the same question about young men: those aged 16–20 have 41% in favour and 45% against; those aged 20–24 have 43% in favour and 45% against; those aged 25–34 have 37% in favour and 53% against; and those aged 35–45 have 27% in favour and 65% against. In 1950, those aged between 18 and 24 had 24% in favour and 61% against; as in the case of young men, there seems to have been

---

* These figures are a slight increase on those in *Exploring English Character*. Then 38% of the men and 14% of the women approved of sexual experience for unmarried young women and 55% of the men and 73% of the women disapproved.

very little change in the views of this age-group. The views of the different social classes follow the same pattern as in the case of young men, with the skilled working class (43 %) and the working class (38 %) being most in favour, and the lower middle class (30 %) and upper working class (22 %) least; but there is no corresponding difference in the views of the inhabitants of the different regions.

These figures suggest that the double standard of sexual morality, by which men are allowed licence which is denied to women, still has fairly wide currency and, it would appear, it is predominantly women who maintain this double standard: 39 % of the women who are in favour of pre-marital experience for men are against it for women: the parallel figure for men is 22 %. An anomalous group of 2 % of both sexes think that sexual experience before marriage is suitable for women but not for men.

Women who support the double standard are liable to invoke generalizations about the differing nature of men and women (some of these will be quoted later in this chapter); whereas men tend to invoke abstract principles of justice, typically with the adage: 'What is sauce for the goose, is sauce for the gander.'*

iv

Those who expressed approval for pre-marital experience for either sex were further asked: 'Should it be restricted to one person or persons he/she loves? or with just anyone he/she feels attracted to?' This question was intended to make the distinction between approval of a love-affair before marriage and approval of (at least hypothetical) promiscuity.

A love-affair before marriage was approved of for a young man by 32 % of our male respondents and 29 % of the female; in the case of a young woman, 31 % of the men and 20 % of the women approved. Here is one further example of men applying the principal of equality and justice and of women discriminating between the 'nature' of the sexes.

It does appear that there is increasing acceptance of a 'real' love-affair before marriage among the younger generation; for a young man having an affair with someone he loves

* A similar distinction is made in *Exploring English Character*, pp. 94, 111.

approval is given by 33 % of those aged 16–20, 37 % of those aged 21–24, 30 % of those aged 25–34, and 26 % of those aged 35–45. Corresponding figures in the case of a young woman are 28 % of those aged 16–20, 32 % of those aged 21–24, 27 % of those aged 25–34, and 19 % of those aged 35–45. Approval of such behaviour in the case of both sexes is highest in the skilled working class and lowest in the upper working and lower middle classes; this is one of the few situations in this survey where the views of the middle class and of the working class are identical.

Promiscuity, sleeping with just anyone he or she is attracted to, is advocated by 29 % of the men and 9 % of the women in the case of young men, and 13 % of the men and 3 % of the women in the case of young women.* Here again there is slightly more approval from our younger respondents: in the case of a young man 24 % of those aged 16–20, 25 % of those aged 21–24, 19 % of those aged 25–34, and 13 % of those aged 35 –45; the corresponding figures in the case of a young woman are 9 % of those aged 16–20, 8 % of those aged 21–34, and 7 % of those aged 35–45. In this situation the views of the working class and the middle class diverge markedly; 22 % of the working class and 17 % of the middle class approve of promiscuity for young men, and 9 % of the working class and 6 % of the middle class in the case of young women. The skilled working class give slightly less approval than the working class without modification, and the upper working class is the most disapproving in both cases, with the lower middle class trailing them very close.

Although approval and practice of promiscuity are not absolutely identical, the 27 % of the men who approve of sleeping with just anyone they are attracted to is near to the 25 % who admitted to more than three partners. The 3 % of women who theoretically approve of a young woman sleeping with just anyone she is attracted to is higher than the 1 % who admitted to more than three partners, but nearly the same as those who admitted to two or more. This quarter of our male respondents and one-thirtieth of our female respondents is the largest group to whom the journalistic phrase 'permissive' can possibly be applied with any accuracy.

† Three per cent of the men and 2 % of the women, very evenly distributed, could not make up their minds between the alternatives.

V

After they had given their views on the desirability of pre-maritual sexual experience, all the informants were meant to be asked why they held the views they advocated; but, owing to an ambiguity* in the lay-out of the questionnaire, a number of the interviewers did not ask those who disapproved of sexual experience before marriage the reasons for their disapproval; no replies were recorded from 20% of the male informants and 37% of the female informants to the question about a young man, and of 27% of the male informants and 45% of the female informants to the question about a young woman. These are not the totals of those disapproving of pre-marital sexual experience, but they do represent a very high proportion of them: the reasons why a quarter of the men and nearly half the women advocate virginity at marriage for young men and two-fifths of the men and two-thirds of the women advocate virginity at marriage for young women are quite inadequately represented.

As a consequence, this survey provides an adequate analysis of the reasons of those who think pre-marital sexual experience desirable, but quite an inadequate one of the reasons for disapproval. Only partial comparisons can be made with the answers to the same questions given in 1950.

The major change in the last twenty years is the increase in the proportion of those who think sexual experience has a good effect on the person's character, making him or her more mature. This is now advanced by 22% of the men and 9% of the women in the case of young men (with much the highest emphasis coming from those under 24); 15% of the men and 3% of the women thought this applied to women also. In 1950 this argument was advanced by only 6% of the men and 7% of the women in the case of a young man, and 3% of the men and 2% of the women in the case of a young woman.

There has also been quite an increase in those who state that

---

* Since the design of the questionnaire was a co-operative effort, I share the responsibility for this ambiguity. Because of the very large percentages who were not questioned about their reasons for disapproving of pre-marital sexual experience, the tabulations of these answers are not reproduced in Appendix Three.

sexual experience before marriage is normal and natural: 9% of the men and 4% of the women in the case of a young man; and 5% of the men and 2% of the women in the case of a young woman; the corresponding figures in *Exploring English Character* were 6% of the men and 2% of the women in the case of a young man and 4% of the men and 1% of the women in the case of a young woman.

The major reason advanced in 1950 in favour of pre-marital experience was to avoid ignorance and maladjustment on the honeymoon; 15% of the men and 9% of the woman thought this justified a young man and 9% of the men and 4% of the women a young woman; in 1969 the corresponding figures were 10% of the men and 7% of the women in the case of a young man, and 6% of the men and 2% of the women in the case of a young woman.

In *Exploring English Character* I wrote:*

What seems to me most noteworthy is the high seriousness with which the great majority of English people approach and regard marriage. Whether pre-marital experience is advocated or reprobated, the effect on the future marriage is the preponderant consideration. Secondly, the high value put on virginity for both sexes is remarkable and, I should suspect, specifically English. Thirdly, it is interesting to note that what might be dubbed the hypochondriacal attitude towards sexual activity has apparently achieved very little currency. This hypochondriacal view, derived from assorted popularizations and vulgarizations of psychology and psychiatry, connects sexual activity with physical and mental health, so that abstinence becomes, as it were, a rather more dangerous type of constipation, and sexual activity a kind of prophylaxis. In some other societies this view would appear to be widely held.

Today these generalizations would need some modification, even though the valuation of virginity in both sexes is still remarkably high (to recall the percentages: 27% of the men and 49% of the women are against sexual experience before marriage for a young man and 43% of the men and 68% of the women in the case of a young woman); but where pre-marital experience is approved of, it is usually as a good thing in itself without considering the effects on the future marriage. This is

* *op. cit.,* p. 97.

particularly marked among those under 24, born since the end of the last war.

The range of attitudes can only be illustrated by quite a large number of quotations. All the informants quoted in this section are married; the views of the unmarried and of the divorced and separated will be given in subsequent chapters. Where informants have differing views on the appropriate behaviour for young men and young women the words 'for women' will be included in square brackets; where these do not appear it will signify that the informant applies the same standards to the behaviour of both sexes.

Married men commend sexual experience before marriage in the following terms:

'It's up to the man himself. It's a normal act and holding himself back until marriage would be abnormal. It would be a strain on a growing boy' (a 29-year-old free-lance caricaturist).

'He should have experience, because it makes sexual life happier. It is physically good for you – healthy body, healthy mind, etc. You should not try to seduce a girl if you are reasonably certain that as a result she will fall in love with you and be hurt, so this depends completely on circumstances. If she will accept it on the same terms, no reason why he should not do it' (a highly educated writer, aged 31).

'The sensible thing is to have it off if you feel the desire. [For young women?] She can't appreciate love with sex unless she has experienced sex without love' (a 35-year-old commercial designer).

'They should sleep with just anyone, but only if he finds someone he likes. It isn't really necessary to have experience before marriage. [For young women?] Just anyone. I'd want them to go with me, wouldn't I, if I were single?' (a 20-year-old building worker).

'Gives him more experience – makes him a better husband and less likely to go off the rails later. [For young women?] Equality these days – in 1969' (a 41-year-old plumber).

'A young man should have experience with just anyone – one or two isn't enough. It's like he's not getting a chance of picking his own partner. He must feel he's picking his own' (a skilled engineer, aged 32).

'It doesn't interfere with marriage at all – I can't think of anyone wanting to marry a virgin! One can have a very much happier married life after having some sex experience. [For young women?]

From the disease part of it – the girl being ignorant about these things – it is better for her to gain experience with a person she is happy with and whom she loves. Gives her a chance without being tied in any way' (a 39-year-old chauffeur courier).

'If more than one person it's lust rather than love. It's inquisitiveness in the first instance; feeling doesn't enter it really. [For young women?] What's good for the goose. . . . The days are gone when a man can go with anyone and expect his wife to be a virgin' (a responsible corporation worker, aged 38).

'One person or persons. It is not all it is made up to be and they should try it. [For young women?] One person or persons, so that they won't get married just for sex' (a 39-year-old insurance executive)*.

'A young man should sleep with just anyone. Young women should not be an old bag, but be reasonable about it. It's quite fair' (a 37-year-old holiday camp attendant).

'Just anyone. It makes them a man when they get married. It doesn't always work out if they are learning when they do get married. [For young women?] One person or persons. It gives them an idea and also gives them confidence when they do get married' (a 44-year-old foreman in a nationalized industry).

'Lots of men I'm sure would like to think young women have not had sexual experience, but this way it gives them a deeper understanding of the relationship, and having been with a few men they are more likely to remain faithful in marriage and not crave excitement' (a 36-year-old chartered accountant).

'Gives them some idea before they get married – most men tend to have several affairs first – probably be disillusioned otherwise – should be some feeling there, though; doesn't enjoy it so much otherwise. [For young women?] Same as above, but more definitely with someone they are in love with. It means more to a woman, so there must be some feeling there for her to want to, or enjoy it' (a 27-year-old painter and decorator).

'It is dangerous if you do it just by attraction – disease, promiscuity. They should have some experience because it gives them an insight into what is going on. They must know about it all before marriage; if not, it can break the marriage. [For young women?] They are entitled to the same freedom as men, provided they are sensible about it (a 41-year-old builder).

* This informant did not have intercourse until three years after his marriage at the age of 26.

Most of our married women informants were a little more circumspect. Thus, the pious Roman Catholic wife of a labourer, aged 32, said:

'Not to the full extent, but must have a little experience. [For young women?] Not to the full extent, but must know if she can stand to be touched by a man.'

'I am not for trial marriages, but I think some marriages fall down for lack of experience. It is only getting married for the icing on the cake, and if the icing doesn't turn out too good, you're just left with the cake. Love must be in it – not just for the experience' (another pious Roman Catholic, the wife of a technical representative, aged 39).

'Nothing more disappointing than if you married a man without any experience. On one's honeymoon you would feel let down. [For young women?] The same reason as a man; it makes a happy basis for marriage if one has experience' (the 27-year-old wife of a printer).

'It is up to him really. It would be better if it were with the woman he was going to marry. [For young women?] I was very inexperienced and I think there is less tension, especially during the honeymoon, if one has some experience before marriage' (the 30-year-old wife of a mechanical engineer).*

'These things need practice; and he should have some experience of sex. [For young women?] To get experience of sex, because everyone is different. It takes some time to adjust sexually, and if you do not know how to set about it, it isn't very satisfying' (the 33-year-old wife of a partner in a building firm).

'Experience does help to start off life – more mature and knows what to do. [For young women?] I know from experience friends who didn't have sex before marriage and are not as happy in their sex life as we are' (the 22-year-old wife of a sales representative).†

'He can't gain experience from books and he needs it for marriage. [For young women?] Yes, to gain experience for marriage, the art of making love. A lot of people think you just get on top and "Bang" but it is an art. To gain this you have to have experience' (the 33-year-old wife of a skilled worker in a hospital).‡

---

* This informant did not have full intercourse before marriage.

† This informant said she had had two partners before she became betrothed.

‡ This informant said she had had no experience at all before her marriage.

'I think it makes you appreciate that when you do get married it's not just for sex, but there's true affection between you. I think you might miss a lot if you only have sex with one person, and it's better before marriage than after' (the 31-year-old wife of a maintenance electrician).

'If you are thinking of getting married you should try your partner out. [For young women?] It helps to know you are more suited to the man you marry' (the 41-year-old wife of a welder).

'It makes them more experienced if, when you get married, you are not marrying a boy. [For young women?] Sometimes they get married and they go to bed, and you find they are quite different from what you thought they were' (the 23-year-old wife of a demolition worker).*

'I think if they intend to marry, it is all right to find out if they are suited. [For young women?] I don't think it's a good thing for any sort of promiscuity, but again, if they are intending to marry, I don't see it is wrong then' (the 37-year-old wife of a bakery supervisor).

'I think the sex side is very important and the ability to satisfy a woman. Therefore he should have some experience – and it is more hygienic with someone he is fond of. I'm a great one for hygiene. [For young women?] I think that it stops them getting married just for sex and again, for hygienic reasons, it is best to be someone you know' (the 33-year-old wife of a design draughtsman).†

All the informants quoted so far represent those who think that the same standards should be applied to men and women. Although, as can be seen, some women advocate this view, it is predominantly a masculine response (see p. 36). The belief that different standards should be applied to the sexual conduct of unmarried young men and unmarried young women is predominantly a feminine response among the English-born, though there are a few Englishmen who advance similar views, as will shortly be illustrated; and for most of our male informants born in Asia or the West Indies it is self-evident that men should have sexual freedom and women should not.

When, in the next group of quotations, there are no square brackets [for young women?] it should be understood that the informant has stated that young women should have no sexual

* This informant had three partners before betrothal.
† This informant said she had had no sexual experience before marriage.

experience, but has not elaborated his or her answer in any way; in a very few instances women have approved of sexual experience for young men, without any elaboration, and have given their reasons for disapproving of it for young women, like the 35-year-old wife of a mechanical fitter who was born in Eire and is a pious Roman Catholic who said: 'A man likes to think of the woman he marries as pure; and then, it is sinning for a woman.'

Since the double standard is so predominantly feminine, we will start with our married women informants:

'Men should have experience with one person or persons; they might get disease if they went with any Tom, Dick or Harry. Women do not need experience' (the 30-year-old wife of a steel-erector).

'No need; men don't need experience. [For young women?] I think women need sexual experience before marriage so that they are prepared. I mean only a short time before marriage (the 21-year-old wife of a scaffolder).

'A young man should have experience with one person or persons so that he understands what he is going in for. [For young women?] Personally, I am a Roman Catholic and I enjoyed being pure so that I could have the full blessing of the Church' (the 21-year-old wife of a machinist).

'It depends on the girl. If a girl allows a man to make love to her then you can't really blame him, and I think it is better for him to have experience. [For young women?] If you've only ever slept with one man you don't know whether any failings are attributable to you or your husband' (the 26-year-old wife of an insurance clerk).*

'Young men should make love with anyone they are attracted to, because then once married he can please his wife more if he has had some experience. [For young women?] She should have a taste before marriage and then she is not so blind to the male anatomy. To some people the male must be awful' (the 26-year-old wife of an industrial executive).

'I think it's natural for a man to want to experiment with sex. As long as the girl is willing and he doesn't make her pregnant it is all right' (the 25-year-old wife of a sheet-metal worker).

'He'd make a better husband. He'd be more experienced in the sexual side which a woman needs. [For young women?] It's not so

* This informant did not admit to any experience outside marriage.

good for a woman to have experience; she can learn from her husband' (the 34-year-old wife of a station foreman).

'Young men should make love to one person or persons; he then understands more how a person feels the first time a person's married and has intercourse, he's tolerant and gives you time. [For young women?] I am still old-fashioned in that way. You should be a virgin when you get married (the 22-year-old wife of a driver).

'Young men should make love with just anyone. He knows how to handle the situation. If two people are married and are both innocent, that's bad. If one has experience he can help his wife to enjoy it. [For young women?] I think I'm a bit old-fashioned about this, because I regret it – because my first experience was not with the man I really love' (the 22-year-old wife of an export manager, married to a Roman Catholic husband).

'I think most men do, and I think it helps them to choose the right woman when they want to settle down. [For young women?] No; you find all this out when you get married' (the 24-year-old wife of a setter operator).

'I think if one is a bit more experienced, I think it makes him less nervous of sexual relations when he eventually marries. [For young women?] No. I think, though, it is up to the individual. Now there are so many contraceptives available; so that makes some difference if the main reason was originally fear of the result. I personally don't approve, though' (the 24-year-old wife of a warehouse man).

'Men are a bit clumsy, and they can learn on other people before marriage. It makes them feel better and they can really "master mind" the act. [For young women?] It is not necessary; you learn quickly enough' (the 28-year-old wife of a warehouse manager).

'Feelings are more genuine if real affection is there – the relationship is mutual and more satisfactory. [For young women?] If fear is not there, maybe Yes' (the Irish-born wife of a docker, aged 44).

'A man is different, and he wouldn't feel a man unless he had sown some wild oats. [For young women?] Just the person that she is to marry; this is just to see if they are physically suited' (the 35-year-old wife of a press operator, born in Edinburgh).

'Because men are built this way, and have not got as much control as women. [For young women?] I was brought up in India to feel it is so important to be a virgin on marriage, so I feel my upbringing has a strong influence on me' (the 24-year-old wife of an industrial engineer).

'Yes; I don't think it matters, if they don't get a girl into trouble, like me. [For young women?] No; but I did' (the 22-year-old wife of a labourer).

'Men are more shy than women. It gives them more confidence and they can probably satisfy their wives when married. [For young women?] Will get a bad reputation, and there is danger of disease' (the 41-year-old wife of a maintenance supervisor).

'To me a man is there to learn you things. [For young women?] I don't think it is right to just go from one to the other. It is different for men. I suppose once a woman has been with a man, other men don't want to go with her. They always know' (the 24-year-old wife of a long-distance lorry driver).

'In most foreign countries, young men are sent to an establishment to gain sex experience and be taught about sex, so that on marriage they know the right way of things. I think this is a good idea as young girls can be hurt by an inexperienced lover. [For young women?] Some men take the attitude that they are getting second-hand goods, and this could go all through the marriage and tend to spoil things' (the 22-year-old wife of a computer engineer).

'Yes – he needs experience for his wife's satisfaction. Just anyone – free to do as he likes – not much danger attached to his character. [For young women?] Yes, as much freedom as a man, but restricted to one person or persons; she gets a bad name otherwise' (the 29-year-old wife of a press operator).

As I have already written, relatively few English-born husbands advocate a double standard of sexual morality, though this does find a few advocates. The views of our fellow-citizens born overseas are typified by a 32-year-old barber from Jamaica who states that young men should have experience with just anyone: 'It doesn't do you any good to stay single and not have experience'; as far as women are concerned he says he does not know: 'It is not so important for a woman.'

English-born male upholders of the double standard can be represented by the following informants:

'Young men should have experience with just anyone. Before you marry you should have your fling. But women should have no experience. Most men would not like to marry a woman who had intercourse with someone else' (a 22-year-old lorry driver).

'It is a question of practice; this is essential; you can't do things with a person you love; the only way to learn is with a person one is not mentally involved with. [For young women?] If she falls in love with the right person she is going to marry he will – or should – have all the experience she will need' (a chief cashier, aged 45).

'Young men should have some experience, because it could be very embarrassing when you are just married. Men should have some experience because, until they have, they do not think women have a climax.* [For young women?] Women have more to lose than a man; that is why it should be with someone they care for' (a 22-year-old swimming instructor).

'Sex before marriage – definitely, if engaged. If not – well it doesn't matter. Use contraceptives. No harm done if they both want it. [For young women?] Only if engaged; if not she's just an old brass' (a lift-erector's mate, aged 25).

'If he doesn't get quite a lot of experience before, he'll want even more after marriage. When you're just a kid, physical attraction is enough to start with. You love to experiment a bit before "love" comes into it. [For young women?] As a safety valve. They are more idealistic than men, and it is better if they think they're in love. They shouldn't make themselves too cheap' (a 28-year-old engineer).

'Otherwise he is as bad as a clumsy man; with anyone, because the one he loves may be a failure in that particular field. I say this from personal experience. [For young women?] Not so important as for a man. Too much makes her a loose woman' (a mildly observant Roman Catholic worker in transport, aged 40).

'It is learning all round and learning all the time. No reason why this should be restricted in any way. It gives him the necessary experience. [For young women?] A girl has more to lose than a fellow. She would otherwise get a bad name and might get into the family way' (a self-employed driver, aged 33).

'One person or persons, merely so that they can appreciate just what a woman does for them – so that it is not just a passing acquaintance and so that they are aware of the person involved in a relationship. [For young women?] No. I think it affects them; I think it is a mental strain to them somehow, or an emotional strain certainly, to do with fears of parents finding out, or worried about convention' (a 36-year-old architectural assistant).

'Just anyone; it is a man's way of proving himself a man and the development of masculine instincts is natural and healthy. [For young women?] One person or persons: better for her to know what

* This informant is mistaken. See Chapter Five, p. 126.

it is all about. A woman risks so much more than a man so it's better that she's "in love"; then if she becomes pregnant it becomes easier to handle – i.e. have baby, possibly marry the man' (a self-employed painter, aged 25).

As I have already explained, a majority of the 27% who disapprove of sexual experience before marriage for men and of the 49% who disapprove of it for women were not asked the reasons for their disapproval, owing to an ambiguity in the instructions to the interviewers. For many, their disapproval was based on religious grounds – a topic which will be explored at greater length in the next section. Such religious objections can be illustrated by the following informants:

'I do not think it is necessary. I can see no reason why sexual experience cannot be obtained with one's wife after marriage. [For young women?] Most men like to have their wives first and they would like to teach their wives how to make love themselves. If a woman has had intercourse before marriage she might feel her husband is not as good as the other man or men' (a 30-year-old schoolteacher, a pious Pentecostal Nonconformist).

'No; because it doesn't help them at all as far as marriage is concerned; it only proves he is capable of the act. I don't think it helps towards a happy marriage; without love it means nothing. [For young women?] The same thing. It is destructive. They are using intercourse as a physical means of satisfaction instead of it being a culmination of the act of love' (the 44-year-old wife of a dairy worker, a very observant member of the Church of England).

'Knowledge they should have, but not experience. Physical contact is not necessary as long as they have full knowledge. [For young women?] Same as above. It gives a source of deliverance of mind after marriage; and it means a woman can slip over and break up the marriage' (a 25-year-old anaesthetist who was born in Pakistan and is an observant Moslem).

'It is not right from the religious viewpoint. Neither a man nor woman should have experience before marriage. On marriage they should go to each other as virgins' (a 29-year-old lorry driver, a very observant Jehovah's Witness).

'The maintenance of virginity is most important, because when marriage takes place the husband has much greater respect for himself if he is in fact a pure virgin. [For young women?] She has greater respect for herself if still a virgin when marriage occurs and her husband has deeper feelings for her if she is in fact pure and virgin on the wedding night' (a 45-year-old draughtsman, a very pious Baptist).

A majority of those questioned who disapproved of pre-marital experience, however, were not observant practisers of whatever religion or sect they claimed membership of, and some did not even claim any religious membership. They were just against pre-marital sexual experience, either on principle or through distaste; and what I find striking is the smugness of many of the replies, particularly from the male respondents. 'I didn't have any experience, and it didn't do me any harm' (a heating engineer, aged 44); 'I didn't have relations before marriage and it has not been a hindrance' (a 33-year-old schoolmaster who describes himself as an agnostic); 'I didn't have and have since done O.K.' (a 40-year-old builder's agent); 'If they think anything of the girl they wouldn't; if my wife had done that I wouldn't have married her' (a 28-year-old tyre-fitter). I think it worth while calling attention to the fact that none of these informants, or the rest of the group of whom they are typical, say that their wives were happy and satisfied, despite their lack of experience; it is always 'I have done O.K.', never 'We'.

A few men and more women advance rather obscure moral arguments against pre-marital experience. Thus, a 23-year-old bank clerk:

'If you sleep around it is not good for one's moral attitude to life. One wouldn't appreciate the act of love when one is married' (a 23-year-old bank clerk).

'I don't see the need if he's going to be married. [For young women?] I feel a virgin has the advantage in married stability' (a 45-year-old lorry driver).*

'It is too dangerous – leads to trouble. [For young women?] I have had a step-daughter of mine in trouble; I know the bad it can do' (a 40-year-old fitter).

For women who do not practise their religion, even when they claim nominal adherence to a creed, the danger of an unwanted pregnancy is a major reason for disapproving of pre-marital sexual experience; as will be shown in Chapter Ten, this is a realistic fear as so many of the young unmarried English boys

* This informant did not have intercourse before his marriage.

and girls do not take any birth-control precautions. A few, too, adduce their own unsatisfactory experiences before marriage as a reason for disapproving of pre-marital sexual experience; thus:

'It is not important; you can learn without actually doing. [For young women?] I just regret it because it was not the man I married. You feel you have given yourself to someone else, and not the man you love' (the 32-year-old wife of a heating engineer).

'Young men should wait for marriage. [For young women?] Looking back, I now see it is wrong and do not agree with it at all – much better to wait till you get married. I did not really understand; I was too young at sixteen' (the 23-year-old wife of a tool-maker).

'I wouldn't like to think his experience was gained at my child's expense. [For young women?] Sake of children; being conceivers morally wrong' (the 30-year-old wife of a systems analyst programmer).

'They will be sorry later in life when he has not kept himself pure for his wife. [For young women?] They will live to regret it. If a baby comes along it spoils everything for a start in married life' (the 38-year-old wife of a welder).

'It's better to wait and meet the right person that they intend to marry. I just don't believe in sex before marriage. [For young women?] Just the same reason. It should not be any different for a man than a woman. I think they should both wait until they are married' (the 23-year-old wife of a plumber).

'No: because I think it is a very cruel thing otherwise, and it is not the way love was meant to be. [For young women?] No: because it is not something to be treated lightly, it is not just giving your body to someone when you feel like it' (the 36-year-old wife of a businessman).

'Not necessary at all – doesn't gain them anything – marriage isn't just that' (the 27-year-old wife of a semi-skilled factory worker).

One informant, the 41-year-old wife of a tool setter, was intellectually prepared to modify her own rigid views; she was unique among those questioned on the reasons for their disapproval:

'I would say no myself, but times are changing. I disagree with the young teen-agers having sex before marriage, but as they get older it is their own business and how they feel about it. I wouldn't like to say Yes or No here. [For young women?] The same applies in reverse. Perhaps it helps, but with immature people they don't know the implications. Again, if they are older it depends on their nature, on their own inclinations, and whether it is a serious affair or not.'

vi

Several cross-correlations were made in an attempt to establish, if it were possible, the influences which determined our informants' attitudes towards pre-marital sexual experience and also their practices.*

The most marked influence on people's views and practices is the active practice of religious observance.† Between 35 % and 42 % of those who visited their church once a month or more frequently were virgins at marriage, compared with 33 % of those who only enter a place of worship for weddings and funerals. The people who said they were without sexual experience at the time of the interview (15 %) consisted of between 27 % and 29 % of those who visited their place of worship monthly or more frequently, and between 10 % and 12 % of those who visited it once or twice a year or less frequently.

The influence of regular church-going is obviously strong in determining the age of starting heterosexual intercourse. Those who first had intercourse before the age of 17 comprise between 3 % and 6 % of those who go to their place of worship monthly or more frequently, and between 10 % and 15 % of those who only go for weddings and funerals, or never. Intercourse before their twentieth birthday was experienced by 21 % of those who attended more than once a month, 33 % of those who attended monthly, 36 % of those who attend once or twice a year, 45 % who only attend for weddings and funerals, and 50 % of those nominal Christians who never enter a church or chapel. These figures, of course, include the 18 % who were married before

* Their attitudes to birth control were also cross-correlated. These findings will be reported in Chapter Six.

† This is in accord with many previous studies of people's sexual views and behaviour. See *Sexual Behavior in the Human Male* by Kinsey, Pomeroy and Martin, Chapter 13, pp. 465–87; *Sexual Behavior in the Human Female* by Kinsey, Pomeroy, Martin and Gebhard, pp. 304–7; *Exploring English Character* pp. 117–18.

their twentieth birthday; but the figures are significant and consistent.

Those who said they had had more than one partner before marriage comprise between 4 % and 7 % of those who visit their place of worship once a month or more frequently, and 21 % of those who attend only for weddings and funerals, or never. Those who said they had had more than three partners before marriage comprise 6 % of those who visit their place of worship monthly or more frequently, and between 10 % and 11 % of those who attend only for weddings and funerals, or never.

Their views are consistent with their practice. Of those who visit their place of worship monthly or more frequently, between 38 % and 44 % are in favour of sexual experience for young men and between 14 % and 28 % in the case of young women; those who go only for weddings and funerals, or never, have between 55 % and 59 % in favour of experience for young men and between 35 % and 42 % in the case of young women.

The attitudes of most of our observant informants are consistent with conventional Christian doctrine concerning the 'sacredness' of sex and its restriction to marriage;* but the very pious Jehovah's Witnesses appear unique in giving religious sanctions to the roles of husbands and wives within marriage. In the words of a 45-year-old baker 'a wife should be loving and in subjection to her husband, provided the husband is not dictatorial'; and the importance of wives being submissive is stressed by all our informants adhering to this sect. The sect is popular in the West Indies, and a 23-year-old woman factory worker from St Lucia, who has been in this country three years, and is a very frequent worshipper, spoke for many of her brethren in stating that the faults wives tend to have is that they resent their subjection to their husbands and try to be boss, and the faults of husbands is that they bully their wives and take

---

* Among the sects represented in significant numbers in our sample, the Methodists and Baptists are particularly restrictive in their views about sexuality outside marriage, and in most cases their acknowledged behaviour is consistent with their views. The views on, and practices of, birth-control of some of our Roman Catholic informants are analysed in Chapter 6.

advantage of their subjection to them. Envisaging a married woman having an affair,* she said: 'If she does it once and repents, the husband must forgive her, but if she goes on doing it the husband may divorce her – that is my religion.' This doctrine is confirmed by a 29-year-old married lorry driver: 'Divorce, but only if adultery is committed; no divorce for any other reason.'

Although the active practice of religion seems to have the most marked influence on sexual behaviour, even nominal adherence to a creed seems to have some restraining influence. It will be recalled† that 23 % of our population stated that they had no religion; and the contrast between this approximate quarter of the population and the majority who retain nominal adherence to some creed, even if they are completely non-observant, is consistent on every level. Thus, of those who had not experienced intercourse before betrothal, 53 % were 'believers', compared with 38 % without religion; 37 % of 'believers' retained their virginity until marriage, in contrast to 23 % without religion. Of those who first experienced intercourse before the age of 17, 9 % were 'believers' and 15 % were without religion; of those who had intercourse before their twentieth birthday 35 % were 'believers' and 47 % were without religion. Of those who admitted to more than three partners before marriage 7 % were 'believers' and 13 % were without religion; of those who admitted to extra-marital love-affairs, 4 % were 'believers' and 7 % were without religion. Forty-eight per cent of the 'believers' were in favour of pre-marital sexual experience for young men and 32 % for young women; the corresponding figures for those without religion are 65 % for young men and 45 % for young women.

In the last paragraph I have placed the word 'believers' in inverted commas, because in the majority of the cases their adherence to the creed they claim appears to be completely nominal; they are willing to put 'C. of E.', and 'R.C.' and the like on forms they fill up or in answer to questions; but they never enter a place of worship, save, for some, on such social occasions as marriages and funerals. But even when religious observance is minimal, echoes of puritanism can be heard in

* See Chapter Eight.
† See p. 10.

many replies. Thus, a 31-year-old postman, who only goes to the C. of E. church for weddings and funerals, disapproves of pre-marital experience 'on religious grounds'; a 26-year-old bank clerk, similarly non-observant C. of E., says of pre-marital experience: 'It is not necessary; it is wrong on religious grounds and spoils the marriage – takes the gloss off. It makes it almost pointless – i.e. marriage.' A 43-year-old lecturer, who says he has no religion, considers the idea of casual adultery 'sinful', and the wife of a driver, aged 29, who also says she has no religion, considers pre-marital intercourse 'not necessary; it isn't moral'. A 40-year-old building trade labourer, who goes to church (C. of E.) once or twice a year is against the birth-control pill because 'everything is put on this earth for a reason. If the Lord intended this He would have done it Himself.'

A minor determinant in the preservation of virginity is geographical immobility. Twenty-two per cent of those who had never moved were virgins at the time of interviewing, compared with 7% who had grown up in a different district to that in which they were interviewed.

In general, living in a rural district seems to limit sexual adventurousness, compared with living in a town. Of those who had grown up in the districts where they were interviewed, 38% from rural and 31% from urban districts did not have full intercourse before marriage; of those who did not marry their first partner 17% were from rural and 26% from urban districts; of those with more than two partners before marriage 14% were from rural, 18% from urban districts.

Among those who were born in other parts of the British Isles but resident in England, the Irish from Eire have the highest rate of any group (57%) marrying as virgins, and the Scots, Welsh and Northern Irish almost the lowest (31%). Only 16% of the Irish from Eire had more than one partner before marriage, compared with 33% of the Scots, Welsh and Northern Irish. In their views of the desirability of pre-marital experience, 46% of the Irish from Eire are in favour for a young man and 19% for a young woman; the parallel figures for the Scots, Welsh and Northern Irish are 57% for young men and 39% for young women.

After marriage, the picture changes somewhat. Six per cent

of the Irish from Eire admitted to adultery,* compared with 3% of the Scots, Welsh and Northern Irish; of course, as Roman Catholics, divorce is not generally available to the Irish from Eire.

The West Indians and Asians hold to the double standard of sexual morality both in theory and practice; but the numbers are so few (17 from the West Indies, 26 from Asia) that the percentages are not very meaningful. In their individual replies to questions about different aspects of marriage it was remarkable how often these informants from overseas invoked religious reasons for the views they held.

Figures of distribution

No intercourse before marriage

Self-ascribed social class Middle 45%; lower middle 41%; skilled working 33%; upper working 39%; working 35%; blank 29%.
Registrar General's categories AB 51%; C1 41%; C2 40%; DE 29%
Regions North-East and North 36%; Midlands 42%; South-East 41% South-West 42%; North-West 30%.
School-leaving age 14 47%; 15 35%; 16 36%; 17 47%.

Married later person with whom had first intercourse

Self-ascribed social class Middle 18%; lower middle 20%; skilled working 18%; upper working 16%; working 20%; blank 17%.
Registrar General's categories AB 12%; C1 16%; C2 20%; DE 20%.
Regions North-East and North 21%; Midlands 15%; South-East 16%; South-West 19%; North-West 26%.
School-leaving age 14 17%; 15 22%; 16 16%; 17 13%.

Married someone else

Self-ascribed social class Middle 17%; lower middle 19%;

* See Chapter Seven.

skilled working 32%; upper working 20%; working 24%; blank 30%.
Registrar General's categories AB 15%; C1 22%; C2 23%; DE 25%.
Regions North-East and North 25%; Midlands 19%; South-East 22%; South-West 23%; North-West 22%.
School-leaving age 14 29%; 15 22%; 16 19%; 17 20%.

How many partners? One

Self-ascribed social class Middle 18%; lower middle 28%; skilled working 25%; upper working 18%; working 23%; blank 21%.
Registrar General's categories AB 10%; C1 18%; C2 24%; DE 24%.
Regions North-East and North 20%; Midlands 19% South-East 21%; South-West 23%; North-West 24%.
School-leaving age 14 20%; 15 25%; 16 18%; 17 16%.

How many partners? Two

Self-ascribed social class Middle 6%; lower middle 4%; skilled working 4%; upper working 1%; working 5%; blank 4%.
Registrar General's categories AB 5%; C1 6%; C2 5%; DE 5%.
Regions North-East and North 4%; Midlands 6%; South-East 4%; South-West 7%; North-West 5%.
School-leaving age 14 5%; 15 5%; 16 5%; 17 3%.

How many partners? Three

Self-ascribed social class Middle 3%; lower middle 1%; skilled working 4%; upper working 4%; working 2%; blank 4%.
Registrar General's categories AB 1%; C1 4%; C2 3%; DE 3%.
Regions North-East and North 3%; Midlands 1%; South-East 3%; South-West 2%; North-West 5%.
School-leaving age 14 4%; 15 2%; 16 2%; 17 2%.

How many partners? More than three

Self-ascribed social class Middle 7%; lower middle 3%; skilled working 16%; upper working 10%; working 11%; blank 18%.
Registrar General's categories AB 7%; C1 7%; C2 10%; DE 12%.
Regions North-East and North 13%; Midlands 8%; South-East 10%; South-West 8%; North-West 9%.
School-leaving age 14 12%; 15 10%; 16 8%; 17 11%.

Age at first intercourse: under 17

Self-ascribed social class Middle 7%; lower middle 6%; skilled working 13%; upper working 7%; working 11%; blank 13%.
Registrar General's categories AB 4%; C1 7%; C2 10%; DE 13%.
Regions North-East and North 10%; Midlands 9%; South-East 10%; South-West 6%; North-West 10%.
School-leaving age 14 7%; 15 12%; 16 8%; 17 8%.

Age at first intercourse: between 17 and 19.11 years

Self–ascribed social class Middle 26%; lower middle 27%; skilled working 32%; upper working 31%; working 33%; blank 6%.
Registrar General's categories AB 19%; C1 26%; C2 32%; DE 30%.
Regions North-East and North 25%; Midlands 29%; South-East 29%; South-West 35%; North-West 29%.
School-leaving age 14 29%; 15 32%; 16 27%; 17 27%.

Age at first intercourse: between 20 and 23.11 years

Self-ascribed social class Middle 37%; lower middle 36%; skilled working 34%; upper working 25%; working 29%; blank 22%.
Registrar General's categories AB 40%; C1 34%; C2 28%; DE 29%.
Regions North-East and North 29%; Midlands 32%; South-East 35%; South-West 31%; North-West 29%.

School-leaving age 14 29%; 15 28%; 16 28%; 17 27%.

Age at first intercourse: over 24

Self-ascribed social class Middle 14%; lower middle 17%; skilled working 12%; upper working 14%; working 10%; blank 17%.
Registrar General's categories AB 21%; C1 17%; C2 11%; DE 9%.
Regions North-East and North 13%; Midlands 12%; South-East 13%; South-West 14%; North-West 14%.
School-leaving age 14 21%; 15 7%; 16 11%; 17 20%.

Age at first intercourse: not yet or never

Self-ascribed social class Middle 8%; lower middle 9%; skilled working 7%; upper working 21%; working 10%; blank 8%.
Registrar General's categories AB 10%; C1 10%; C2 8%; DE 13%.
Regions North-East and North 8%; Midlands 12%; South-East 8%; South-West 9%; North-West 11%.
School-leaving age 14 3%; 15 8%; 16 17%; 17 7%.

Do you think that young men should have had some sexual experience before marriage?

Self-ascribed social class Middle: Yes 48%, No 40%, D/K 10%; lower middle: Yes 44%, No 44%, D/K 9%; skilled working: Yes 56%, No 34%, D/K 7%; upper working: Yes 45%, No 41%, D/K 13%; working: Yes 54%, No 35%, D/K 9%; blank: Yes 58%, No 38%, D/K 5%.
Registrar General's categories AB: Yes 42%, No 47%, D/K 6%; C1: Yes 46%, No 41%, D/K 11%; C2: Yes 53%, No 36%, D/K 9%; DE: Yes 59%, No 32%, D/K 8%.
Regions North-East and North: Yes 54%, No 36%, D/K 10%; Midlands: Yes 47%, No 39%, D/K 12%; South-East: Yes 55%, No 35%, D/K 8%; South-West: Yes 51%, No 29%, D/K 13%; North-West: Yes 50%, No 44%, D/K 6%.

If Yes, should it be restricted to one person or persons he loves, or with just anyone he feels attracted to?

Self-ascribed social class Middle: one person 30%, just anyone 15%, D/K 3%; lower middle: one person 26%, just anyone 14%, D/K 4%; skilled working: one person 34%, just anyone 19%, D/K 3%; upper working: one person 29%, just anyone 14%, D/K 4%; working; one person 30%, just anyone 21%, D/K 2%; blank: one person 30%, just anyone 24%, D/K 2%.

Registrar General's categories AB: one person 29%, just anyone 13%, D/K 0%; C1: one person 24%, just anyone 18%, D/K 3%; C2 one person 32%, just anyone 18%, D/K 3%; DE: one person 35%, just anyone 22%, D/K 2%.

Regions North-East and North: one person 30%, just anyone 21%, D/K 2%; Midlands: one person 29%, just anyone 15%, D/K 3%; South-East: one person 30%, just anyone 22%, D/K 2%; South-West: one person 30%, just anyone 19%, D/K 5%; North-West: one person 34%, just anyone 13%, D/K 2%.

Do you think young women should have some sexual experience before marriage?

Self-ascribed social class Middle: Yes 32%, No. 58%, D/K 9%; lower middle: Yes 29%, No 62%, D/K 9%; skilled working: Yes 43%, No 48%, D/K 8%; upper working: Yes 25%, No 62%, D/K 11%; working: Yes 36%, No 53%, D/K 10%; blank: Yes 35%, No 61%, D/K 5%.

Registrar General's categories AB: Yes 28%, No 64%, D/K 7%; C1: Yes 34%, No 57%, D/K 9%; C2: Yes 36%, No 53%, D/K 10%; DE: Yes 39%, No 49%, D/K 11%.

Regions North-East and North: Yes 36%, No 54%, D/K 10%; Midlands: Yes 36%, No 53%, D/K 10%; South-East: Yes 35%, No 55%, D/K 9%; South-West: Yes 36%, No 50%, D/K 12%; North-West: Yes 34%, No 58%, D/K 8%.

If Yes, should it be restricted to one person or persons she loves, or with just anyone she feels attracted to?

Self-ascribed social class Middle: one person 25%, just anyone 6%, D/K 2%; lower middle: one person 20%, just anyone 6%, D/K 2%; skilled working: one person 32%, just anyone 8%, D/K 3%; upper working: one person 17%, just anyone 5%, D/K 3%; working: one person 25%, just anyone 9%, D/K 2%; blank: one person 23%, just anyone 12%, D/K 0%.

Registrar General's categories AB: one person 21%, just anyone 6%, D/K 0%; C1: one person 23%, just anyone 9%, D/K 2%; C2: one person 26%, just anyone 8%, D/K 3%; DE: one person 28%, just anyone 9%, D/K 2%.

Regions North-East and North: one person 23%, just anyone 10%, D/K 2%; Midlands: one person 28%, just anyone 5%, D/K 3%; South-East: one person 24%, just anyone 9%, D/K 1%; South-West: one person 24%, just anyone 12%, D/K 1%; North-West: one person 28%, just anyone 4%, D/K 3%.

3 Symmetrical marriage: The modern pattern

i

Throughout most of our history, and in most of the known world, the ideal roles of husband and wife have been envisaged as *complementing* one another: the husband should be the provider, strong and aggressive outside the home and completely dominant within; the wife should be the home-maker and mother, succouring and submissive, easily tearful.* These complementary roles were envisaged as God-ordained and 'natural': 'He for God only, she for God in him'; 'When Adam delved and Eve span'; 'Men must work and women must weep' and many more saws, proverbs and quotations illustrate this traditional view of male and female characters. Contempt was felt for those couples who did not fit this complementary picture, particularly for couples where the wife 'wore the breeches' and the husband was 'hen-pecked'.

Within the household, it was considered to be a bad marriage if the husband did any housework which was not dependent on his greater physical strength and imputed mechanical skills (such as carrying coal or mending fuses); a typical 28-year-old working-class wife from Enfield complained in 1950 of husbands being 'afraid of being thought a cissy; mine hates people to know he helps at all in the house; won't push pram',† and a woman who didn't spend all her time looking after her home and her children but went 'gadding about' was a bad wife and a bad mother.

These traditional views of the complementary roles of

---

* For a detailed discussion of sex roles, see Margaret Mead: *Male and Female* (London and New York, 1949)
† *Exploring English Character*, p. 135.

husband and wife were completely dominant twenty years ago: I could then write:

Somewhat over-simplifying the picture, one might say that in English marriage character makes for the woman's happiness and the man's unhappiness; and domestic behaviour and skills excite a man's approval and (to a lesser extent) the woman's condemnation.*

The appreciation of a wife's skills as housekeeper, cook, and mother, and of a husband's understanding, thoughtfulness and generosity; the fears that a wife would nag and gossip and act stupidly and a husband be lazy, untidy and mean with money; these still play a major role, particularly with our older informants. But for our younger informants, particularly those aged between 25 and 34 and in the Registrar General's C2 (skilled manual) category, this traditional complementary ideal has been replaced by an ideal of equality, of husband and wife doing everything together, of minimal separation of interests or pursuits outside working hours, which I am here calling the ideal of symmetrical marriage. In a symmetrical relationship A responds to B as B responds to A; the differences of temperament, of function, of skills are all minimized.†

Very important components in the ideal of a symmetrical marriage are comradeship, doing things together, and articulateness. Thirty per cent of our husbands and wives 'always' go out together and another 39% 'usually' do so; this is especially the habit of the skilled working class, followed by the lower middle and middle classes. In the working class husbands and wives are more likely to go out 'separately and together equally'; and the small groups who 'usually' or 'always' go out separately are also chiefly found in the working class and those who will not

* *Exploring English Character*, p. 129.
† What I am calling 'symmetrical marriage' seems to be the same as what Goldthorpe, Lockwood, Bechhofer and Platt call 'companionate' marriage in *The Affluent Worker in the Class Structure*, p. 108 (Cambridge University Press, 1969). These authors add in a footnote: 'The changing pattern of marriage is one topic which has been curiously neglected in recent research into working-class social life. While our own study cannot help much to fill the gap, it does serve to indicate that the development of new normative expectations in regard to marital relationships may well be of major importance in understanding new working-class life-styles in general.'

classify themselves. Only a tiny minority of 13% do not take their holidays together, and 5% of these do not have holidays; of the remainder 5% 'usually' take their holidays together, and 1% each take them 'separately and together equally', 'usually separately' and 'always separately'. This minority tend to be couples who are both working and self-employed and in the Registrar General's AB category.

ii

Table Two shows in summary form the answers which our informants gave to the question 'What do you think tends to make for a happy marriage?' and compares their answers with those given to the same question in 1950. A few of the categories in this table have a number of synonymous components: thus 'equanimity' includes 'good temper' and 'sense of humour'; 'comradeship' includes 'discussing things together, going out together, doing things together'; 'sexual compatibility' includes a 'satisfactory sex life'; 'financial security' includes 'no money difficulties'; a 'happy home life' includes 'good housekeeping and/or cooking' and 'non-interference from in-laws'.

Comparing the answers given in 1950 and those in 1969 to the same question, it is interesting to note the virtual disappearance of material circumstances as essential to a happy marriage. Today's young couples seem to take for granted having a home of one's own, which bulked so large in 1950; although the housing problem is not yet completely solved, and probably will not ever be while the laws about rented property encourage immobility, it now barely preoccupies the younger married groups; and with separate dwellings available for most young couples, the interference of 'in-laws' is also seldom mentioned. Similarly, financial security and the absence of debts plays a much smaller role today than in 1950; relative prosperity is, as it were, almost taken for granted.

Psychologically interesting is the relative disappearance of the importance of equanimity, good temper or a sense of humour; the apprehension that one of the spouses (more often the husband) will have a bad temper or be 'moody' (a key phrase in contemporary England to describe somebody of uncertain temper without implying any judgement; 'moodiness' is apparently

Table two

What do you think tends to make for a happy marriage?
Since the respondents in *Exploring English Character* named more
qualities, the figures from this survey should be increased by 22 %
for strict comparability.

	This survey				Exploring English Character		
	Total percentage	Married only	Men	Women	Total percentage	Men	Women
Give-and-take, consideration	28%	29%	24%	31%	39%	36%	42%
Discussing things, understanding	28%	29%	26%	30%	35%	32%	38%
Love, affection	19%	17%	20%	18%	24%	21%	27%
Equanimity	4%	4%	3%	4%	24%	20%	29%
Mutual trust, mutual help, no secrets	20%	20%	21%	19%	27%	26%	30%
Comradeship, doing things together	29%	30%	27%	30%	15%	12%	18%
Children	14%	14%	17%	11%	15%	17%	12%
Shared interests	13%	13%	13%	14%	13%	10%	16%
Sexual compatibility	5%	5%	7%	3%	11%	12%	9%
Financial security – no debts	5%	5%	7%	4%	15%	16%	13%
Home of one's own	1%	1%	1%	0%	6%	6%	5%
Happy home life	5%	5%	7%	3%	8%	8%	10%
Total percentages	172%	173%	174%	168%	253%	216%	248%

envisaged as a temperamental attribute, as little amenable to modification as any other genetic trait); for most of the younger married English today this is not a risk which is often envisaged.

A satisfactory sex-life is also apparently taken for granted more frequently today than in the past; men mention this much more frequently than women, but the percentage doing so is only about half that of twenty years ago.

Give-and-take or consideration, discussing things together and understanding, love and affection and mutual trust all hold nearly the same importance today as they did in 1950; and, although mentioned less frequently, so do shared interests and children. It is interesting that in both surveys men, particularly men of the working class, mention the importance of children much more frequently than do women;* tender fatherhood seems to bring more conscious rewards than does motherhood, because, as can easily be understood, mothers are much more aware of the work and the limitation of outside interests inherent in the care of young children than are the fathers.

The great change since 1950 is the emphasis given to comradeship, to doing things together; today this is mentioned by nearly a third of all our respondents, compared with barely half that number twenty years ago. It is this changed emphasis, together with the high valuation of articulateness, which would seem to justify the term 'symmetrical marriage' as a statement of the contemporary ideal. Key terms in the phrasing of this ideal are 'togetherness' and 'communication'. Although the first term is almost certainly transatlantic in origin and the second was used popularly in the U.S.A. several years before it received wide currency here, both have become basic intellectual concepts for the younger married men and women of England today.

Only a rather large battery of quotations can illustrate the ways in which our informants handled these concepts. They were also asked: 'What do you think tends to wreck a marriage?'

---

* Ann Cartwright, in *Parents and Family Planning Services*, based on interviews with young parents, states: 'Rather more fathers than mothers hoped they would have more children, 54% compared with 47%' (p. 140). Her Table 59, page 142, shows that more fathers than mothers were pleased at the latest pregnancy.

(a topic which will be discussed at length in Chapter 4) and in a few instances I have quoted the respondent's answer to this question too, when it seems to be an elaboration of the same theme.

A 23-year-old self-employed painter and decorator says that what makes for a happy marriage is 'plain simple togetherness'; in his view what can wreck a marriage is 'money worries and husband drinking too much'. A 35-year-old divorced and remarried representative uses the same phrase: 'Togetherness – i.e. taking wife out, appreciation of her, enough housekeeping, recognizing her moods, etc.'

The 23-year-old wife of a warp-knitter advises: 'Working together, planning things together, talking about things'; the 41-year-old wife of a senior sales executive, a pious Roman Catholic, born in Eire: 'Doing things together as often as you possibly can; it keeps you close to each other'; the 28-year-old wife of an ink-maker: 'If you work at the marriage and do everything together and love each other. Trust each other.' The 29-year-old wife of an automobile designer advises: 'Going out together and having free time'; what she thinks can wreck a marriage is 'Not interested enough in the wife's affairs at home; not going out together often enough'. The 24-year-old divorced and remarried wife of a steel-fixer: 'Doing things together and talking over your plans together; both taking a fair share in everything to make things run smoothly.'

Identical, or very similar, phrases were used by nearly a third of our informants; wives put a little more emphasis than did husbands on the dominant value of companionship; but it is a recurring theme with both sexes.

So, too, is the importance of articulateness, of communication. The 28-year-old wife of a warehouse manager said that what would make for a happy marriage is when you are 'able to communicate with each other, and being considerate towards each other; tolerance of faults'. She thought that what could wreck a marriage is 'lack of consideration and communication; that's the main factor'. The 30-year-old wife of a foreman bricklayer said: 'We try to decide and agree on everything together, and I think this is the best way to a happy marriage'; the 41-year-old wife of an engineering foreman: 'Partnership in everything. If you can talk to each other instead of holding it all in, you're on the way to a happy marriage'; the 45-year-old wife of a postman: 'Working together; the ability to talk to each other about everything'; and the 22-year-old wife of a police constable: 'If one loves each other enough to be able to discuss all matters in the open'; the 33-year-old wife of a company director, born in Eire: 'You do everything together – you have discussions without arguments; you respect each other's point of view'; the 32-year-old wife of a mechanical engineer: 'Being able to discuss all your problems with one another, completely interested in each other, prepared to sit down and listen to each other; the sexual side of marriage is important, compatibility there.'

Many husbands give similar advice: a 37-year-old widowed and remarried holiday-camp assistant thinks a marriage will be happy 'if you can talk out all your problems, try to see each other's point of view and not get irritated'; a 22-year-old swimming instructor: 'Being sexually happy and discussing things together – bringing things out in the open.' He thinks a marriage can be wrecked by 'failure to discuss things with one another'.

A value, and phrases, which today's young couples stress nearly as much as did their elders twenty years ago, are give-and-take and consideration. The reiteration of these phrases is apparently comforting and felt to be sufficient; the majority of the respondents who used them elaborated very little. The 36-year-old wife of a self-employed builder: 'Give and take. Getting along together, and the sharing of pleasures together. Making their pleasures yours (fishing)'; the 28-year-old wife of a tool-maker: 'Understanding – trust – love – give and take; don't expect too much of your partner'; the 21-year-old wife of a sugar-beet processor: 'Giving and taking. Fitting in with each other's wishes. Understanding one another.' What she thinks will wreck a marriage is 'incompatibility; forced marriages often fail because they get started off on the wrong foot'.

A 35-year-old self-employed building contractor said: 'You have to work together to keep it happy. It can be hard work; you must all give up. You have to have give-and-take; it is not all romance and roses'; similarly, a 32-year-old storekeeper: 'Give-and-take; a good understanding; able to see one another's point of view.'

Give-and-take fades into shared interests as a value; to a great extent this is a semantic rather than a logical division of categories. Indeed the 28-year-old wife of a sub-contractor, a pious Roman Catholic born in Eire, uses both phrases: 'Giving and taking and the willingness to share the responsibilities, and of all things the most important is to be able to see each other's point of view'; but a more usual phrasing is that of the 37-year-old wife of a herdsman, a pious member of the Church of England: 'Sharing everything – doing everything together – being interested in the same things'; or the 29-year-old wife of a motor mechanic: 'When you treat everything as though you were both one person.'

A 34-year-old window cleaner said: 'One shares everything – never think of myself first – my children come first and then *me* and my wife'; or the 35-year-old wife of a sculptor: 'Recognition of the whole family unit as opposed to any one member being more important than another.' The 30-year-old wife of a carpenter: 'If you are both more or less the same temperament, enjoy a joke, and have the same ideas on alcohol and things like that. If one is for it and one against, that does not do.'

A 31-year-old solicitor's clerk advises: 'You must know your partner well before marriage – general frankness – fair proportion of pastimes and activities in common. Got to love someone really, more than anyone who is likely to come along.' A 39-year-old trade-officer affirms: 'I am a strong believer in a woman not having time on her hands to get bored. My wife is placid and I am moody, so we complement each other – I tend to dominate.' This view of the value of conflicting temperaments is echoed to a certain degree by the 21-year-old wife of a senior engineer: 'You've got to be suited – liking things the same, though you can be exact opposites too – you can't say how; I like going out; we never stay in.' What this woman thinks could wreck a marriage is 'when you get fed up with each other and don't go out, get shut indoors with children all the time'. She has only been married one year, and has no children to date.

A 33-year-old anaesthetist, born in Pakistan, thinks a marriage will be happy 'if they understand each other and try to dissolve defects and correct each other. Give responsibility in their respective fields of individual prospect. Keep to religion.' What he thinks can wreck a marriage is 'less understanding between the two people; too much independence from each other; too much free mixing with other people'.

Mutual trust and the absence of secrets between husband and wife is another quality which is valued nearly as much by our contemporary informants as by those of twenty years ago; sometimes this is carried to remarkable lengths. Thus, a 38-year-old official in local government replied: 'Children, definitely children. Giving and sharing and having no secrets. We open each other's letters.' A 32-year-old engineer, a fairly pious Roman Catholic: 'You have got to be one together. No such thing as being two of you – being one in mind and body.' A 33-year-old schoolmaster, who describes himself as an agnostic: 'Trust; same views on religion and same sexual appetite.'

Mutual trust and the absence of secrets seems to be particularly stressed by those who are active in their religious observances, whatever these may be. The 41-year-old wife of a council school-keeper, who is an ardent Spiritualist said: 'You must really love your husband, and you have both to pull the same way. You have got to be able to talk, and so solve these problems. There should be no secrets between husband and wife'; the 41-year-old wife of a senior lecturer in economics, a pious member of the Church of England: 'Be absolutely true to one another. A Christian attitude helps – both having the same faith and trying to practise it'; but in contrast the 32-year-old wife of a surveyor, an observant Methodist, said: 'Mutual trust. Unselfishness on both parts, realizing both are individuals and both have a life to lead – you don't have to live in each other's pockets. I have music and I go to church; he doesn't, but he doesn't mind me going.'

Although equanimity and good temper are stressed much less today than they were twenty years ago, they are still mentioned on occasion. Thus, the 33-year-old wife of a fence-erector: 'Just getting on together; if you don't get on together you'll be having rows all the time. It would get on your nerves.' This woman, when asked what she thought would wreck a marriage, replied: 'I wouldn't know; mine is very happy. Another woman or another man, I would think, but I don't really know.' The 26-year-old wife of an assistant manager: 'Love and understanding, but it's hard work. You've got to understand little things and have patience; not get irritable because you're tired.' The 30-year-old wife of an insurance clerk: 'Tolerance is all I can say. This black-and-white line that some people make – you know, "This is right, and that's it" and not thinking they could be wrong – that couldn't be a happy marriage.' The 33-year-old wife of a clerical worker: 'Being able to agree and understand each other; able to make up their difficulties after a fall-out.'

A 44-year-old butcher commended: 'A sense of humour. Nice when the wife shows interest in her husband's activities. Good cooking.' Even more succinctly, a 32-year-old barber who was born in Jamaica said that what makes for a happy marriage is 'Laughter'; what he thinks could wreck a marriage is 'the wife not treating her husband gently'.

The traditional values of a happy home life, financial security, sexual compatibility and children still find their advocates, though they are markedly fewer than they were twenty years ago. A 31-year-old fitter: 'In my case I have a good wife, two nice children, a good family unit'; or a 28-year-old postman: 'Good home, nice children, nice wife, happy financially, no worries, being in love with your wife.' For the wives the comforts of home are even more material: the 27-year-old wife of a grocery owner: 'To eat well and get sufficient rest and be well; general well-being'; for her what can wreck a marriage is 'lack of sleep and drinking'. The 32-year-old wife of a painter and decorator: a marriage will be happy 'if dinner is ready and everything satisfactory when he comes home at night, if his wife is always in for him'.

The importance of children is stressed by a 29-year-old lorry driver, a pious Jehovah's Witness: 'Love and the comfort and happiness that children bring. Interests which apply to both partners. Must be a united family.' Some of our women respondents qualify their answers somewhat on this topic; thus, the 30-year-old wife of a printing operator: 'Children, definitely, I think, though they do get on your nerves a lot . . .'; or the 34-year-old wife of a power-press operator, a pious Roman Catholic born in Eire: 'I think children do hold it together; pull with one another; both give and take.'

Sexual compatibility was mentioned relatively seldom. This cannot be because of the other questions about sexual behaviour

in the questionnaire, because the questions on marriage pre-
ceded them; it would seem that today's younger couples tend
to take sexual compatibility for granted in a way their parents
never could. Among the few bringing up the topic spontaneously
are a 36-year-old butchery manager: 'A deep and consistent
sex relationship. Equality and give-and-take attitude, children
and family life'; a 41-year-old airport porter: 'Satisfactory
sex life – if that is right one would tend to agree on every other
subject'; a 28-year-old greengrocer, a pious Jehovah's Witness:
'In our own love, our worship together shows us that God has
put us together to be married, to love one another, to be reasonable with one another, to be kind and considerate and work for
one another's interests.'

Among the few women spontaneously mentioning this topic
is the 24-year-old wife of a long-distance lorry driver: 'If you
get on well in every way – sex – if you're all right that way, and
both give and take a little'; and the 32-year-old wife of a scrap-
merchant: 'Keep yourselves together as much as you possibly
can, and never refuse him when he wants sex.'

The importance of financial security was also mentioned
spontaneously relatively seldom; like sexual compatibility, this
would appear to be practically taken for granted by today's
younger married people. The 27-year-old wife of a deck-hand
said: 'I think if you marry someone sensible that has saved
money when he was single, you have a good beginning. Better
to get married and wait a bit until you have children – not to
have to get married.' What she thinks could wreck a marriage
is 'if your husband is possessive, or if you have money troubles –
it leads to arguments'. The 27-year-old wife of a council gardener: 'Have trust and a weekly wage to depend on always'; the
33-year-old wife of a design draughtsman: 'Enough money to
live on – understanding between you, doing things together'; a
22-year-old woman who was deserted by her husband and is
living on social security: 'Start off on the right foot – able to
afford things that you want. Both willing to struggle to get
what you want and both do the same to help.' A 45-year-old
lorry driver: 'A desire to understand each other and get along
together; a steady budget and both thrifty and having children.'

iii

Table three

What are the three most important qualities a husband/wife should have?

	This survey				Exploring English Character		
	Total percentage 276%	Married only	Men	Women	Total percentage 308%	Men	Women
Understanding, consideration	39%	42%	24%	52%	27%	23%	33%
Love, affection, kindness	33%	35%	22%	44%	20%	22%	17%
Faithfulness	12%	11%	12%	12%	21%	21%	21%
Intelligence	4%	3%	6%	2%	14%	18%	8%
Sense of humour	15%	16%	11%	18%	20%	16%	24%
Patience, level-headed	14%	15%	13%	16%	9%	11%	8%
Tolerance	10%	11%	8%	11%	11%	9%	14%
Equanimity good temper	12%	13%	10%	13%	9%	7%	10%
Thoughtfulness	6%	6%	1%	10%	14%	2%	28%
Generosity	11%	12%	2%	19%	10%	4%	19%
Fairness, justice, not keeping secrets	6%	6%	3%	8%	10%	6%	13%
Economical	7%	4%	2%	5%	10%	16%	1%
Love of home, co-operation	10%	12%	6%	14%	7%	6%	7%
Moral qualities	9%	8%	12%	7%	17%	13%	24%
Personal qualities	15%	13%	28%	4%	20%	26%	12%
Good mother, love children	17%	16%	34%	1%	10%	18%	—
Good father, love children	8%	9%	3%	12%	7%	3%	13%

Table three (continued)

	This survey				Exploring English Character		
	Total percentage	Married only	Men	Women	Total percentage	Men	Women
Good housekeeper	18%	18%	37%	1%	17%	29%	1%
Good cook	7%	6%	14%	—	12%	21%	—
Good worker, ambitious	5%	5%	2%	8%	6%	2%	12%
Share responsibility, share interests	8%	8%	8%	8%	5%	0%	11%
Treat wife as person	3%	3%	2%	4%	3%	2%	4%
Virility, strength	1%	1%	1%	2%	6%	3%	9%
No answer, don't know	6%	4%	7%	5%	5%	5%	5%

Table Three summarizes the answers given to the question 'What are the three most important qualities a husband/wife should have?' in 1950 and 1969. Three phrases used in this tabulation need a little expansion to be fully comprehensible. 'Moral qualities' comprise those traits which in a religious context might be called virtues: good principles, sincerity, integrity, Christian purpose, a good honest outlook, and the like. 'Personal qualities' refer to traits with social and physical (not moral) significance: 'keeping oneself attractive and smart', 'good conversationalist', 'good manners and good company', cleanliness, dressing well, beauty and the like. 'Equanimity' covers all the variations of tact, good temper, not getting angry, keeping his/her cool and the like.*

In 1950, as the table demonstrates, husbands and wives put a

* Cf. *Exploring English Character*, p. 125.

lot of emphasis on moral and economical qualities: a sense of humour, fairness, faithfulness, moral qualities, personal qualities, intelligence, economical and being a good cook; in 1969 the emphasis had been shifted to psychological qualities: understanding, love and affection, patience, equanimity, shared responsibilities and interests and, emphatically for the husbands, being a good mother. This shift in emphasis to husbands and wives being people who like one another rather than as efficient executants of their roles as bread-winner and house-wife would appear to confirm the shift to the ideal of symmetrical marriage.

The value of a husband being understanding and considerate can be exemplified by the following typical quotations. The 40-year-old wife of an under-manager, a pious member of the Salvation Army, replied: 'I think he should discuss things with his wife: be considerate'; the 41-year-old wife of a council storekeeper, an ardent Spiritualist: 'I feel he should understand you and also he should have love for you and should be able to talk things over; no secrets between you.' The 31-year-old wife of a maintenance electrician: 'Understanding, plenty of money, kindness, a loving nature'; the 29-year-old wife of an automobile designer: 'Consideration; get on well with children; interest in home'; the 30-year-old wife of a printing operator: 'Be understanding over anything which may upset you and that sort of thing; have a reasonable attitude towards money; be a good father.'

Good nature and affection from husbands are commended in the following phrasings. The 32-year-old wife of a mechanical engineer: 'Patience with a woman; to have understanding so that all problems can be discussed and have a love of home'; the 24-year-old wife of a programme analyst: 'I must come first – before the car; be sociable towards my friends as well as his; to help in the home where necessary'; the 35-year-old wife of a painter and decorator: 'Kindness; being able to share everything together; consideration for his wife'; the 37-year-old wife of a herdsman, a pious member of the Church of England: 'Being able to put up with you if you are not in too bright a mind; help in the house and garden; share it all together and be a good father'; the 39-year-old wife of a poultry-farmer: 'Good natured in every way: loving, affectionate, considerate; doesn't mind what I do – easy-going.'

A few of today's wives put primary emphasis on the importance of the man's traditional roles as father and bread-winner: the 23-year-old wife of a warp-knitter: 'He should put his wife and children before anyone else; he should not go out separately: he should have no secrets'; the 44-year-old wife of an accountant: 'Have an interest in the family; sense of humour; you want them to be considerate'; the 38-year-old wife of a department-manager: 'Honesty; kindness; with the children to be good with them – my son and husband are like brothers'; the 31-year-old wife of a labourer in wood: 'Be at work; treat you well – not knock you about; like the children'; the 30-year-old wife of a driver, a pious Roman Catholic: 'Not too sexy; bring good money home; love children'; the 32-year-old wife of a surveyor: 'Apart from loving his wife, which one assumes he must do as he married her; kindness; not be mean with money; a sense of humour.'

Relatively recent immigrants to our shores, who grew up in a different culture, have naturally acquired idiosyncratic attitudes towards sex and marriage; but though, in some cases, they accept that the husband should have more freedom than the wife, their views on the qualities of a good husband do not differ markedly from their hosts. The India-born wife of an industrial engineer, aged 24, who had not seen her husband before her marriage, demanded that a husband be: 'In a position to offer security; patience; and understanding'; the 38-year-old wife of a labourer, who came from Jamaica eleven years ago: 'Good and kind to his wife; look after the family; to comfort his wife, to share your troubles and do everything necessary that a husband should do'; the 32-year-old wife of a company director, born and educated in Eire: 'Honesty – not telling silly stupid lies; not to break promises; be able to be respected by his wife.'

As Table Three showed, today's young husbands put far more emphasis than the earlier generation did on a wife's skills as mother and housekeeper; contemporary styles of marriage have tended to involve the husband far more in the domestic routines than did the more traditional pattern which held that the 'husband's place' was away from the kitchen range and the baby's cot or pram; and so I tend to interpret this male preoccupation with traditionally feminine skills as one more sign of symmetricality and companionship in marriage, and not as a harking back to an idealized period when women 'knew their place'.

Men tend to be much more terse than women when discussing the qualities they wish their wives to have. A 38-year-old wages clerk: 'Being a good mother and being able to be thrifty'; a 33-year-old driver: 'Good mother; good partner; economical manager'; a 43-year-old garage owner (a non-observant Catholic whose twenty years of marriage have been childless): 'A good mother and able to have children; a good cook; an interesting sex-partner'; a 42-year-old male nurse (who has had seven children in his eighteen years of marriage): 'Ability to cope with children – if she has any; pleasant'; a 35-year-old brewery worker: 'Good housekeeper; good manager financially; good cook and trustworthy'; a 41-year-old plumber; 'Good cook; good manager; good mother'; a 45-year-old lorry driver: 'Adaptable; good with money in the house; pleasing personality; the ability to establish equal relations'; a 32-year-old storekeeper (who has had one child in ten years of marriage): 'A good manager; good with children; homely'; a 38-year-old cemetery foreman: 'Affection for her husband and children; pride of achievement in keeping out of debt: working together'; a 33-year-old self-employed taxi-driver: 'Very domesticated; very good with children; should be smart'; a 28-year-old electrical engineer: 'Good cook; keep good clean house; stimulate exciting sexual relations.' (This man, incidentally, has had a very active sex life both before and outside marriage.)

Inspection of Table Three will show that most husbands put far less emphasis on understanding and consideration or love and affection than did the wives. Examples of those who did mention these qualities are a 28-year-old postman:'Understanding; good at running a home; romantic'; a 37-year-old widowed and remarried holiday-camp attendant: 'Pleasant; manage on what money we have; understanding her husband's point of view'; a 23-year-old painter and decorator: 'Understanding and a certain amount of obedience'; a 39-year-old chauffeur-courier: 'Love must be foremost, physically and mentally; understanding; patience'; a 41-year-old airport porter: 'To be a woman first, a housewife second; be a good mother and a good and clean housekeeper'; a 32-year-old engineer, a moderately pious Roman Catholic: 'Must be feminine; mature; gentle; and love me'; a 40-year-old estimating engineer, an observant member of the Church of England: 'Loving and amicable; be understanding; be of the same religious faith'; a 45-year-old draughtsman, a pious Baptist: 'Feminine woman; good mother; good home-maker.'

I have mentioned the religious affiliation and practice of the last three informants, because it does appear as though the active practice of religion does have a bearing on the expectations of husbands about their wives and the qualities they value. This would be difficult to demonstrate statistically from the material available for the followers of the traditional Christian faiths; but, perhaps because the sample contains relatively few members, the Jehovah's Witnesses consistently hold dogmatic views on the roles and duties of husband and wife; a very articulate member of this sect, a 43-year-old baker, said that a wife should be: 'Good mother and tolerant; loving; and in subjection to her husband, provided the husband is not dictatorial'; a second member of the sect, a 28-year-old greengrocer: 'Principled love, not erotic love; intelligently willing; a good worker and submissive'; and a third, a 29-year-old lorry driver: 'Cleanliness; a good worker: respect for her children.'

The few members of Asian creeds also tend to invoke religious sanctions for the qualities wives should have: a 33-year-old anaesthetist, a Moslem from Pakistan: 'Obedient; sincere; respect for the whole family'; a 41-year-old lorry driver, a Buddhist from Ceylon: 'Good mother; home loving, i.e. good housekeeper; honest, i.e. faithful.' Immigrants from Christian countries, on the other hand, seem to have much the same values as their hosts; a 37-year-old self-employed tailor from Cyprus: 'Personality; good manners; good-looking'; a 45-year-old fitter from Guyana: 'Feminine; good looks; good housekeeper'; and a 32-year-old barber from Jamaica: 'Give comfort; be reliable.'

A few of the husbands seemed to use this question, as so many did the question about the faults wives tend to have (discussed in Chapter Four), to make implicit criticisms of the wives they'd got; thus, a 29-year-old electrical engineer: 'Should be broad-minded about the husband's work, his being late; be prepared to let him out for a drink with the boys; considerate, trying to be cheerful'; a 38-year-old tyre builder: 'Good mixer socially; good at handicrafts; tolerance'; a 22-year-old grocery assistant: 'Should always agree with husband; should always do as husband wishes; should always be faithful'; a 24-year-old furnaceman: 'Cleanliness; loyal to her husband; a good cook';* a 30-year-old self-employed builder: 'Thrift; cleanliness; an interest in outdoor sports.'

Figures of distribution

> In the following analyses, I am treating a deviation of 3 % or more from the national total as probably significant.

What makes for a happy marriage and age

Those aged 16–20 emphasize love (27%) and have 3% saying they don't know. They under-emphasize give-and-take (21%) and comradeship (25%)

Those aged 21–24 emphasize discussing things together (31%) and love (26%) and have 3% saying they do not know. They under-emphasize give-and-take (24%), mutual trust (17%) and comradeship (26%).

Those aged 25–34 are entirely on the average.

Those aged 35–45 emphasize give-and-take (31%) and under-emphasize love(16%).

The qualities a husband/wife should have and age

Those aged 16–20 emphasize love and affection (44%), personal qualities (20%), faithfulness (10%) and the man being a good worker (9%); 10% said they did not know the answers. They under-emphasize understanding (33%), generosity (6%) love of home (7%), sense of humour (10%) and the wife being a good housekeeper (15%).

Those aged 21–24 emphasize personal qualities (19%) and have 9% not replying. They under-emphasize understanding

* In view of the discussion in Chapter Six, it may be worth noting that these last two informants regularly use withdrawal as a technique of birth-control.

(36%), sense of humour (12%), tolerance (6%) and fairness
(3%).

Again, those aged between 25 and 34 are entirely on the
average; and those aged 35–45 only differ from the average in
the emphasis they put on tolerance (13%).

What makes for a happy marriage and social class

The middle class emphasize discussing things together (31%).

The lower middle class emphasize give-and-take (32%) and
under-emphasize love (15%) and children (9%).

The skilled working class emphasize love (22%) and under-
emphasize give-and-take (24%).

The upper working class emphasize give-and-take (32%),
discussing things together (31%), mutual trust (23%) and
equanimity (8%). They under-emphasize a happy home life
(2%), shared interests (6%), love (16%) and comradeship
(22%).

The working class put very strong emphasis on children (17%)
and under-emphasize discussing things together (24%).

Those who refuse to place themselves in a social class heavily
emphasize comradeship (36%) and under-emphasize love
(13%) and children (9%).

The qualities a husband/wife should have and social class

The middle class put heavy emphasis on understanding (45%)
and tolerance (13%); they relatively seldom mention the technical skills of women as wives and mothers: good mother and
good housekeeper (11% each), good cook (4%).

The lower middle class emphasize love (37%), faithfulness (16%),
sense of humour (20%), being a good mother (23%) and a
good housekeeper (22%). They seldom mention equanimity
(9%), fairness (3%) and have very few (3%) who did not answer.

The skilled working class show high appreciation of feminine
skills: good mother (24%), good housekeeper (24%), personal
qualities (23%). They under-emphasize understanding (34%),
patience (11%) and being a good father (3%).

The upper working class put great emphasis on patience (25%) and also emphasize faithfulness (16%), sense of humour (21%), moral qualities (12%), personal qualities (18%), being a good housekeeper (22%). They under-emphasize understanding (31%), love (29%), equanimity (9%), generosity (6%), love of home (4%), shared responsibilities (4%).

The working class emphasize the wife's skills as a good house-keeper (21%) and a good cook (10%). They under-emphasize understanding (35%) and tolerance (6%).

Those who will not place themselves socially put heavy emphasis on personal qualities (25%) and good housekeeping (23%); they also value economical (11%), intelligent (7%) and virile (5%) spouses. They under-emphasize understanding (33%), love (26%), patience (8%), generosity (6%), moral qualities (6%) and the man being a good worker (2%).

What makes for a happy marriage and the Registrar General's categories

AB emphasize discussing things together (31%) and under-emphasize children (10%).

C1 emphasize discussing things together (31%) and under-emphasize comradeship (26%) and children (11%).

C2 is entirely on average.

DE emphasize love (22%) and children (21%); they under-emphasize give-and-take (25%) and discussing things together (25%).

The qualities a husband/wife should have and the Registrar General's categories

AB emphasize understanding (44%) and sense of humour (24%). They under-emphasize personal qualities (12%), good mother (9%), good housekeeper (8%), love of home (7%), good cook (3%) and economical (1%).

C1 emphasize understanding (45%), sense of humour (18%), tolerance (15%) and intelligence (7%). The only quality to which they pay little attention is to the wife being a good cook (3%).

C2 is entirely on average.

DE put great emphasis on feminine skills: good housekeeper (26%), good cook (10%), personal qualities (18%). They under-emphasize understanding (30%), sense of humour (11%), equanimity (9%), generosity (8%), tolerance (6%) and thoughtfulness (3%). To a certain extent the AB and DE categories are mirror-images of each other.

What makes for a happy marriage and the regions

The North-East and North under-emphasize love (14%) and shared interests (8%).

The Midlands under-emphasize discussing things together (31%) and mutual trust (17%).

The South-East emphasize give-and-take (31%), discussing things together (31%) and sexual compatibility (8%).

The South-West emphasize give-and-take (33%), mutual trust (26%), comradeship (32%), children (18%), shared interests (21%); they under-emphasize discussing things together (23%).

The North-West heavily emphasize discussing things together (34%) and under-emphasize give-and-take (18%); respondents from this region hardly make any mention of equanimity or sexual compatibility.

The qualities a husband/wife should have and the regions

The North-East and North emphasizes personal qualities (19%), tolerance (13%) and economical (8%); they under-emphasize understanding (35%), equanimity (6%) and moral qualities (6%). This region has the highest percentage (10%) of informants who did not know the answer to these questions.

The Midlands do not emphasize any quality and under-emphasize being a good mother (14%).

The South-East is entirely on the average.

The inhabitants of the South-West seem to hold most strongly to the traditional views of the functions of husband and wife; they praise the good mother (21%), the good housekeeper (21%), love of home (14%), being a good worker (10%), shared responsibility (11%), thoughtfulness (10%), economy (8%); they under-emphasize understanding (36%) and patience (10%). Only 2% of the inhabitants of this region felt unable to answer the questions.

The people of the North-West emphasize patience (24%), good housekeeping (21%) and thoughtfulness (15%); they under-emphasize love (30%), a sense of humour (12%) and equanimity (9%).

4 *The pitfalls of marriage today*

i

The contrasts between the ideals of marriage today and those of twenty years ago are maintained in our respondents' replies to the question 'What do you think goes to wreck a marriage?'; their views are internally consistent. Table Four shows in summary form the negative factors emphasized today and those emphasized twenty years ago.

Very few of today's younger couples fear the deprivation of having no house of one's own, which bulked so large twenty years ago; and, now that they no longer have to share a house, the interference of in-laws is seldom mentioned. Financial insecurity has also diminished in importance; there are far fewer mentions of poverty or extravagance; though disagreements about money are mentioned (the handling of money within the family will be analysed in greater detail in section ii of this chapter), the material causes for marital unhappiness are not today considered to play an important role.

It is also interesting to note that sexual incompatibility is mentioned far less frequently, as are the fears of too many children or no children; today's younger couples are sexually far more sophisticated than their parents. Drunkenness is far less of a menace, and the wives have far less fear of their husbands having a bad temper, of domestic quarrels and fights. The untruthfulness and lack of trust which bulked so large twenty years ago plays a very small role today.

The one defect which maintains all its importance is selfishness and its synonyms of no give-and-take and intolerance; for today's young couples, as for their parents, it is the second most frequently cited cause for the breakdown of a marriage. Twenty years ago it was surpassed by lack of trust and untruthfulness;

Table four

What do you think tends to wreck a marriage?

	This survey				Exploring English Character		
	Total percen- tage	Mar- ried only	Men	Women	Total percen- tage	Men	Women
Lack of trust, untruthfulness	6%	7%	6%	7%	33%	33%	33%
Selfishness, no give-and-take, intolerance	25%	26%	25%	25%	28%	28%	29%
No house of one's own, bad manage- ment, in-laws	4%	2%	5%	4%	21%	22%	19%
Temper, arguing, quarrelling, fighting	10%	10%	11%	9%	20%	15%	26%
Sexual incompati- bility, fear of more children, no children	10%	10%	11%	9%	22%	25%	22%
Lack of affection, love, general irritation	7%	7%	7%	8%	6%	6%	6%
Poverty, extrava- gance, money disagreements, wives working	17%	19%	15%	19%	25%	25%	26%
Neglect, bad communication, spouse going out	30%	31%	26%	33%	15%	11%	20%
Infidelity, jealousy	25%	25%	29%	22%	14%	14%	13%

Table four (continued)

	This survey				Exploring English Character		
	Total percentage	Married only	Men	Women	Total percentage	Men	Women
Conflicting personalities, no common interests	12%	11%	13%	12%	8%	8%	8%
Drunkenness	7%	7%	7%	7%	10%	9%	12%
Don't know	2%	2%	2%	1%	—	—	—
Total percentage	155%	157%	157%	156%	210%	204%	219%

today bad communication, or neglect, or one spouse going out without the other, tops the list. Wives mention this defect much more frequently than husbands. Today's husbands put far more emphasis on infidelity and jealousy than did their fathers; this defect is particularly feared by the young and by members of the skilled working and working classes and people living in the rural South-West; it is mentioned much less frequently by members of the middle class and people living in the two Northern regions.

The fear that the two spouses may have conflicting personalities and no common interests has gained in importance over the last twenty years; this fear is voiced most frequently by the young (it would, clearly, render a symmetrical marriage impossible) in the lower middle and upper working classes.

The 26-year-old wife of an overseas service engineer put the case against bad communication very clearly: 'Not enough understanding between a couple, so that they cannot talk to each other – a barrier between them. Perhaps it's the way they were brought up – their own parents' attitude to each other – or else it was not a proper marriage in the first place.'

Other formulations of the same theme are: 'Lack of understanding between one another inasmuch as you don't talk

G

things out. I have a feeling that when a man sees attractive girls at work and goes home to a rather plain wife, it tends to upset things' (the 31-year-old wife of a maintenance electrician); 'Not enough trust between the parties; not willing to share responsibilities; if one goes out alone and not together' (the 35-year-old wife of a sheet-metal worker); 'Lack of give-and-take; lack of seeing each other social as well as in the home; lack of mutual understanding – e.g. money' (the 35-year-old wife of a press operator); 'When the husband doesn't treat his wife as an equal; when he is the boss and she has to do everything he says; when there is no real understanding between them' (the 25-year-old wife of a sheet-metal worker); 'The sameness of everything. You've got to keep each other's interest by finding new things to do, either together or apart. It is the tediousness of marriage which can wreck it; you must find new outlets all the time to keep the freshness; you think you know each other so well – maybe you don't' (the very observant Roman Catholic wife of a technical representative, aged 39).

Although bad communication was mentioned more frequently by wives than by husbands, more than a quarter of the husbands called attention to this danger. For example: 'Not being interested in the same things and not being able to discuss things together; going out separately too much' (a 26-year-old factory supervisor); 'Lack of interest in communicating with each other; refusal to discuss mutual personal problems and to take action to remedy them' (a 30-year-old teacher, a very observant Pentecostal Nonconformist); 'Boredom with one another; sexually frustrated, with one too demanding or too unresponsive; taking each other for granted. A lot of people get married at the wrong time, too soon' (a 31-year-old solicitor's clerk); 'Lack of partnership; woman refuses to give way where a man will give way; and lack of mutual trust' (a 45-year-old local government officer); 'Working wives don't have enough time for housework; the house gets untidy; this causes friction and the wife doesn't spend enough time with her husband' (an electrical engineer, aged 29).

The complaints about infidelity and jealousy are mostly fairly terse; thus 'unfaithfulness; always falling out; husband going out on his own' (a 22-year-old grocery assistant); 'No children; they seek different sex mates; introverted, pursuing their own careers and social activities' (a 43-year-old garage owner*); 'Disloyalty; cruelty to wife; a disagreeable sex-life' (a 24-year-old furnaceman); 'Adultery is one without a doubt; sometimes women do this because they do not have enough to occupy themselves. That is usually brought on by husband's selfishness' (a 36-year-old architectural assistant); 'Insecurity and equality in the home; court orders too easily given and wives ready to cut loose from marriage' (a 45-year-old lorry driver).

Wives, too, complain about infidelity and jealousy, though not quite as frequently as do husbands. 'The man going out with another woman: it happened in our family' (the 26-year-old wife of a lens polisher): 'Unfaithfulness and money problems and cruelty' (the 31-year-old wife of a photogravure retoucher); 'Just if a third party should come along and one of the couple should be a flirty type' (the 34-year-old wife of a planning engineer); 'A husband having a girl-friend, because then the husband hasn't enough money for the wife or enough time and tenderness for his wife' (the 38-year-old wife of a labourer who was born in Jamaica and has been in this country eleven years); 'Going out separately; if they go out separately they might meet somebody else' (the 23-year-old wife of a warp-knitter); 'It is the places people go; especially if you go alone, you are often tempted away from home life' (the 36-year-old wife of a self-employed builder).

Conflicting personalities was the third theme which has gained in importance over the last twenty years: 'Different temperaments – one being too possessive and selfish' (the 44-year-old wife of a docker, born in Eire†); 'After a time people might find they cannot live together or they are not suited and they just cannot put up with each other any longer' (a 38-year-old wages clerk); 'Not being ideally suited in the first place; both to have the same temperament; looking at other women when out alone' (the 39-year-old wife of a representative); 'Intolerance of each other; lack of money sometimes; and incompatibility' (the 31-year-old wife of a mechanical engineer);

* This informant's marriage of 23 years had been childless. He admitted to more than three post-marital partners.
† The interviewer noted that, after the end of the interview, this informant said 'divorce is too easy'.

'The combination of wives demanding too much attention and husbands going out on their own leading to quarrels' (the 20-year-old wife of an insurance agent).

For both sexes selfishness is a major cause for the wreck of a marriage, but most informants treated this as self-evident and elaborated very little. Among the few who did were a 45-year-old draughtsman, a pious Baptist: 'Selfishness – i.e. one partner wanting to do as they please without regard to the other's wishes or feelings'; a 34-year-old machine-tool fitter: 'Too much of the good life; I mean spending so much money on enjoyment that there is nothing left for essentials'; 'Doesn't help and share the jobs; all jobs should be shared if a wife is out at work' (the 24-year-old wife of a naval electrician); 'Not pulling one's weight and not seeing the other person's point of view' (the 24-year-old wife of a steel-fixer).

Quarrelling, arguments, and other signs of bad temper are also usually treated succinctly. 'Continual bickering; being unable to get on together' (the 31-year-old wife of a long-distance driver); 'Constant argument; jealousy; overspending of money; trying to keep up with the Joneses' (a 38-year-old cemetery foreman); 'Rows about money; not agreeing on things like how many children you want, things like that' (the 20-year-old wife of a lorry driver); 'Arguing all the time; not agreeing on the basic things like money and children; not really liking each other to start with – falling in love without liking each other as well' (the 38-year-old wife of a bank clerk); 'Quarrelling instead of falling in with each other's ideas' (the 30-year-old wife of a foreman bricklayer); 'Arguing all the time, not agreeing on how to bring up the children' (the 28-year-old wife of an inkmaker); 'Rowing too much – nagging wives and men can nag too; meanness with money, saying "that's mine, that's yours"' (a 35-year-old self-employed building contractor).

'Sexual relations is a major fault' (a 42-year-old self-employed man with a car-hire business) is a typical phrasing of the complaints about sexual incompatibility. This topic, it will be recalled, has greatly diminished in importance over the last twenty years, but a few respondents use much the same phrases as their mothers did, or might have; 'Mainly sex; husbands need so much of it and go out to find it' (the 20-year-old wife of a gas-fitter); 'Sex – if one or other doesn't give in to partner's needs' (the 23-year-old wife of a toolmaker); 'Sex problems – un-understanding of husband, especially after young babies are born' (the 23-year-old wife of a R.E.M.E. craftsman).

A 36-year-old chartered accountant made the rather interesting and idiosyncratic point that what could wreck a marriage is 'lack of cleanliness. I had a friend who knew a leading divorce judge and he said that this was a basic factor – lack of cleanliness, order, personal cleanliness were what would drive people out to commit adultery, etc.'

Arguments about money, rather than absolute or relative poverty, are instanced, particularly, by wives, as behaviour which could wreck a marriage. 'Lack of money – that is number one' (the 33-year-old wife of a design draughtsman). 'If the husband doesn't give the wife enough money – a lot of quarrels stem from money – if he earns it and keeps too much for himself' (the 30-year-old wife of a carpenter); 'Finance can cause misunderstanding; my husband thought I was squandering the money, so I let him do the shopping for a week and we have no more discussion' (the 32-year-old wife of a meter-reader); 'Not shortage of money but squabbling about it; I think money is a great evil if there isn't understanding about it; a husband taking it for granted it is all right for him to go out alone' (the 41-year-old wife of an engineering foreman); 'Bad housing, inadequate, overcrowding, things those squatters are on about – husband wants to get out of the way; lack of finances. Seems material, but they are basic things' (the 32-year-old wife of a surveyor); 'Husbands going out in the evening alone and spending too much money which should be spent in the home' (the 32-year-old wife of a welding inspector); 'Greed over money – making money too important and having rows over it; putting money before happiness' (the 26-year-old wife of an assistant plant-hire manager); 'Money could if you get yourself into a lot of debt, if a chap drinks a lot' (the 30-year-old wife of a print operator); and, as a contrast, the views of the 41-year-old wife of a senior sales executive, a pious Roman Catholic born in Eire: 'The wife becoming financially independent is one of the main reasons when she goes out to work.' Her views are shared by a 41-year-old lorry driver, who was born in Ceylon: 'Both husband and wife working – being too sociable instead of spending more time at home.'

ii

Because of the self-evident importance of the handling of money within the family (I have only quoted a very small sample of the respondents who mentioned disputes about money as a cause for the breakdown of marriage), we asked all our married

Table five

Financial arrangements in marriage

Totals add up to less than 100% because the unmarried were included in the tabulations.

	Give/receive housekeeping	Give/receive whole pay packet	Joint bank account	Other
Self-ascribed class				
Middle	54%	7%	18%	6%
Lower middle	45%	12%	21%	6%
Skilled working	54%	15%	8%	7%
Upper working	51%	13%	10%	—
Working	53%	16%	6%	3%
Blank	37%	19%	12%	8%
Registrar General's Classifications				
AB	51%	2%	31%	5%
C1	45%	6%	23%	5%
C2	57%	15%	8%	4%
DE	47%	18%	3%	5%
Regions				
North-East and North	47%	20%	15%	2%
Midlands	50%	12%	14%	4%
South-East	54%	6%	13%	7%
South-West	57%	13%	8%	3%
North-West	45%	23%	8%	3%

respondents what arrangements they made. Much the most general is for the husband to 'give' his wife a housekeeping allowance; 27% of the husbands and 37% of the wives named this arrangement. Six per cent of the husbands and 10% of the wives cash cheques on a joint account, and it is interesting to note, as Table Five shows, that this custom has now been adopted by some people in all social classes and all regions, though understandably it is more common among the more prosperous who receive a monthly salary rather than a weekly wage and – rather incomprehensibly – is much less popular in the two Western regions than in the rest of the country. Thirdly, 8% of the husbands hand over their whole pay-packet to their wives, unopened, and 7% of the wives receive the entire pay-packet and give their husbands some back as pocket money for their own private spending; this arrangement is most common among the working classes in the two Northern regions and is very unusual in the South-East. Finally, 2% of the husbands and 3% of the wives have various other idiosyncratic arrangements; this is usually because they are self-employed and not in receipt of a regular wage or salary.

Examples of these idiosyncratic arrangements are given by a plumber's 41-year-old wife: 'We work out all expenses together – pay these – then share the remainder between us'; the 27-year-old wife of the owner of a grocery store: 'We get grocery and greengrocery from the business and share the money he takes from the business'; the 24-year-old wife of a clerical accounts worker, who was born in Spain: 'My husband pays all the bills for the flat; I buy all the food so I do not in fact have housekeeping'; the 41-year-old wife of a sales executive who was born in Eire, a very observant Roman Catholic: 'For personal spending we cash cheques on a joint account; my husband does all the shopping for the house; I hate shopping'; a 29-year-old free-lance cartoonist: 'We budget on a Friday evening and then I draw cheques for her on a Saturday morning; I take charge of the money'; a 45-year-old chief cashier: 'I pay for everything myself; I do most of the shopping myself.'*

* This informant's marriage seems fairly unsatisfactory; he complained of wives who want to 'change the man to the ideal man they had in mind; when they cannot achieve that they become a nagger; frigidity'. He hardly ever has marital intercourse, but considers this to be normal.

More than one wife out of six who receive housekeeping allowances do not know what their husbands earn;* in contemporary England one's income would appear to remain an unviolable secret, especially for men. Our interviewers received refusals to answer the question on approximate income from 4% of the male and 2% of the female respondents; by contrast only 1% of either sex refused to answer the question on techniques of birth control and 5% that on frequency of intercourse.

Some wives don't seem disturbed about the ignorance in which they are kept; thus, the 45-year-old wife of a pump-fitter: 'I don't know; I've always had enough housekeeping so I haven't bothered to find out'; or the wife of a working man, aged 44, who doesn't even know her husband's occupation ('works in acid; don't know what he does'!) 'I've no idea; I've never seen his packet';† but in other cases the arrangement is obviously very unsatisfactory. Thus the 41-year-old wife of a long-distance driver: 'He gives housekeeping when he feels like it; that is why I go out to work. I never go out except to work – I work on a night shift'; or the 41-year-old wife of a welder who wished that 'husbands would give wives pocket money'; and there were some poignant incidents‡ of separated or deserted wives being left practically penniless.

Cross-correlations demonstrate that the way domestic finances are handled has a marked influence on the values, the hopes and fears, of marriage.§ When a housekeeping allowance is 'given' or received attributes concerned with money play a very much larger role than they do when the handling of the household money is more evenly shared through the husband handing over his pay-packet or a joint bank account. Both those who 'give' and receive a housekeeping allowance place

---

* The actual figures are 55% of 1,037 married women receive housekeeping allowances; 199 respondents said they did not know the 'income of the head of the household'; of these 51% were wives receiving housekeeping allowances and 35% of the remainder were unmarried youngsters.
† This informant complained that 'husbands drink too much. They go out on their own too much. They don't treat sport as they used to; they go to football matches and all they do is try to make a fight and break things and then come home in a bad mood.'
‡ See Chapter Eight p. 178.
§ For the percentages, see the 'figures of distribution' at the end of this chapter, pp. 107-8.

poverty as the first cause of a wrecked marriage; the husbands want their wives to be economical, good mothers and good housekeepers, and fear they will be extravagant, and bad housekeepers; the wives want their husbands to be understanding and generous and fear they will be mean with money.

These traits play relatively little part in the hopes and fears of married couples with other financial arrangements. When the whole pay-packet is handed over both husbands and wives stress the importance of comradeship in making for a happy marriage; infidelity is what they think could wreck a marriage. The husbands who hand over their whole pay-packets appreciate their wives' technical skills as good housekeeper, good mother, and good cook, and fear they may not be technically competent. The wives who receive the whole pay-packet hope their husbands will be understanding, affectionate, patient and home-lovers and fear they will be selfish, lazy and untidy.

Similarly, with a joint bank account, the husbands consider that comradeship and financial security make for a happy marriage and think selfishness, infidelity or poverty could wreck it; their wives emphasize the value of give-and-take and discussing things together; they too fear selfishness and poverty. The husbands hope their wives will be patient, neat and personable ('personal qualities') and fear they may be bad housekeepers or have 'moral faults'; the wives hope that their husbands will be understanding, loving and with a sense of humour and fear they will be lazy and untidy.

This summarizing of the numerous and elaborate cross-correlations suggests to me that the ideal of 'symmetrical marriage' is very difficult to attain unless financial knowledge and responsibilities are shared; when the husband keeps complete control of the money, and especially when he hides from his wife the total of his earnings, the marriage is likely to follow the traditional complementary pattern with traditional quarrels and misunderstandings.

iii

As the previous section has indicated, respondents were asked 'What are the three chief faults wives/husbands tend to have?;

Table six

What are the three chief faults husbands/wives tend to have?

Faults of husbands in parentheses.

	This survey			*Exploring English Character*		
	Total percentage	Men	Women	Total percentage	Men	Women
	229% 227%			251%		
Selfishness inconsiderate	16% (39%)	16% (38%)	16% (41%)	35%	16%	38%
Lack of intelligence of communication	4% (4%)	5% (3%)	3% (4%)	22%	24%	20%
Bad temper, moody	8% (8%)	6% (6%)	10% (10%)	12%	11%	13%
Childishness, fussiness	5% (3%)	8% (2%)	3% (4%)	4%	2%	9%
Complacency	2% (4%)	3% (4%)	1% (3%)	7%	1%	16%
Moral faults	4% (6%)	5% (5%)	4% (6%)	12%	11%	13%
Jealousy, lack of trust	7% (5%)	7% (3%)	7% (6%)	9%	12%	8%
Domineering, bossy	18% (12%)	18% (12%)	18% (12%)	12%	16%	9%
Nagging, moaning	41% (6%)	28% (4%)	54% (7%)	18%	29%	4%
Gossip, natter	8% (1%)	10% (1%)	7% (0%)	12%	23%	0%
Extravagance, keeping up with the Joneses	25% (4%)	25% (5%)	26% (4%)	11%	17%	2%

Table six (continued)

	This survey			Exploring English Character		
	Total percentage	Men	Women	Total percentage	Men	Women
Mean with money	2% (15%)	1% (11%)	3% (19%)	8%	1%	17%
Letting self go, slovenly	11% (3%)	13% (4%)	9% (2%)	8%	13%	1%
Over-anxious	5% (1%)	6% (1%)	5% (1%)	7%	13%	0%
Bad housekeeper	11% (1%)	14% (1%)	8% (1%)	5%	10%	1%
Too houseproud	5%	2%	6%	5%	8%	0%
Bad parent	7% (8%)	9% (8%)	6% (9%)	5%	5%	5%
Frigid, put children before spouse	5% (1%)	3% (1%)	7% (1%)	3%	3%	3%
Taking spouse for granted	7% (21%)	5% (23%)	9% (19%)	10%	3%	18%
Lazy, won't help	5% (16%)	5% (15%)	5% (17%)	5%	10%	1%
Untidy, demanding	4% (7%)	3% (4%)	5% (10%)	7%	0%	17%
Drinking, gambling, infidelity	5% (26%)	7% (34%)	3% (19%)	6%	8%	3%
Goes out on own, won't entertain spouse	7% (24%)	6% (27%)	7% (22%)	3%	—	6%
No answer, don't know	17% (12%)	21% (12%)	14% (12%)	23%	25%	20%

but, owing to an ambiguity in the instructions to the interviewers,* both male and female informants were questioned on the faults of husbands and wives instead of, as I had intended, women being questioned about husbands and vice versa as was done for the question about the most important qualities.†
This produced the rather curious sidelight that the English are more conscious of, or at any rate more articulate about, the stereotyped faults of their own sex than they are of those of the other. Thus more women mentioned that wives could be nagging, extravagant and frigid than did men; more men said that husbands could be mean with money, unfaithful, neglectful, take their wives for granted and drink or gamble excessively than did women. One could say that most of our informants generalized about the faults of their own sex and particularized about the faults of their spouses. This gave quite a lot of insight into the stresses of individual marriages, but it makes the interpretation of the tables (dealing with total figures) confusing and ambiguous.

Table Six shows in summary form the complaints made about husbands and wives today, and those made twenty years ago. The complaints that husbands are selfish, mean with money and take their wives for granted and that wives nag and let themselves go remain much the same; there is a considerable decrease in the complaints of both sexes about their spouse's lack of intelligence and their moral faults (such as irresponsibility, lying, greed and similar vices) and some decrease in the complaints that husbands are complacent, bad tempered and untidy and that wives gossip too much and are over-anxious; and there are marked increases in the complaints that wives are extravagant, bad mothers or bad housekeepers and that husbands are lazy and (above all) go out on their own and won't entertain their wives. There would appear to be some shift from complaints about the characters of husbands and wives to complaints about their behaviour, which is congruent with the hypothesis of symmetrical marriage. Formerly, if husbands and wives 'got on together' this was sufficient for a satisfactory

---

* I must certainly take my share of the responsibility for this ambiguity. See footnote, p. 38.

† See Chapter Three, p. 72.

marriage; today they must do things together if the marriage is to be satisfactory, especially for the wives.

As in most similar researches with which I am acquainted, the women tend to be both more voluble and more precise. The Scottish-born wife of a press operator in a copper works, aged 35, complains of a husband 'taking his wife for granted, as regards always being there for housework, cooking, etc., always having their own enjoyment and always going out as a matter of course. They forget that she is still a woman and forget to give her compliments; she still needs courting after marriage.' Variants on this theme are: 'Taking a wife's place for granted; taking all the decisions by himself; being autocratic' (the 30-year-old wife of an insurance clerk); 'Leaving their wives alone too much; neglecting them in other ways too, forgetting birthdays, etc.; taking them for granted' (the 21-year-old wife of a sugar-beet processor); 'Expecting too much of the wife when she has young children; not talking enough to his wife and leaving her too much on her own' (the 23-year-old wife of a self-employed builder); 'Not able to see when a woman needs a rest; thoughtlessness; inability to converse' (the 27-year-old wife of a grocery-store owner); 'I think they might become completely immersed in business; they may not think that their wives want to be taken out and be quite content to put their feet up after their hard day's work; some spend too much time out with the boys and neglect their families' (the 41-year-old wife of a lecturer in economics, a pious member of the Church of England).

This jealousy of their husband's men friends, voiced by the last informant quoted, is fairly general; it is sometimes linked with jealousy of the attention the husband gives to his car. Thus the 35-year-old wife of a blind fixer complains of husbands 'dropping off to sleep in the chair, not listening when you talk to them; they talk on and on when talking to other men'; 'Going out without their wives, putting their mates before their wives' (the 30-year-old wife of a steel erector); 'Going out drinking with pals; spending too much time on the car; being rather thoughtless and inconsiderate' (the 24-year-old wife of a self-employed builder); 'Going out for half an hour and coming back three hours later' (the 44-year-old wife of an accountant);*

* This informant said of herself 'I'm too soft with the kids'.

'Don't understand that a wife should be irritable when they get home; don't think wives need to go out; don't take wives and children for enough holidays' (the 29-year-old wife of a gas-fitter); 'Selfishness – going out too much – gambling and spending money; not taking their wives out enough' (the 34-year-old wife of a power press operator, born in Eire and a very observant Roman Catholic).

Selfishness and inconsiderateness still give rise to many wives' complaints, and these are sometimes joined with the jealousy of a husband paying attention to other people or other things; thus, the wife of a computer engineer, aged 22: 'Just not caring; selfish – putting car first; bad manners'; 'They tend to think they have more privileges than the wife' (the 29-year-old wife of a motor mechanic); 'They are very determined – they'll get their own way if it kills them; they can be untidy about the house, thinking the wife is a servant' (the 20-year-old wife of a lorry driver); 'Wrapped up in themselves and their work; irritability and no time to amuse the children when the mother is busy' (the 30-year-old wife of a worker in a mine); 'They are selfish, very possessive and they like to have their own way most of the time' (the 27-year-old wife of a deck-hand); 'They don't realize how closed a life a woman has in her home and don't take her out and try to broaden her interests; they tend not to realize how far money goes – that is one of the things they tend to row about; most men tend to be selfish over hobbies and interests' (the 31-year-old wife of a maintenance electrician); 'Not considering his wife; go out and leave her; working late, not to phone their wives' (the 22-year-old wife of a driver); 'Expect too much from their wives sometimes; don't understand how difficult it is when you first have a baby, mentally and physically; aren't sympathetic enough' (the 25-year-old wife of a sheet-metal worker); 'A lot of men think they're not, but they are very selfish and like their own way, although they say they don't' (the 38-year-old wife of a department store manager); 'Perhaps a little too much ego sometimes, but I think this is general of all males; not always realizing how much a woman does in the home and perhaps thinking they are the only breadwinner, deep down' (the 36-year-old wife of a man with his own business).

Husbands' laziness and untidiness are also frequently commented on. 'Lazy; going out drinking and spending too much' (the 30-year-old wife of a driver, a pious Roman Catholic); 'Untidiness; dipping biscuits in tea; being late for meals or to take you out' (the 35-year-old wife of a self-employed building contractor); 'To live in a public house, never at home nights; lazy husbands, if they don't dig vegetable garden there'd be no vegetables; cruel to children and animals' (the 37-year-old wife of a herdsman); 'Watching T.V. too much – especially Saturdays; lack of enthusiasm re redecorating, etc.; lack of responsibility' (the 28-year-old wife of a tool-maker); 'Watch telly too much; some husbands should do more to help with the garden; I know of quite a few cases of unfaithfulness' (the 30-year-old wife of a printing operator); 'Just irritating ways, walking over clean carpets with dirty shoes, that sort of thing; not listening to his wife when she's talking; not being under-standing enough' (the 39-year-old wife of a railway foreman); 'Sleeping in his chair during day or evening; difficult to get up in the morning; having to be persuaded to have a bath and change underclothes' (the 27-year-old wife of a council gardener); 'As far as I am concerned he works too bloody hard and I don't get his company' (the 35-year-old wife of a service manager); 'Untidy, fussy with food if only children before marriage' (the 24-year-old wife of a naval electrician); 'Selfishness; they cannot stand pain – when they have a cold they are half dead; they never help in the house' (the 32-year-old wife of a gardener); 'To expect and rely on the wife to do everything for him as his mother did; a husband who goes out a lot on his own; laziness with jobs round the house' (the 41-year-old wife of a plumber).

Even when they are not kept in ignorance about a husband's earnings, many wives disapprove of the way the men deal with money. 'Too dominant; very selfish; spend their money too freely and thoughtless about the marriage' (the 22-year-old wife of a police constable); 'Stingy with money; not taking wives out enough; laziness in general' (the 28-year-old wife of a ware-house manager); 'Drinking too much; leaving wives alone too much and keeping their wives short of money' (the 45-year-old wife of a postman); 'Not giving enough money to cope; a man who lives at betting shops or pubs' (the 36-year-old wife of a self-employed builder); 'Selfishness; going out on their own;

mean with money' (the 20-year-old wife of an insurance agent); 'Unpunctuality for meals; meanness with money; going off and leaving their wives alone when they go out together for an evening' (the 36-year-old wife of a scrap-merchant); 'Too much interest in football or cricket; meanness; non-co-operative' (the 32-year-old wife of an electricity meter reader).

The old complaints of complacency and bad temper are still sometimes dwelt on; the 44-year-old wife of a dairy-worker complains: 'They are always right; some men tend to take things for granted; irritable first thing in the morning – it upsets the day'; 'They can natter if things don't go their way; the tea always has to be on the table or the question is asked "Why?" they think about themselves a lot and some are mean' (the 24-year-old wife of a filleter); 'If they're moody, drinking too much, selfish' (the 32-year-old wife of a metallurgist)*; 'Lack of patience; not always as helpful in the home as they should be; not listening enough to the wife's point of view' (the 26-year-old wife of a factory supervisor).

There is occasional criticism of the husband's inadequacies as a father. 'Not enough authority where the children are concerned' (the 33-year-old wife of a sheet-metal worker); 'Being selfish; not helping enough in the house: arguing in front of the children' (the 28-year-old wife of an ink-maker); 'Impatience with children; don't share everything, including money; don't like their wives to go out alone' (the 44-year-old wife of a clerical worker in the G.P.O.); 'Rather untidy; doesn't always understand how I treat the children; thinks I make too much of the children' (the 38-year-old wife of a bank clerk).

Very few wives made complaints with directly sexual overtones. Among the few who did was the 27-year-old wife of a municipal engineer: 'Away from home too much; expressing admiration of other women to wives; do not show the appreciation they may well feel for their wife and family'; 'Far too much eyes for other women; they forget you all grow old; they never seem to be contented – you never know what they want' (the 38-year-old wife of an air radio instructor); 'Smoking too much having girl friends; hitting wives and bad words' (the

* This informant remarked to the interviewer: 'I can never save.'

38-year-old wife of a labourer who was born in Jamaica and has been here eleven years).

The husbands who make complaints with sexual overtones are liable not to be above suspicion themselves. A 43-year-old garage owner said that wives 'talk too much; liable to be promiscuous; smoking in children's company' but admitted later in the interview that he had had more than three partners since his marriage. A similar admission was made by a 37-year-old holiday-camp assistant, who had been widowed and remarried, who complained that wives are 'too quick to notice what their husband does and get a wrong impression'. No similar admission was, however, made by a butchery manager, aged 36, who complained of wives 'making up to other men; a habit of going out on her own; indifferent to husband's needs; being out when he returns from work'.

Many men complained of women's extravagance. 'Moaning; can't get enough done; when you've paid your money up you're like a prisoner' (a 37-year-old painter and decorator); 'Gossip too much; too nosey; pre-judge people; too possessive; greedy for money, etc.; keeping up with the Joneses' (a 31-year-old solicitor's clerk); 'Too finicky, e.g. shopping; gossipy; don't enjoy themselves' (a 38-year-old tyre-builder); 'Too many clothes: expect too much in this day and age and more than is good for them, such as worldly goods' (the 42-year-old business manager of a car-hire firm, separated from his wife); 'Relying too much on mother's judgement; taking on too much hire purchase; smoke cigarettes, but perhaps deny their family necessities' (a 29-year-old lorry driver, a very observant Jehovah's Witness); 'Spending more money than they can afford – going out to work while they have young children, and not looking after her home' (a 41-year-old lorry driver, born in Ceylon).

Several husbands grumbled about their wives' stupidity, and even (it would appear) on occasion that they were women. 'They're just women – difficult to understand' (a 35-year-old technical manager); 'Leaving off top of toothpaste; so-called woman's intuition' (a 33-year-old driver); 'Negligence in reading instructions; lack of mechanical ability; insufficient breadth of interest' (a 36-year-old grammar-school master); 'In arguments they have to have the last word; not able to understand husbands at times' (a 28-year-old postman); 'Care-lessness about everything, house and family; ignorance, general' (a 37-year-old tailor, born in Cyprus); 'Tendency to repeat themselves in conversation; over-worrying about her husband; fussing and anxiety; shops uselessly, i.e. without any intent' (a 36-year-old architectural assistant).

These complaints shade into complaints about their wives' incompetence; 'Can't cook; no idea about housekeeping; no good at looking after children' (a 33-year-old self-employed taxi-driver); 'Poor mothers, bad housekeepers, inability to work together' (a 42-year-old postman); 'Do not stick to family work, do not do household jobs properly, are not religious minded; mix too much with other people which breaks up mat-rimonial life' (a 33-year-old anaesthetist, born in Pakistan); 'Not prepared to get up in the morning; family neglect; resis-tance to co-operate in sex' (a 45-year-old local government officer).

The traditional complaints that wives domineer or nag are voiced by quite a few husbands. 'Too domineering; they don't like men going out with their pals; they go out too much on their own' (a 34-year-old machine-tool fitter); 'Too domineering; always want more money; don't always do the things you want them to do' (a 22-year-old grocery assistant); 'Possessiveness; bad raging temper; too domineering' (a 23-year-old self-em-ployed painter and decorator); 'Domineering, selfish, always want to get more out of husband; think more of themselves than the household; spend too much on themselves' (a 35-year-old brewery worker); 'They nag too much; forget husband has to work hard for money' (a 32-year-old engineer); 'Nagging; I do not like to see women smoking' (a 38-year-old wages clerk); 'A woman who is a nagger; pressing for extra money for un-necessary things; failing to grow up with the children' (a 45-year-old lorry driver); 'They nag a lot, that's all, but they have usually got a good reason' (a 41-year-old plumber); 'Nagging, particularly husbands; wives tend to think about themselves too much and are not often willing to share his activities; pok-ing fun at the husband in public' (a 30-year-old school-teacher, a pious Pentecostal Nonconformist); 'One who makes a fool of their husband in public' (a 40-year-old builder's agent); 'They attach themselves to their mothers too strenuously; chatting about useless things and wanting to know other people's business; they make an awful fuss about their own ailments, although they are much tougher than men' (a 39-year-old self-employed chauffeur-courier).

iv

I do not think it is an unfair deduction to assume that the majority of our informants (I have only quoted a small, but I hope typical, sample) used the generalized questions about the chief faults that husbands or wives tend to have to make quite specific complaints about their own spouses. A few people rejected this opportunity, and I think their marriages can be interpreted as outstandingly successful.

Among these happy husbands is a 43-year-old slaughter-house manager, married for twenty-one years and with one child, who replied: 'My wife is a fine woman and I cannot honestly state any faults'; he named as the qualities a wife should have 'good housekeeper, good mother, a good nature' and clearly considered that his wife was described in these terms. A 32-year-old storekeeper said: 'As in my estimation my wife has no faults, I am unable to have any idea of the faults that wives have'; and a 38-year-old clerical assistant in local government: 'Tiny silly little things; my wife would be pleased to hear this, but I don't think she has any big faults, things that really matter'; a 38-year-old cemetery foreman answered 'too house-proud, over-zealous' and when the interviewer pressed for a third defect answered: 'No; I'm very happy'; a 43-year-old baker, a pious Jehovah's Witness, said: 'Nothing that really matters; hates sewing';* and a 32-year-old engineer, a moderately observant Roman Catholic: 'My wife doesn't have faults; don't know of any others.'†

* This informant named as the qualities a wife should have: 'Good mother and tolerant; loving and in subjection to her husband, providing the husband is not dictatorial.'
† This informant named as the qualities a wife should have: 'Must be feminine, mature, gentle and love me.' When asked what a husband should do if he found his wife having an affair with another man (see Chapter Eight) he replied: 'They say if love is strong enough it could be forgiven; I think I could forgive, but there wouldn't be the same sparkle as there was before.'

Examples of contented wives are the 23-year-old wife of a plumber who replied to the question about the faults of husbands: 'I can't say; I have no worries like that. I suppose some men aren't considerate to their wives; perhaps mean over money'; the 28-year-old wife of a building sub-contractor, born in Eire (as was her husband), an observant Roman Catholic: 'We get on so well, I can't think of any'; the 29-year-old wife of an automobile designer in the Midlands: 'I've not given much thought to this because I am happy myself; I feel these questions can only be answered by dissatisfied couples'; the 24-year-old wife of a warehouseman: 'I can't think of any; my husband is good to me and I don't take notice of other husbands; sometimes not talking at times when he is home from work can annoy me';* the 35-year-old wife of a painter and decorator: 'When you don't have these problems it's hard to say'; the 21-year-old wife of a work-study engineer: 'Too much work to do at work and brought home; I can't think of anything else';† the 40-year-old wife of an under-manager, a very observant member of the Salvation Army: 'I can't say: my husband hasn't got any faults; I don't know about other husbands';‡ the 26-year-old wife of an insurance clerk: 'Not talking to their wives enough; I don't know what else; my husband is perfect': the 23-year-old wife of a warp-knitter: 'My husband hasn't got any faults.' The same answer was given by the 37-year-old wife of a smelter, who was born in India and did not see her husband before her arranged marriage. Another Indian-born woman, the 24-

---

*This informant met her husband at a teen-age coffee bar; they married when she was twenty, and they have one child.

† This informant met her future husband at a swimming club when she was 14; they courted for six years without having intercourse; they now have it six times a week. When asked about what a husband or wife should do if they found their spouse having an affair with another, she replied: 'He ought to moan, but my husband couldn't care less; he wants me to be happy in all I'm doing; no, he wouldn't mind. [For a wife?] I'd go mad; I'd tell him so, but I know what he'd say. He wouldn't think much of it if I told the girl off; he'd tell me anyway, but I wouldn't like it.'

‡ This informant's answer to the question about what a wife should do if she found her husband having an affair with another woman was: 'I don't know; it doesn't apply to me; it wouldn't happen to me!' She and her husband had known each other all their lives, got married when she was nineteen and have five children.

year-old wife of an industrial engineer, said: 'I do not know how to answer this; I do not really know much about husbands and wives in this country; I cannot think what faults husbands have.'

Figures of Distribution

(Note: as in Chapter Three, I am treating a deviation of 3% from the national total as probably significant).

What can wreck a marriage and age

Those aged 16–20 emphasize infidelity (28%), conflicting personalities (18%) and bad temper (15%). They under-emphasize poverty (8%) and sexual incompatibility (5%). Five per cent say they don't know.

Those aged 21–24 do not emphasize any factor but under-emphasize selfishness (20%).

Those aged 25–34 are entirely on the average.

Those aged 35–45 emphasize selfishness (29%) and under-emphasize neglect (26%).

What can wreck a marriage and social class

The middle class emphasize selfishness (30%) and under-emphasize infidelity (22%).

The lower middle class emphasize conflicting personalities (30%) and sexual incompatibility (13%).

The skilled working class emphasize infidelity (28%) and under-emphasize selfishness (22%).

The upper working class emphasize selfishness (28%), conflicting personalities (17%) and lack of trust (10%); they under-emphasize neglect (26%) and poverty (14%).

The working class emphasize infidelity (29%) and under-emphasize selfishness (20%).

Those who will not place themselves in a social class emphasize bad temper (15%) and sexual incompatibility (13%); they under-emphasize neglect (27%), selfishness (20%), and lack of trust (3%); 5% of this group did not answer the question.

What can wreck a marriage and the Registrar General's categories

AB emphasize selfishness (35%) and sexual incompatibility (13%); they under-emphasize neglect (27%), infidelity (20%), bad temper (5%) and drunkenness (4%).

C1 emphasize selfishness (30%), conflicting personalities (15%) and lack of affection (10%); they under-emphasize neglect (26%).

C2 is entirely on average.*

DE emphasize infidelity (29%) and drunkenness (10%); they under-emphasize selfishness (20%).

What can wreck a marriage and the regions

The North-East and North under-emphasize neglect (26%), infidelity (22%) and selfishness (21%).

The Midlands under-emphasize poverty (14%) and sexual incompatibility (6%).

The South-East emphasize poverty (22%) and sexual incompatibility (14%).

The South-West emphasize infidelity (37%), neglect (36%), conflicting personalities (15%), drunkenness (11%), no house of one's own and in-laws (8%). They under-emphasize selfishness (18%).

The North-West emphasize selfishness (34%) and lack of trust (9%); they under-emphasize infidelity (22%), poverty (9%), bad temper (6%), sexual incompatibility (4%) and lack of affection (3%).

Domestic financial arrangements and attitudes towards different aspects of marriage.

Husbands who 'give' a housekeeping allowance consider the most important factor making for a happy marriage children (19%); they under-emphasize love (16%). The most

---

* It will be recalled that this category was also entirely on the average in their views of what made for a happy marriage – see Chapter Three, pp. 78, 80. In our population of the younger English married people, C2, the skilled manual working class aged between 25 and 34 would seem to set the pattern of the hopes and fears concerning marriage today.

important factor tending to wreck a marriage is sexual incompatibility (13%); they under-emphasize conflicting personalities (8%). In considering the desirable qualities in a wife they emphasize economical (8%), personal qualities (26%), good mother (38%), good housekeeper (39%) and good cook (13%); they under-emphasize love (22%), understanding (21%), fairness (3%), generosity (2%) and thoughtfulness (1%). When considering the faults of a wife they emphasize extravagance (29%), gossip (11%), bad housekeeper (16%) and bad mother (10%); they under-emphasize lack of intelligence (3%) and too house-proud (1%).

Wives who receive a housekeeping allowance consider the most important factors making for a happy marriage give-and-take (32%) and comradeship (32%); they under-emphasize love (16%) and children (11%). The most important factors tending to wreck a marriage are neglect (36%), and poverty (20%); they under-emphasize selfishness (21%). In considering the desirable qualities in a husband, they emphasize understanding (54%), generosity (21%), fairness (9%), love (44%), sense of humour (18%), good temper (15%), thoughtfulness (11%) and love of home (16%). When considering the faults of a husband they emphasize meanness with money (20%), bad temper (11%), untidiness (11%) and nagging (9%); they under-emphasize the husband going out on his own (21%) drinking (21%) and taking the wife for granted (18%).

Husbands who hand over their whole pay-packet and get some back consider the most important factors making for a happy marriage comradeship (32%), children (20%) and a happy home life (9%). The factor tending to wreck a marriage is infidelity (29%); they under-emphasize conflicting personalities (8%). In considering the desirable qualities of a wife, they emphasize good housekeeper (52%), good mother (38%), good cook (13%), personal qualities (26%) and love of home (22%). When considering the faults of a wife they emphasize moral faults (9%), being over-anxious (8%), being a bad housekeeper (17%) and a bad mother (10%); they under-emphasize nagging (28%), domineering (12%) and lack of intelligence (1%); they do not mention bad temper or childishness.

Wives who receive the whole pay-packet and give some back consider an important factor in a happy marriage is comradeship (34%); they under-emphasize give-and-take (24%) and sexual compatibility (2%). As factors wrecking a marriage they under-emphasize neglect (25%), quarrelling (6%), sexual incompatibility (5%) and lack of affection (3%). The only quality in a husband that they emphasize is that he should be a good worker (10%). When considering the faults of a husband they emphasize selfishness (43%), laziness (19%), untidiness (14%) and extravagance (7%); they under-emphasize domineering (11%) and complacency (1%).

Husbands with a joint bank account consider important factors making for a happy marriage comradeship (34%) and financial security (11%); they under-emphasize give-and-take (23%). Factors tending to wreck a marriage are selfishness (32%), poverty (20%), infidelity (32%), sexual incompatibility (13%) and lack of affection (10%); they under-emphasize neglect (21%), drunkenness (4%) and bad temper (7%). When considering the qualities of a wife they emphasize personal qualities (25%), patience (19%) and sharing responsibilities (12%); they under-emphasize sense of humour (12%) and economical (1%). In considering the faults of wives they emphasize moral faults (8%) and being a bad housekeeper (17%); they under-emphasize nagging (30%), bad temper (4%), jealousy (3%) and being too house-proud (2%).

Wives with a joint bank account consider important factors in a happy marriage give-and-take (39%), discussing things together (34%) and shared interests (16%); they under-emphasize mutual trust (16%) and children (7%). They emphasize the factors tending to wreck a marriage of selfishness (35%) and poverty (23%); they under-emphasize neglect (25%) and infidelity (21%). When considering the qualities of a husband, they emphasize understanding (53%), love (40%), sense of humour (25%), patience (20%) and love of home (13%); they under-emphasize being economical (1%). In considering the faults of husbands they emphasize laziness (19%) and untidyness (10%); they under-emphasize drinking and gambling (15%) and lack of intelligence (1%).

Faults of a husband and age

Those aged 16–20 emphasize taking the wife for granted (26%), and jealousy (8%) and under-emphasize untidiness (2%). Fifteen per cent of this age-group didn't know the answer.

Those aged 21–24 emphasize the husband going out on his own (27%) and under-emphasize mean with money (12%) and being a bad father (5%). They too have 15% not answering.

Those aged 25–34 emphasize laziness and sleepiness (19%).

Those aged 34–45 are on the average.

Faults of a wife and age

Those aged 16–20 emphasize the wife being domineering and bossy (26%) taking the husband for granted (16%) and jealousy (11%); they under-emphasize nagging (35%), extravagance (20%), selfishness (13%), bad housekeeper (5%), going out on her own (3%), drink (2%) and moral faults (1%). They have 25% saying they do not know the answer.*

Those aged 21–24 emphasize nagging (45%) and letting herself go (14%) and under-emphasize extravagance (20%) and being a bad housekeeper (8%)

Those aged 25–35 emphasize nagging (44%) and extravagance (28%).

Those aged 35–45 emphasize selfishness (19%) and being a bad housekeeper (14%).

Faults of a husband and social class

The middle class emphasize selfishness (42%) and taking the wife for granted (25%) and under-emphasize drinking and gambling (19%).

The lower middle class emphasize selfishness (46%) and under-emphasize drinking and gambling (19%).

They have 9% don't knows.

*It is worth noting the difference of 'don't knows' in the questions about the faults of husbands and wives, which suggest that English young women envisage marriage more realistically than do young men of the same age.

The skilled working class emphasize drinking and gambling (31%) and untidiness (10%) and under-emphasize selfishness (35%).

The upper working class emphasize taking the wife for granted (26%) going out on his own (31%), laziness (23%), domineering (16%), being a bad father (15%) and extravagance (9%); they under-emphasize drinking and gambling (23%), mean with money (10%) and bad temper (5%).

The working class emphasize drinking and gambling (34%) and under-emphasize selfishness (35%) and taking the wife for granted (17%).

Those who will not place themselves socially emphasize drinking and gambling (34%) and jealousy (8%); they under-emphasize selfishness (35%) going out on his own (16%), taking the wife for granted (15%), mean with money (11%), lazy (11%), untidiness (4%) and complacency (1%).

Faults of a wife and social class

The middle class emphasize nagging (44%) and domineering (21%); 13% say they do not know.

The lower middle class emphasize domineering and bossiness (24%), taking their husbands for granted (11%) and jealousy (10%); they under-emphasize that she goes out on her own (3%) or is untidy (1%).

The skilled working class emphasize letting herself go (15%) and untidiness (10%); they under-emphasize extravagance (22%).

The upper working class emphasize bad housekeeper (22%), letting herself go (17%), bad mother (10%) and bad temper (10%); they under-emphasize nagging (36%), domineering (14%), gossip (5%), going out on her own (4%) and jealousy (3%).

The working class emphasize extravagance (30%); they under-emphasize selfishness (13%) and domineering (15%); 20% say they do not know.

Those who will not place themselves socially under-emphasize nagging (36%), extravagance (19%), selfishness (10%), domineering (11%), letting herself go (8%) and being a bad housekeeper (8%).

Faults of a husband and the Registrar General's categories

AB emphasize selfishness (51%) and domineering (15%); they under-emphasize going out on his own (19%), drinking and gambling (12%) and laziness (12%).

C1 emphasize selfishness (47%), taking the wife for granted (29%) and domineering (17%); they under-emphasize drinking and gambling (19%).

C2 emphasize drinking and gambling (29%).

DE emphasize drinking and gambling (35%) and going out on his own (31%); they under-emphasize selfishness (29%) and taking the wife for granted (14%).

Faults of a wife and the Registrar General's categories

AB emphasize domineering (22%), selfishness (21%), childishness and fussiness (21%), lack of intelligence (8%) and being overanxious (8%); they under-emphasize being a bad housekeeper (8%), gossip (5%), going out on her own (3%) and drinking (1%).

C1 emphasize selfishness (19%) and have 14% saying they don't know.

C2 is on the average.

DE emphasize extravagance (28%) and gossip (11%); they under-emphasize domineering (15%) and selfishness (10%); they have 21% saying they don't know.

Faults of a husband and the regions

The North-East and North under-emphasize selfishness (34%), taking the wife for granted (18%), mean with money (11%), lazy and sleepy (12%), domineering (8%) and untidy (4%); they have 18% don't knows.

The Midlands emphasize gossip (28%) and under-emphasize selfishness (34%), taking the wife for granted (16%) and mean with money (12%).

The South-East emphasize selfishness (42%) and taking the wife for granted (24%); they under-emphasize drinking and gambling (21%).

The South-West emphasize drinking and gambling (35%), going out on his own (29%), laziness (21%), bad temper (11%), moral faults (11%), untidiness (11%), jealousy (8%) and complacency (7%); they under-emphasize selfishness (33%); they have 8% don't knows.

The North-West emphasize selfishness (50%), drinking and gambling (32%), domineering (16%), letting himself go (11%) and untidiness (10%); they under-emphasize bad temper (5%) and moral faults (3%); they have only 3% don't knows.

Faults of a wife and the regions

The North-East and North emphasize gossip (14%); they under-emphasize nagging (37%), letting herself go (6%), bad housekeeper (6%) and going out on her own (4%); they have 18% don't knows.

The Midlands emphasize bad temper (11%) and taking the husband for granted (10%); they under-emphasize nagging (37%) and letting herself go (8%).

The South-East emphasize nagging (47%).

The South-West emphasize nagging (49%), extravagance (36%), going out on her own (13%), jealousy (12%), bad temper (11%), gossip (11%) and laziness (8%); they under-emphasize domineering (11%) and selfishness (10%); they have 11% don't knows.

The North-West emphasize selfishness (29%), domineering (24%), letting herself go (19%), bad housekeeper (18%), bad mother (10%), laziness (10%), over-anxious (9%) and untidy (7%); they under-emphasize extravagance (20%), gossip (5%), too houseproud (2%) and frigid (2%); they have 9% don't knows.

Tables 30–35

5 *Sex in marriage*

i

Sixty-five per cent of our male informants and 67% of the female consider sexual love very important in marriage; 32% of the men and 28% of the women consider it fairly important; tiny groups – 2% of the men and 4% of the women – consider it not very important and 1% of both sexes consider it not at all important.

Twenty years ago* 58% of the men and 51% of the women thought sexual love very important, 35% of the men and 39% of the women fairly important; and 5% of the men and 6% of the women not very important; in that survey too there were the anomalous 1% of both sexes who stated that it was not at all important.

Besides the differences in absolute percentages, what strikes me as suggestive is the changed position of the two sexes during the last twenty years; in 1950 7% more men than women thought sexual love very important, in 1969 2% more women than men; in 1950 there were 4% more women than men opting for the tepid choice of 'fairly important', in 1969 4% more men. Since the two samples are not strictly comparable, not too much can be read into these figures; but they do seem to add confirmation to the changing view of female sexuality and woman's 'natural' behaviour, which will be documented in section iv of the present chapter.

Only 4% of our married sample refused to answer the question 'About how often do you have intercourse?'; the remainder answered very precisely indeed. Unfortunately, there was some confusion about the questioning of the unmarried; earlier

* *Exploring English Character*, p. 94, Table 48.

ii

Table seven

Rates of intercourse of younger English married couples

In the first, third and fourth columns the total include the 37% of our unmarried respondents (roughly 200 out of 590) who answered this question: see also Table Eighteen, Chapter Ten.

Rates of intercourse	Total percentage	Percentage married respondents	Men	Women	Absolute numbers
Daily or more often	1%	2%	1%	2%	25
6 times a week	—	1%	1%	1%	11
5–6 times a week	—	—	1%	0%	7
5 times a week	1%	1%	1%	0%	15
4–5 times a week	1%	2%	1%	2%	26
4 times a week	2%	3%	3%	2%	40
3–4 times a week	5%	6%	4%	5%	84
3 times a week	7%	10%	8%	7%	152
2–3 times a week	6%	9%	6%	8%	140
Twice a week	14%	20%	16%	16%	307
Once or twice a week	6%	7%	5%	8%	110
Once a week	14%	19%	15%	16%	295
2 or 3 times a month	5%	6%	6%	5%	198
Less often	8%	7%	8%	7%	97
Not consistent	5%	4%	8%	7%	48
Never	9%	1%	8%	5%	13
Refused	5%	4%	5%	4%	47
Not asked	11%	—	—	—	—

in the interview every informant had been asked at what age they first had sexual intercourse;* of those who denied ever having had intercourse, some were questioned again by the interviewers and others were not; these latter account for nearly all the 11 % not asked. The tables, of course, include the unmarried (and the 43 individuals who were divorced, separated or widowed) which explains the difference between column one (total percentage) in table Seven and column two (percentage of married respondents); the tables from which the analyses in the following pages are made are based on these total 'weighted' figures; but those replying 'never' and those not asked are excluded from all the calculations.

To the best of my knowledge, there is no comparable analysis of marital intercourse of a whole national population, scientifically sampled, for any other society; and what I think is worth calling attention to is the very close correspondence between the figures given by men and those given by women. Since heterosexual intercourse involves both sexes, the answers given by a random sample should coincide or very nearly; since this has in fact occurred, there is a very strong suggestion that the answers are reliable. There does not appear to be any conspicuous male phallic boasting, which one cannot avoid suspecting in some other groups of figures.

It will also be noticed that there is a very wide range of answers given by our informants about their contemporary rates of marital intercourse. Their actual phrasings were used and coded. For purposes of analysis I found it convenient to divide people into three groups: those with a high rate of intercourse of three times a week or over, representing 24 % of the married population (20 % of the total population having intercourse); those with a medium rate of more than once a week but less than three times a week, representing 36 % of the married population (39 % of the total population having intercourse); and those with a low rate of once a week or less, representing 37 % of the married population (30 % of the total population having intercourse). The actual median for married English men and women aged between 16 and 45 is two acts of intercourse a week (between one and two acts of intercourse when the unmarried who are having intercourse are included);

* See Chapter Two, pp. 31–33.

the groups indicating once or twice a week, twice a week or two to three times a week are very close to the national median.

Analysis by age and social class gives very little further information about these variations in the frequency of sexual activity. There is a slight tendency for the high rates to be more frequent between the ages of 21 and 34, and for the low rates to be in the youngest and oldest groups, but there are so many exceptions in both directions that the difference is questionably significant. There is a similar slight tendency for high rates to be more frequent in the skilled working class and upper working class. All the evidence suggests that the differences in frequency of intercourse have a genetic, physiological basis, possibly combined with differing social circumstances.

This research completely fails to bear out the generalization made by Kinsey and his associates* that sexual activity declines consistently from adolescence onwards and that the young are inevitably more potent than their elders. It should of course be borne in mind that Kinsey was eliciting reminiscences from his volunteer informants and we were asking about current behaviour from our randomly selected sample of informants; that Kinsey was dealing with all 'outlets' (masturbation being statistically the most important) and we exclusively with heterosexual intercourse, and almost entirely with marital intercourse; but if age were a determinant of the level of sexual activity, one would have expected the analysis of our sample by age to demonstrate this. It signally fails to do so.

By cross-correlations within the limits of the information provided by the questionnaire we attempted to determine what factors were correlated with high and low frequencies of intercourse. Much the most convincing of these is that with the age of adolescence, the earlier the adolescence the higher the rate of sexual activity.†

Our women informants were asked: 'At what age did you become physically a woman?'; and only 1% of the women did not give a precise answer. Men were asked: 'At what age did you become sexually a man?'; 2% of the men refused to answer this

---

* *Sexual Behavior in the Human Male*, by Kinsey, Pomeroy and Martin (Saunders and Co., 1948) Chapter 7, pp. 218–62, 'Age and Sexual Outlet'. Marital intercourse is dealt with on pp. 253–7.
† This finding is in agreement with Kinsey, *op. cit.*, pp. 303–8.

question and 5% said they did not know. The remainder gave precise answers, and although we are only dealing with re-collections, there is a marked congruence between the answers of our informants and the findings of Dr J. M. Tanner and his associates based on physical measurements and observation.*

Very briefly, 1% of the men and 2% of the women named some age under 11; 6% of the men and 32% of the women said they had become physically mature under the age of 13; a further 34% of the men and 40% of the women between the ages of 13 and 14 years 11 months; 30% of the men and 17% of the women between the ages of 15 and 16 years 11 months; 14% of the men and 5% of the women between the ages of 17 and 18 years 11 months; 9% of the men and 5% of the women named some age over 19.

The late figures appear somewhat ambiguous; there may have been some confusion in our informants' minds between the attainment of physical maturity and the experiencing of hetero-sexual intercourse, or maybe the fallibility of memory accounts for the somewhat improbable replies. It was above all our oldest age-group, those aged between 35 and 45, who named the later ages; in this group there were 10% who named some age over 19 (and none who named some age before 11), com-pared with 5% or 6% of their juniors.

At the age of 15, the present legal school-leaving age, 40% of the men and 72% of the women stated they had reached puberty; this represents 61% of those aged between 16 and 24; 58% of those aged between 25 and 34; and 49% of those aged between 35 and 45. Forty-nine per cent of the men and 27% of the women named some age over 15; this represents 33% of those aged between 16 and 20; 34% of those aged between 21 and 24; 36% of those aged between 25 and 34; and 44% of those aged between 35 and 45. These figures do seem to confirm Dr Tanner's findings of a continual shift towards earlier puberty; with the rather large age-groups which we are using the break appears to come between those under and those over the age of 35; those who reached puberty after the end of World War Two did so earlier than their seniors.

The age of puberty also seems to be correlated with

* See *Education and Physical Growth* (University of London Press, 1961) and *Growth at Adolescence* (Blackwell, Oxford, 1962) by J. M. Tanner.

I

self-ascribed social class; of those who stated they had reached puberty before they were 15 years old, 56% said they were lower middle class, 50% middle, 47% skilled working, and 44% upper working and working classes. Of those who named some age over 17, 17% said they were working class and skilled working, 16% middle, 15% upper working and 13% lower middle.

Table eight
Age of puberty and frequency of intercourse

Age at puberty	Low rates of intercourse – once a week and under (omitting 'not consistent'). 27% of total	High rates of intercourse; three times a week and over. 18% of total
Under 11	10%	49%
11–11.11	17%	26%
12–12.11	22%	18%
13–13.11	25%	17%
14–14.11	28%	17%
15–15.11	30%	17%
16–16.11	26%	16%
17–17.11	30%	23%
18–18.11	43%	10%
Over 19	43%	12%

Table Eight correlates the age of puberty with frequency of intercourse; and, as can be seen, there is a tendency for those who reached puberty before the age of 14 to have high rates of intercourse and for those who reached it after the age of 17.11 to have low rates. Although early puberty and greater sexual potency seem to be correlated, there are no clear correlations between early puberty and promiscuity either before or after marriage; but there does seem to be a tendency for those who reach puberty early to marry early.

We further correlated frequency of intercourse with school-leaving age and current income. Table Nine demonstrates

Table nine

Age of school-leaving and frequency of intercourse

Age of school-leaving	Low rates of intercourse – once a week and under (27%)	High rates of intercourse – three times a week and over (18%)
14	44%	11%
15	28%	25%
16	23%	17%
17	19%	28%
(18)	(12%)	(24%)

There are so few who left school over the age of 17 that the percentages are not very meaningful.

the tendency for high rates of intercourse to be correlated with education prolonged beyond the legal minimum; but the picture is somewhat confused by the fact that those who left school at fourteen are necessarily the older group of informants.

As far as current income is concerned, the high rates of intercourse seem to be concentrated among the relatively prosperous, with incomes between £1,300 and £2,600 a year, and are infrequent among those with low incomes of £520 a year or less or over £2,600. Here, again, interpretation is complicated by the fact that the low incomes are mostly those of people under 20 and the high incomes those of people over 35.

With all these provisos, it would still appear justifiable to state that there is a tendency for high rates of marital intercourse to be correlated with early puberty, education prolonged beyond the minimum, and moderate financial prosperity. Those who leave school at the minimum legal age and who classify themselves as working class (DE in the Registrar General's category) have the greatest proportion of people leading a varied sex-life,* with more partners outside marriage, but they would not appear to have a more active one within marriage. The myth that the working class is more sexually potent than the middle classes, which has been upheld by quite

* See Chapter Two, p. 31, and Chapter Six, p. 159.

a few novelists (mostly of middle-class origin) and informs some contemporary radical propaganda, would not seem to have any factual basis.

iii

Immediately after the question about frequency of intercourse, our informants were asked: 'Do you think this is about average for people like yourself? Or more? Or less than average?'; and I find it interesting and revealing that whatever their actual rate of intercourse, down to once weekly, at least three-quarters of our informants consider themselves average. Only when the frequency drops to two or three times a month or less often, do a majority of informants think they are below average; but the lowest figure for any group, no matter how seldom they have intercourse, is 39% considering themselves average.

There is little consistency in the views of those who think their performance departs from the average. Ten per cent of those with high rates of three times a week or more consider themselves below average; 8% of those who have intercourse once a week or less frequently consider themselves above the average.

This belief in one's own averageness can be interpreted as a sign of mental health; it would suggest that the younger married people in England are not tormented by neurotic fears of sexual inadequacy which would seem to be widespread in some other societies. Alternatively, it can be interpreted as a sign of smugness or self-satisfaction; very few of our informants, certainly less than one per cent of those answering this question, replied that they had not enough information, which was the only possible accurate reply. The majority would appear to be completely sure that they are representative of the norm, without any intellectual curiosity and with few doubts; two thirds of our informants seem prepared to embody that legal fiction, the man or woman 'on the Clapham omnibus' whose values are so frequently invoked by judges in legal cases dealing with implied sexual misbehaviour.

To illustrate the wide gamut in the belief in one's averageness I will cite a few informants from both ends of the scale who consider their sexual lives average: the wife of a bus conductor, aged 20½, married for two years, who has intercourse about twice a day; a 22-year-old electrician's mate, who started intercourse at 16 and married his first partner and has intercourse daily; a 27-year-old painter and decorator who has intercourse six times a week; the 22-year-old wife of a computer engineer who has intercourse six or seven times a week; a 20-year-old painter, who had a very active sex-life after the age of 19, and has been married six months, has intercourse daily; a 32-year-old barber, born in Jamaica, who has intercourse daily; a 24-year-old woman, whose marriage lasted six months and is now divorced, had intercourse twice daily while she was married. In contrast, a 39-year-old skilled upholsterer who did not have intercourse before his marriage at the age of 36, and now has it three or four times a month; the 27-year-old wife of a factory worker, virgin at her marriage, who now has intercourse once a month; the 45-year-old wife of an engineer has intercourse 'once in three weeks – too busy'; a 45-year-old fitter welder, born in British Guyana, once a month; a 45-year-old chief cashier 'hardly ever'; a 37-year-old holiday-camp assistant has intercourse 'six or eight times a month; it goes in cycles; miss two or three weeks then three or four nights in a row'; the list could easily be continued.

The majority of those who think their performance more than average do so with some justification: for example, a 37-year-old painter and decorator, a pious Roman Catholic, who has intercourse nightly; a 35-year-old commercial designer, who developed an interest in girls at 14 and started intercourse at 16 and still has intercourse nightly; the 21-year-old wife of a senior engineer, who was virgin at marriage and now has intercourse six times a week; the 23-year-old wife of a craftsman in the armed forces has intercourse six or seven times a week;* the 39-year-old wife of a technical representative, a pious Roman Catholic who uses the rhythm method of birth control, has intercourse 'within the safe period as much as we desire it; for the ten or twelve days of the safe period, perhaps every day then'; but on the other hand the 41-year-old wife of a welder,

* This informant thinks sex 'not very important' in marriage; she had one partner before betrothal.

who has intercourse once a fortnight also thinks this is more than average.*

Quite a few marriages appear to be nearly sexless; it is above all the wives who reveal this. The 41-year-old wife of a railway clerk answered: 'Seldom, if I am honest'; the 33-year-old wife of a company director, born in Eire: 'once in a blue moon – really, almost never'; the 39-year-old wife of a representative said that four years after she was married she had to see a psychologist and has intercourse 'once a month, I should think, now'†; the 38-year-old wife of an insurance clerk, whose nineteen years of marriage have been childless, answered 'never'.

It is above all the wives, too, who reveal the use of sexual intercourse as a weapon in a bad marriage. The 41-year-old wife of a long-distance driver answered: 'Never, if I can help it; about twice a month against my will'; the 34-year-old wife of a station-master: 'Now not for about three months, owing to the present situation of a strained marriage'; the 22-year-old wife of a labourer: 'Off and on – depends if we quarrel or not'; the 35-year-old wife of a service manager: 'When I'm lucky, about once a week': the 45-year-old wife of a skilled engineer: 'Not very often if I have my way.'

Finally, one example of the very few respondents who said he did not know whether he was average or no. This is a 43-year-old office manager who first had intercourse when he married at the age of 25, and first replied: 'I prefer to let my wife decide'; when the interviewer pressed for a more precise answer, he said two or three times a month.

iv

In an attempt to ascertain whether there had been any change in the views about female sexuality in the last twenty years, we repeated a question from *Exploring English Character* in which informants were presented with a choice of four statements about 'most women' and were asked to choose the one with which they most agreed and the one with which they most disagreed. The four statements were: 'Most women don't care much about the physical side of sex'; 'Most women don't

---

* This informant said that she was assaulted when she was 17, but did not willingly have intercourse until marriage at the age of 26.
† This informant thinks sex 'not at all important' in marriage.

have such an animal nature as men'; 'Most women enjoy the physical side of sex as much as men'; 'Most women enjoy sex more than men'. This, however, seems a difficult type of question to answer; whether informants are filling in a form themselves or are presented with a card by the interviewer, a considerable number appear to find it impossible to restrict themselves to a single choice.

Table ten

	Most agree with				*Most disagree with*			
	1969		1950		1969		1950	
	Men	*Women*	*Men*	*Women*	*Men*	*Women*	*Men*	*Women*
Most women don't care much about the physical side of sex	7%	18%	16%	26%	50%	34%	55%	39%
Most women don't have such an animal nature as men	25%	29%	38%	48%	14%	18%	21%	13%
Most women enjoy the physical side of sex as much as men	56%	54%	63%	51%	4%	7%	10%	8%
Most women enjoy sex more than men	7%	4%	15%	4%	27%	48%	39%	57%

In both surveys figures add up to more than 100%, as informants appear unable to restrict themselves to the choice of a single sentence.

As Table Ten shows, there has been very little change in the overall pattern over the years. Then, as now, men tended to emphasize women's physical enjoyment of sex more than do women, and women woman's more 'spiritual' nature than do men; and the repudiations follow a similar pattern. Roughly half the population consider that the enjoyment of men and women is similar; a very small proportion (and that more male than female) believe that women enjoy sex more than men, and women repudiate this notion most emphatically; and nearly half the women and a third of the men claim that women are more 'spiritual' and with a less 'animal' nature.

However, if one breaks down the answers in the present survey by age, it does appear that there has been a real change in the estimation of female sexuality among those born since the end of World War Two. Thus, approval of the two statements claiming that women are more 'spiritual' is voiced by 33% of those aged between 16 and 24, 38% of those aged between 25 and 34 and 47% of those aged 35 and 45. Disagreement with the two sentences that women enjoy sex as much as, or more than, men was voiced by 37% of those aged 16–20, 34% of those aged 21–24, 46% of those aged 25–34 and 50% of those aged 35–45. The statement that most women enjoy the physical side of sex as much as men was approved by 57% of those aged 16–20, 59% of those aged 21–24, 58% of those aged 25–34 and 51% of those aged 35–45.

Socially, the belief in woman's more 'spiritual' nature is held most strongly by those considering themselves lower middle class and least by those considering themselves upper working and skilled working class. These two latter classes are much more certain that women enjoy sex just as much as men than are the members of the other social classes, including those who call themselves working class without modification.

In 1950, I was not allowed to ask a concrete question about female orgasm* because the editors thought that it might cause unnecessary offence, and would anyhow be too embarrassing for the young women coding the questionnaires! With the great diminishment in verbal prudery in the intervening twenty years, no objection was ever raised about asking a question on this topic but the wording was found to be difficult. Pilot interviews showed that the word 'orgasm' was not recognized by quite a number of the people questioned; and eventually we settled on the rather cumbrous but explicit phrasing: 'When a man and woman are making love, do you think that women have a real physical climax to the act of love-making in the same way as men?'

Eleven per cent of the men and 14% of the women said that

* See *Exploring English Character*, p. 26 and footnote 13, p. 33.

they did not know the answer to this question;* 77 % of the men and 59% of the women answered in the affirmative and 11 % of the men and 26% of the women in the negative. The very marked contrasts in the beliefs of men and women about female orgasm seem to me noteworthy. It is predominantly male doctors, psychologists and other researchers into the human sexual response who have stressed the importance of orgasm for female sexual satisfaction; there is quite a lot of evidence to suggest that this is a cultural construct, not basically founded on the imperatives of female anatomy;† and the figures just cited suggest that it is more important for men than for women to believe in female orgasms in England.

The positive answer is very evenly distributed among the different age-groups, except that 31 % of those aged between 16 and 20 said that they did not know; but the negative answer, that women do not have a climax, has a distribution analogous to that disclosed in the choice of questions about female sexuality; 9% of those aged between 16 and 20, 16% of those aged between 21 and 24, 23 % of those aged between 25 and 34, and 22 % of those aged between 35 and 45. Once again, the change in the attitude to female sexuality seems most marked in those born after the end of World War Two.

Socially, those calling themselves middle class or working class without modification have fewer believers in female orgasm than members of the intervening classes; and the middle class has the highest percentage (23 %) answering in the negative; the upper working and working classes have a higher percentage of 'don't knows'.‡ Regionally, the two Southern regions have a markedly higher proportion of positive answers than the rest of the country.

Those who said that a woman has a 'real physical climax' were asked if this were true of all women, of most women or of some women; and here, once again, the responses of the two

* These total percentages include the unmarried.
† See *Male and Female*, by Margaret Mead, pp. 216–19.
‡ This is one of the situations where there is a marked contrast between self-classification by social class and the Registrar General's categories (see figures of distribution at the end of this chapter). In the Registrar General's categories it is the DE group which has the lowest percentage of positive answers and the highest percentage of negative. I cannot find a plausible explanation for this discrepancy.

sexes are revealingly contrasting. Thirteen per cent of the men*
and 2 % of the women chose the answer 'all women', 45 % of the
men and 31 % of the women chose 'most women'; and 18 % of
the men and 27 % of the women chose 'some women'. These
figures would seem to confirm the hypothesis that men have the
greater psychological need to believe in female orgasm.

Apart from the young and inexperienced, age seems to make
little difference to these replies; the older respondents chose
'some' more and 'most' less than their juniors, but the differences
are questionably significant statistically. Nor is there much
variance by social class; the skilled working class has the highest
proportion choosing 'all' and the upper working and working
classes the highest proportion choosing 'most'; the middle class
has the lowest proportion choosing 'all' and the lower middle
class the lowest choosing 'most', but in all cases it is only a
difference of 3 % or 4 % from the total. The two Western regions have the highest proportions of those choosing 'most',
the South-East the highest proportion choosing 'some'.

A few women corrected the phrasing of the question. Thus,
the 26-year-old wife of a factory supervisor:† 'Yes, but not always,
even in one woman'; the 23-year-old wife of a self-employed
builder, who had several partners before her marriage: 'No,
not as often as men'; the 33-year-old wife of a charge-hand: 'No:
some might do, not always like men.' The 41-year-old wife of
a senior sales executive, who was born in Eire and goes to daily
Mass, replied: 'Yes, I really don't know about other people; I
don't discuss the subject.'

Most of the people with very high rates of marital intercourse
(five times a week or more frequently) believe that women do
have orgasms; but some of the men who have had a very varied
sex-life, with numerous partners both before and after marriage,
do not.‡ A few wives, whose marriages would appear to be not
very satisfactory, answered 'don't know' to this question.

* Among the most positive were young unmarried men without any
heterosexual experience.
† This informant has been trying to conceive for the last twelve months
before the interview.
‡ This latter observation should not be considered a generalization. I
was surprised by about five men who said they had had more than three
partners before marriage and several after and denied that any women
had physical climaxes.

Figures of distribution

How important do you think sexual love is in marriage?

By age 16–20: very important 59 %, fairly important 34 %; not very important 4 %, not at all important 1 %.

21–24: very important 72 %; fairly important 25 %, not very important 2 %; not at all important 1 %.

25–34: very important 65 %; fairly important 32 %; not very important 3 %; not at all important 0 %.

35–45; very important 65 %; fairly important 30 %; not very important 3 %; not at all important 1 %.

By self-ascribed social class Middle class: very important 66 %; fairly important 30 %; not very important 3 %; not at all important 0 %.

Lower middle class: very important 69 %; fairly important 28 %; not very important 5 %; not at all important 0 %.

Skilled working class: very important 69 %; fairly important 28 %; not very important 3 %; not at all important 0 %.

Upper working class: very important 66 %, fairly important 31 %; not very important 1 %; not at all important 2 %.

Working class: very important 64 %; fairly important 31 %; not very important 4 %; not at all important 1 %.

'Blank': very important 64 %; fairly important 29 %; not very important 3 %; not at all important 1 %.

At what age did you become physically a woman? At what age did you become sexually a man?

By age 16–20: under 14.11 60 %; 15–16.11 37 %; over 17 4 %.

21–24: under 14.11 48 %; 15–16.11 38 %; over 17 12 %.

25–34: under 14.11 43 % 15–16.11 37 %; over 17 23 %.

35–44: under 14.11 32 %; 15–16.11 36 %; over 17 31 %.

By self-ascribed social class Middle: under 14.11 43 %; 15–16.11 33 %; over 17 23 %.
Lower middle: under 14.11 42 %; 15–16.11 39 %; over 17 18 %.

Skilled working: under 14.11 43%; 15–16.11 36%; over 17 20%.

Upper working: under 14.11 42%; 15–16.11 37%; over 17 23%.

Working: under 14.11 40%; 15–16.11 40%; over 17 21%.

Blank: under 14.11 38%; 15–16.11 33%; over 17 26%.

When a man and woman are making love, do you think that women have a real physical climax to the act of love-making in the same way as men?

By age 16–20: Yes 58%; No 9%; D/K 31%

21–24: Yes 68%; No 16%; D/K 16%.

25–34; Yes 71%; No 23%; D/K 5%.

35–45: Yes 70%; No 22% D/K 7%.

By social class Middle: Yes 66%; No 23%; D/K 10%.

Lower middle: Yes 72%; No 16%; D/K 11%.

Skilled working: Yes 72%; No 17%; D/K 10%.

Upper working: Yes 68%; No 15%; D/K 16%.

Working: Yes 67%; No 19%; D/K 13%.

Blank: Yes 70%; No 15%; D/K 14%.

By Registrar General's categories AB: Yes 68%; No 18%; D/K 13%.

C1: Yes 71%; No 16%; D/K 12%.

C2: Yes 69%; No 19%; D/K 11%.

DE: Yes 62%; No 22%; D/K 14%.

By regions North-East and North: Yes 68%; No 19%; D/K 11%.

Midlands: Yes 62%; No 18%; D/K 20%.

South-East: Yes 70%; No 20%; D/K 9%.

South-West: Yes 75%; No 16%; D/K 9%.

North-West: Yes 65%; No 20%; D/K 13%.

If YES, would you say All women? or Most women? or Some women?

By age 16–20: all 9%; most 37%; some 12%.

21–24: all 8%; most 40%; some 20%.

25–34: all 8%; most 38%; some 25%.

35–45: all 6%; most 37%; some 26%.

By social class. Middle class: all 5%; most 38%; some 22%.

Lower middle: all 7%; most 34%; some 30%

Skilled working: all 10%; most 38%; some 23%.

Upper working: all 7%; most 39%; some 23%.

Working: all 7%; most 39%; some 22%.

Blank: all 14%; most 36%; some 20%.

By Registrar General's categories AB: all 8%; most 36%; some 22%.

C1: all 9%; most 38%; some 24%.

C2: all 8%; most 38%; some 23%.

DE: all 7%; most 37%; some 21%.

By regions North-East and North: all 11%; most 38%; some 19%.

Midlands: all 6%; most 34%; some 23%.

South-East: all 8%; most 36%; some 26%.

South-West: all 8%; most 45%; some 21%.

North-West: all 4%; most 45%; some 15%.

6 Birth Control

i

When the questionnaire was being planned and the interviews administered, much the most authoritative source on contemporary practices of birth control was the very recently published *Textbook of Contraceptive Practice** by Drs John Peel and Malcolm Potts. This work had to rely on data derived from numerous studies of small local groups, in Britain and the United States, most of them drawn from the clients of hospitals, birth-control clinics and the like. There was not at that time any nation-wide study of contraceptive practice available to them.

Between the appearance of their book and the writing of this chapter in November 1970, there have appeared two studies of large samples of the birth-control practices of married women: the Population Investigation Committee started a programme based on interviewing 2,300 married women in Britain in 1967, and the preliminary results were published in *Family Planning*, January 1969; and Ann Cartwright's *Parents and Family Planning Services*,† based on interviews with 1,495 mothers and 257 fathers, was published in the autumn of 1970.

Although the samples are carefully composed, they are not comparable to that used here. The Population Investigation Committee's sample is entirely composed of women, considerably older than our sample – the oldest group of women were married in 1941; Miss Cartwright's sample, with six times as many mothers as fathers, was based entirely on interviews with women and men who had very recently become parents and nine-tenths of the mothers and four-fifths of the fathers were

* Cambridge University Press, 1969.
† Routledge and Kegan Paul, 1970.

under 35.* I think it can therefore still be claimed that this study of the contemporary practices of a stratified random sample of men and women in England between the ages of 16 and 45 has no analogue in any other published research.

Only twelve married people refused to answer the question: 'Do you regularly use any birth-control methods? If yes, which?' Thirty-nine per cent of our married† respondents said that they did not practise any form of birth control, and 57 % that they did so.‡ Twenty-five informants had either been sterilized themselves or had sterilized spouses (predominantly hysterectomies, and a few vasectomies) and it is not quite clear whether the tabulators counted these people as using a birth-control technique or no; since this is less than 2 % of our married population, it does not affect the over-all figures significantly.

The rejection of birth control is much the most marked in those who consider themselves working class without qualification (41 %), those who refuse to place themselves in a social category (42 %), in the Registrar General's DE group (46 %) and regionally in the North-West (50 %) with its high concentration of Roman Catholics. The acceptance of some technique of birth control is marginally highest in those considering

* The most marked difference between these two surveys and the present is the very much lower proportion saying they had never employed any contraceptive technique. In the Population Investigation Committee's sample the figure was 12·6 % of married women, but this refers to the whole of their married lives, and not necessarily to contemporary practice. In Miss Cartwright's study (Table 9, p. 16) the corresponding figures are 7 % who had never used any contraceptive method, and 18 % at the time of the interview; these, of course, are all young fertile women. Compared with the present study, Miss Cartwright reports a much higher percentage using withdrawal (21 %) and the safe period (6 %); otherwise there is considerable congruence between her results and those discussed in this chapter.

† For the unmarried, see Chapter Ten, p. 216. It may be remarked here that the unmarried are much more likely to take the risk of an unwanted pregnancy than are the married.

‡ Taking the population as a whole, including the unmarried, the replies of the two sexes correspond closely, which suggests that the answers are reliable. Forty-eight per cent of the men and 51 % of the women said they did use some form of birth control; 36 % of the men and 38 % of the women that they did not; 9 % of the men and 8 % of the women, who had previously indicated that they had no sexual experience, were not questioned again.

themselves skilled working class, lower middle class and middle class and living in the South-East and North-East.

The sheath, or french letter, is still much the most popular technique of birth control; it is used by 29% of our married population. It is particularly favoured by the older respondents:* 11% of those aged 16–20, 25% of those aged between 21 and 34, and 31% of those aged between 35 and 45 prefer this method. It is most used by those calling themselves skilled working class and lower middle class and least by those calling themselves upper working class: regionally there is some concentration in the South-East and South-West.

The next most-favoured technique is the pill, used by 19% of our married population, with some concentration in the younger groups: 5% of those aged 16–20, 15% of those aged 21–24, 22% of those aged 25–35 and 10% of those aged 34–45.

The use of the pill increases very markedly as incomes increase;† only 10% of those with incomes under £666 a year use the pill, between 13% and 14% of those with incomes between £666 and £1,300 a year, and between 20% and 22% of those with incomes above £1,300 a year. Congruently with these figures, the highest proportion of pill-users are found in the Registrar General's AB category and those calling themselves middle and lower middle class. Regionally, the pill is employed much more in the North-East and South-East than in the rest of the country.

The concentration of the use of the pill among the more prosperous is probably due to the fact that at present it is necessary to get a doctor's prescription, which has to be paid for, before the pill can be obtained; the more prosperous and better educated are probably more accustomed to paying for a private consultation than are the mass of the population, for whom medical service should be 'free'. There is also, apparently, a belief that french letters are cheaper than the pill with a

---

* These totals also include the unmarried. The sheath is practically the only birth-control device used by the unmarried who are having intercourse; 17% use it at least intermittently, but, in the typical words of a 22-year-old self-employed taxi-driver, 'generally take a chance'. See Chapter Ten, p. 216.

† This is confirmed in Cartwright, *op. cit.* p. 22.

prescription;* this is probably not factually true, except for those with a very low rate of intercourse. There would also appear to be a widespread, if not very articulate, belief among the working classes that it is the husband's prerogative to determine whether any form of birth control should be used and that it is unseemly, almost unwomanly, for the wife to take the initiative. Several of our unskilled working-class wives gave verbal approval to the pill if 'the husband cannot control himself' (a periphrasis for withdrawal) though they did not themselves use it. Rubbers, of course, can be purchased without any medical prescription.

Like the pill, the diaphragm or cap† (and a few soluble pessaries) is used predominantly by the middle classes and the Registrar General's AB category (10%, contrasted with 1% DE) and those aged over 25. In total, 6% of our married population employ the diaphragm.

Five per cent of our married population practise withdrawal, with some concentration in the upper working and lower middle class; 3%, very evenly distributed throughout the population, had been fitted with an intra-uterine device, a coil or loop; and 1% employed the safe period. This last tiny group seem to be confined to the very poor.‡

ii

Adherence to a religious sect would appear to influence the choice of birth-control methods used rather than its practice; there is only a difference of 2% in the use of some birth-control method between those who claim adherence to a creed and those who say they are without religion. For church members the sheath is the most popular technique, used by 26% of the believers (29% Church of England, 10% Roman Catholic) but only by 20% non-believers. Withdrawal is used by 4% of those who claim some creed (with a heavy concentration of 11% Methodists and 10% Baptists) and by 3% non-believers. In

---

* In 1969, no birth control appliances were available on the National Health, with the possible exception of hysterectomy and the coil (i.u.d.). See below, p. 135.

† This is confirmed in Cartwright, *op. cit.*, p. 195, Table 80.

‡ A few individuals who are not Roman Catholic use this method.

K

contrast, the pill is used by 18% of those who say they have no religion and 13% of those who belong to a sect (including 14% Church of England and 10% of the Roman Catholics). Two per cent of Roman Catholics use the safe period and 47% use no birth-control techniques at all; members of the Church of England (like the total population) have 35% using no birth-control technique.

Among the 10% of our Roman Catholic respondents who use the pill are several regular communicants; although they had no apparent hesitation in giving this information to the interviewers, it would seem more prudent not to identify them nor quote them directly. Only 5% of the Roman Catholics voiced direct religious objections to the pill, among them a 44-year-old priest, who said:

'On balance, the invention of the pill is a good thing medically, but not in discussion to use it generally. Birth control in years to come will be out-dated by a more natural rhythm method which will be perfected.'

In contrast, an observant bank official, aged 39 said:

'Being Roman Catholic, I have had guidance on this. As it happens, my wife is unable to have children so it doesn't affect us; but if it is used for family planning – i.e. birth control rather than birth prevention – then I think it is a very good thing. I think we will eventually reach the stage when it is available to everyone.'

Fifty-two per cent of the Roman Catholics questioned* approved of the pill in general terms, even though they may qualify this approval in the typical words of the 41-year-old wife of a senior sales-executive, who was born in Eire and goes to daily Mass: 'A good thing in general, but not for people like me, of my faith.'

On the other hand, the Roman Catholics seem much less apprehensive about the potential medical dangers of the pill (9%) than are the members of the Church of England (15%) or the Methodists (24%); in general, those who claim adherence to a creed are somewhat more apprehensive (14%) than those who say they have no religion (10%); these latter are more enthusiastic about the pill (65%) than are the believers (57%).

* For the views of the whole population on the pill, see below, pp. 138–140.

iii

As can be expected, there is a correlation between the use of some birth control technique and the size of the family. Some form of birth control is used by 46% of our childless informants, 50% of those with one child, 64% of those with two children, 60% of those with three children, 49% of those with four, and 53% of those with five or more children.

The most significant difference seems to be in the use of the sheath: it is employed by 21% of the childless fathers, 27% of those with one child, 36% of those with two, 28% of those with three, 20% of those with four, and 16% of those with five or more children. There is nothing like so marked a variation with the other birth-control techniques;* and it would therefore appear that the large 'problem' families are due more to the fathers' selfish refusal to take precautions† (their wives often use the phrase 'control themselves') than to the mothers' hyper-fertility.

Sterilization of oneself or one's spouse is heavily concentrated in the large families of five or more children (8%, contrasted with 3% of those with three or four children and 1% of those with one or two) and it seems possible that this operation is generally performed in hospital. One of the few vasectomies reported was performed on the husband, a self-employed builder, of a 24-year-old woman who had had three children in her five years of marriage.

The picture is less clear with the intra-uterine device. The coil has been fitted to 5% or 6% of the mothers of three, four and five or more children, 3% of those with two, and 1% of those with one; there is no evidence to indicate whether the fitting was done in hospital or at a birth-control clinic.

* The actual figures for the pill are 18% childless, 14% one child, 20% two, 23% three, 13% four, 18% five or more; for the diaphragm 6% childless, 3% one child, 6% two children, 6% three children, 9% four children, 3% five or more; for withdrawal 2% childless, 9% one child, 5% two, 3% three, 3% four, 8% five or more children.
† This is confirmed in Cartwright, *op. cit.* Her figures for the use of the sheath (p. 21, table 11) is 32% of families with one child, 30% two children, 25% three children, 26% four children, 10% five children, 7% six children, 3% seven or more children. On page 27 she writes that a high proportion of the mothers of large families said their husbands were opposed to birth control.

iv

Before I started reading the questionnaires of this research, I had shared the very widespread belief that withdrawal, or *coitus interruptus*, was inherently undesirable and liable to produce psychological and physiological tensions in those who consistently practised it. But this method was preferred by some of the respondents who, on the basis of the full information in the interview, I would consider among the happiest of all the married people I was analysing: for example, a 43-year-old slaughter-house manager who said after twenty years of marriage: 'My wife is a fine woman and I cannot honestly state any faults'; or the 30-year-old wife of a foreman bricklayer who had known her husband from childhood: 'We try to decide and agree on everything together, and I think this is the best way to a happy marriage'; a 24-year-old married furnaceman, who has intercourse four times a week, and said in answer to the question about the components of a happy marriage: 'considerate to partner, sex life in unison and children'; or the 44-year-old wife of a dairy worker who said: 'If a woman is happily married, she won't go out looking for another man; I know it's considered modern these days but I disapprove of it.'*

There were also some users of withdrawal who showed some of the neurotic symptoms I had expected: thus, a 44-year-old timber-yard worker replied to the question on frequency of intercourse: 'The wife has had a nervous breakdown, so only four times in the last six months'; or a 45-year-old chief cashier who complained that wives want 'To change the man to the ideal man they had in mind; when they can't then they become a nagger; frigidity. [What goes to wreck a marriage?] Sex due to mental stress; instead of attracting each other, one becomes frigid'; or a 22-year-old grocery assistant, very recently married to a wife met on a blind date, who considered that wives 'should always agree with her husband, always do as her husband wishes, should always be faithful' and sees as faults of wives that 'they are too domineering, always want more money, and don't always do the things you want them to do'.

Rather than relying on my impressions of the 92 questionnaires of the respondents who used this technique, I thought it preferable to cross-correlate the views on what makes for

* For views on adultery, see Chapters Seven and Eight.

happiness or unhappiness in marriage (analysed in Chapters Four and Five) and on female sexuality (analysed in Chapter Six) with the different techniques of birth control.* I paid particular attention to such indications of neurosis as that the wife was over-anxious or too house-proud, that the husbands took their wives for granted, and the like.

According to these cross-correlations, the users of the sheath are representative of the whole married population being analysed; and the four techniques contrasted are the pill, the coil, the diaphragm and withdrawal. By these standards, the use of the diaphragm is the most clearly implicated with neurosis; it will be recalled that this technique is almost entirely confined to the middle-aged and middle class. The users of withdrawal put more emphasis on the importance of discussing things together and comradeship as components of a happy marriage than do the users of any other birth-control technique; and perhaps most significant of all, they have the highest percentage of any group believing in female orgasm: users of the sheath have 76%, users of the diaphragm 77%, users of the coil 67%, users of the pill 73% and users of withdrawal 82% believing in female orgasms. Consequently, the prejudice against *coitus interruptus* does not seem to be rationally founded.†

* For details, see figures of distribution at the end of this chapter, pp. 145–6.
† Peel and Potts, in their *Textbook of Contraceptive Practice*, p. 51, write: 'It has recently become less fashionable to condemn coitus interruptus as a physically and psychologically injurious technique. In the past a variety of disturbances have been attributed to its use, including prostatic hypertrophy and impotence in men and pelvic congestion and frigidity in women. There are no reliable data to suggest a causal relationship between method and symptoms. On the other hand there is some evidence that the use of the method, especially where it is insisted upon by one partner despite the explicit objections or wishes of the other, may lead to tension and a consequent deterioration of sexual relationships.

'Requiring neither prior preparation nor medical supervision and costing nothing, coitus interruptus is widely practised without apparent harm and with considerable success. If there are no good grounds for recommending it, neither are there any obvious grounds for discouraging it among couples who have already decided on the method and appear to be relatively happy with it. An official Indian family planning manual which in its earlier editions condemned the practice, now advises: "It is condemned by some doctors, but try it. You won't suddenly become a nervous wreck. If you notice bad effects you can easily give it up." This seems to be as much and as little as the medical adviser will need to say.'

Table eleven

On balance do you think that the invention of the pill for birth control is a good or bad thing?

Category	Total	Men	Women	Married	Single
Good without qualification	59%	62%	55%	58%	60%
Good for over-population, family planning	11%	12%	11%	11%	13%
Good for woman's peace of mind – lessens anxiety, tension	6%	4%	7%	6%	4%
Qualified approval	3%	2%	4%	3%	3%
Still too early to judge	5%	4%	6%	6%	4%
Specific mention of danger of thrombosis, coronary	2%	1%	2%	2%	1%
Vague mention of medical side-effects, medically imperfect	11%	10%	12%	12%	8%
Bad because unnatural, encourages promiscuity	3%	3%	3%	3%	2%
Bad without qualification	15%	12%	18%	15%	12%
No answer/refused	3%	4%	2%	2%	6%

Very small numbers – less than 1% in either case – said the pill was a good thing for poor parents and that it was bad from the religious point of view.

v

Although only 18% of our married population (15% of the total population) actually use the pill, no less than 97% of the total were willing and eager to give their views in answer to the question: 'On balance, do you think that the invention of the pill for birth control is a good or a bad thing?' Since no answers were suggested, I worked out categories on a 10% sample;

Table Eleven shows the categories and the emphases of men and women.

Absolute hostility to the pill is most marked among our older respondents, aged over 35, in the semi-skilled and un-skilled DE Registrar General's categories. It is the older groups, too, who make the most mention of vaguely apprehended medical side-effects. Its relevance to the population explosion is most mentioned by the young, those under twenty, and by members of the lower middle class. Its value in providing a woman with peace of mind is most emphasized by members of the middle class, and is hardly mentioned at all by people in the DE Registrar General's category and those living in the two Northern regions. Taking all the grounds for disapproval, these are mentioned markedly more in the two Northern regions than in the rest of the country; approval is highest in the South-East.

The actual users of the pill are 95 % in favour of it; 5 % are apprehensive of the medical side-effects. However, considerable intellectual approval is also given by those using other birth-control techniques: 63 % of those using the sheath, 72 % of those using the diaphragm, 73 % of those using the coil, and 58 % of those practising withdrawal. It is interesting to note that those who practise withdrawal seem more content with their tech-nique than any other group.

Many of our informants quoted their own experiences to explain their approval or disapproval of the pill. Among those happy with it were the 25-year-old wife of a boiler assistant:

'Good. It relieves the fear of pregnancy; it is 100% safe against pregnancy; relieves you of any pre-preparation which can be off-putting.'

'Good; I take it. I like it because it is no trouble – you pop one in your mouth and it's done with and you are safe' (the 26-year-old wife of a boat-builder).

'Good. I was very biased against it medically when I first heard about it – but nothing based on real scientific knowledge. In all other respects it makes the love side of marriage so much freer, it can only be a good thing' (the 24-year-old wife of a school-teacher a pious Nonconformist).

'It saves a lot of worry. It is much easier to use than the other methods. I find it keeps me better tempered; I don't get the irritability I used to get' (the 32-year-old wife of a police sergeant).

'There is always this dreadful fear, perhaps, after two children. . . . You can't afford a thing. . . . The pill is so easy to use and so pleasant to use' (the 33-year-old wife of a company director, born in Eire).

'It's excellent; I have been on them four years now and I feel marvellous. It's a lot of nonsense that's talked about thrombosis. I have always felt better on the pill, and I certainly don't want any more children' (the 41-year-old wife of a lorry driver).

'On the whole it is a good thing. It eases tensions and because of its safety, if one is attracted by somebody and has an affair, it takes away the risk of pregnancy' (the 23-year-old wife of a service craftsman).

'A good thing – I am not a person that likes risk, and I think that for the first time a woman can enjoy sex without fear; also there are no children that were unwanted in the first place, and it is the children who suffer' (the 24-year-old wife of an assistant draughtsman).[*]

'Sex plays a tremendous part in marriages and the pill gives you absolute freedom which is essential' (a 30-year-old teacher, an observant Pentecostal).[†]

'It is a good thing, from my experience; I get more satisfaction and I feel the wife does' (a 36-year-old butchery manager).

'A good idea. You can relax more. You are not worried about becoming pregnant. It isn't a worry all the time – you know – Am I pregnant this month? Lots of people can't afford lots of children and the pill is perfect for planning your family' (the 21-year-old wife of a plumber).

'It's marvellous – in this day and age when a young couple need a good start you can have intercourse without the fear that you might fall pregnant' (the 26-year-old wife of an assistant plant-manager).

'It takes away an awful lot of tension – there is another tension; I have doubts about the side effects, but for contraception it is marvellous' (the 41-year-old wife of an engineering foreman).

---

[*] This informant added: 'Until I had my first child he used to use a sheath, until I started on the pill.'
[†] This informant said: 'We use the pill for a certain time, but my wife cannot use it too long, then I use a sheath.'

For some of our informants the pill had undesirable after-effects. Thus, the 31-year-old wife of a transport planner:

'I think it's good if it suits you. You are completely protected against having a baby. I took it and it had bad effects on me. I didn't want to have anything to do with my husband; I think if I'd gone on with it I'd have been mental.'

'I use a cap. I used to have the pill but had to come off it for health reasons. It gave me blood-pressure' (the 36-year-old wife of a shop proprietor).

'Bad thing; I used to take it, it is like a drug. Even if you want a child you don't want to come off them. My marriage started breaking up because my husband wanted a child and I kept putting it off. I wouldn't go back on it again. I used to be irritable when I took them, and never felt the same as I used to. I still don't feel the same after stopping them' (the 20-year-old wife of a long-distance lorry driver).

'On the whole it's good, because I'm thinking of the population explosion. It affects me badly – it gives me pre-menstrual depression all the time. My husband says it works because it makes women frigid!' (the 33-year-old wife of a design draughtsman).

'It's a bad thing; my wife had a heart attack through it' (a 40-year-old drop stamper).

'A bad thing – I wouldn't ever dare take it myself. I think it upsets your body. They gave them to my daughter for painful periods and it made her have periods twice a month' (the 37-year-old wife of a herdsman).

'It takes the element of risk out of sex, but it is a good thing for limiting the family. It has made me less able to enjoy sex' (the 25-year-old wife of a machinist).*

'I've been on it for five years, and I'm still terrified of it. The side-effects can be bad, but I don't want any more children and this is the surest way' (the 39-year-old wife of a railway foreman).

A considerable number of informants, with no personal experience of the pill, voice these vague fears of side-effects,

---

* The interviewer added: 'This sounds odd, but the element of risk made her enjoy it more.' This informant admitted to three partners before marriage and two after; she says she has never been in love and does not believe that women have orgasms.

presumably exacerbated by discussions in the public press and on television. It is interesting to note that a number of young husbands say: 'I wouldn't let my wife take it' and young wives: 'My husband wouldn't let me use it'; it would appear that many husbands still arrogate to themselves, and many wives concede, the right to determine the measures which will protect the woman's health and, of course, the birth-control techniques, if any, which the couple will use.

Some of these fears are obviously based on a confusion between the birth-control pill and thalidomide.* 'A terrible thing – deformed babies, etc. It's awful' (a 44-year-old butcher); 'A bad thing because I think if you do have a baby while you're taking the pill it will harm the child' (the 44-year-old wife of a storeman); several informants made similar remarks.

Some of the fears are really grotesque. 'Bad thing; should be given to men; unbalances nature, making women more aggressive. Getting more like men, the women that have the pill' (a 39-year-old roof-tiler); 'The pill is dangerous to health; people put on weight and their legs swell' (the 42-year-old wife of the manager of a large factory); 'I know lots of people round here on it and they don't look very well' (the 32-year-old wife of a gardener); 'I wouldn't value it at all at present; it's the woman who has to take the pill and have the abortion; how about sterilization for men? I'm anti-medicine generally' (the 32-year-old wife of an architect).

Despite their apprehensions, a few informants approve of the pill for others: 'I think for under-developed countries and the world as a whole it is good, but I think there might be medical questions which need answers before I would trust it' (the 44-year-old wife of a civil service administrator); 'I'd never use the pill myself because it may be harmful, but it will be useful in India and places like that' (the 45-year-old wife of a petrol-pump attendant).

Most of our informants who commented on the relevance of the pill to the population explosion were not so cynical. They are typified by a 36-year-old chartered accountant who said: 'It's something that can be manufactured cheaply and got out to under-developed countries so we will all be able to feed ourselves in a hundred years' time.' It is above all our younger

* Peel and Potts, *op. cit.*, p. 117, report the same confusion.

respondents who develop this theme; and it is they, too, who stress that the pill prevents the birth of unwanted babies.

The virulence of those who disapprove of the pill because it might lead to promiscuity rather surprised me. 'It makes it too easy for single girls to have a sex life' (the 26-year-old wife of a technologist); 'Good for married people but I don't agree for single people; it gives them no moral fibre' (the Edinburgh-born wife of a press operator, aged 35); 'Conception is a woman's only protection; it might make her too weak and fall' (a 45-year-old sales representative).

Some replies demonstrated oddly contrasting views about 'nature'. On the one hand there are those who think the pill more 'unnatural' than other birth-control techniques: 'I think it is unnatural to interfere with the way the body works, and I wouldn't take it' (the 28-year-old wife of an ink-maker, who uses a diaphragm); 'Bad thing; don't like what it does; interferes with the organs of a woman' (a 23-year-old bank clerk who uses a sheath); 'I wouldn't like them because it's interfering with nature' (the 36-year-old wife of a bricklayer's labourer, who uses withdrawal). In contrast, 'It must be good; from the point of view of being married it does allow you to be absolutely natural. Using any other method stops you relaxing and being spontaneous; I think this is bad' (the 26-year-old wife of an insurance clerk); 'It is a more sure method of contraception than any other; it is more natural' (the 24-year-old wife of an overseas service engineer).

Figures of distribution

Do you regularly use any birth-control methods? If YES, which?

> Totals are less than 100% because the unmarried, without sexual experience, are included in the calculations.

By self-ascribed social class Middle class: Yes 49%; No 31%; sheath 27%; diaphragm 4%; coil 3%; pill 15%; withdrawal 4%; other 3%.

Lower middle class: Yes 49%; No 32%; sheath 31%; diaphragm 5%; coil 2%; pill 14%; withdrawal 5%; other 2%.

Skilled working class: Yes 49%; No 33%; sheath 32%; diaphragm 2%; coil 2%; pill 12%; withdrawal 4%; other 1%.

Upper working class: Yes 40%; No 24%; sheath 20%; diaphragm 4%; coil 3%; pill 8%; withdrawal 7%; other 0%.

Working class: Yes 39%; No 41%; sheath 20%; diaphragm 3%; coil 1%; pill 14%; withdrawal 4%; other 1%.

Blank: Yes 48%; No 42%; sheath 23%; diaphragm 6%; coil 1%; pill 15%; withdrawal 2%; other 2%.

By Registrar General's categories AB: Yes 54%; No 31%; sheath 26%; diaphragm 10%; coil 3%; pill 18%; withdrawal 4%; other 3%.

C1: Yes 53%; No 31%; sheath 30%; diaphragm 5%; coil 3%; pill 16%; withdrawal 3%; other 2%.

C2: Yes 51%; No 37%; sheath 28%; diaphragm 4%; coil 2%; pill 16%; withdrawal 5%; other 3%.

DE: Yes 38%; No 46%; sheath 20%; diaphragm 1%; coil 1%; pill 13%; withdrawal 5%; other 0%.

By regions North-East and North: Yes 50%; No 36%; sheath 25%; diaphragm 5%; coil 1%; pill 20%; withdrawal 6%; other 1%.

Midlands: Yes 44%; No 40%; sheath 23%; diaphragm 5%; coil 2%; pill 11%; withdrawal 9%; other 2%.

South-East: Yes 57%; No 30%; sheath 32%; diaphragm 5%; coil 3%; pill 18%; withdrawal 2%; other 3%.

South-West: Yes 46%; No 40%; sheath 29%; diaphragm 4%; coil 2%; pill 11%; withdrawal 4%; other 1%.

North-West: Yes 36%; No 50%; sheath 18%; diaphragm 3%; coil 1%; pill 11%; withdrawal 4%; other 1%.

By income

> I am omitting from this tabulation the four lowest income categories, since the absolute numbers are so few, and are composed principally of juveniles, many without sexual experience. The categories and absolute numbers are: less than £312 per annum, 10 people; £312–£416 17 people; £416–£520 24 people; £520–£666 53 people.

£666–£884 per annum: Yes 38%; No 42%; sheath 22%; diaphragm 1%; coil 0%; pill 12%; withdrawal 4%; other 0%.

£884–£1040 per annum: Yes 48%; No 39%; sheath 25%; diaphragm 4%; coil 2%; pill 14%; withdrawal 7%; other 2%.

£1,040–£1,300 per annum: Yes 54%; No 37%; sheath 31%; diaphragm 3%; coil 2%; pill 15%; withdrawal 5%; other 0%.

£1,300–£1,820 per annum: Yes 61%; No 31%; sheath 32%; diaphragm 7%; coil 3%; pill 20%; withdrawal 5%; other 0%.

£1,820–£2,600 per annum: Yes 61%; No 29%; sheath 33%; diaphragm 8%; coil 3%; pill 22%; withdrawal 5%; other 2%.

Over £2,600 per annum: Yes 65%; No 31%; sheath 26%; diaphragm 13%; coil 8%; pill 22%; withdrawal 1%; other 5%.

Techniques of birth control and attitudes to marriage

> In these cross-correlations I am treating a variation of 4% or over from the totals given in Chapters Four and Five as probably significant.

What are the chief faults wives tend to have? Uses of the diaphragm emphasized that wives were over-anxious (11%) and under-emphasized that they went out on their own (1%), were bad mothers (1%) or lazy (1%).

Users of the coil emphasized that wives were extravagant (39%), their moral faults (12%) and being a bad mother (15%) and under-emphasized their domineering (12%), nagging (37%) and being too house-proud (0%).

Users of the pill emphasized their childishness (9%) and nagging (48%) and under-emphasized domineering (19%).

Users of withdrawal emphasized extravagance (32%), selfishness (21%), lack of intelligence (8%) letting herself go (15%), being a bad housekeeper (16%) and drinking (9%). They under-emphasized the complaints that wives could be over-anxious (2%) or too house-proud (1%).

What are the chief faults husbands tend to have? Users of the diaphragm did not emphasize any factor and under-emphasized nagging (2%).

Users of the coil emphasized domineering (20%) and taking his wife for granted (27%) and under-emphasized selfishness (34%) and drinking (17%).

Users of the pill did not emphasize or under-emphasize any factor.

Users of withdrawal emphasized jealousy (9%), drinking (34%) and laziness (23%) and markedly under-emphasized selfishness (34%) and taking his wife for granted (12%).

What do you think tends to wreck a marriage? Users of the diaphragm emphasized selfishness (31%) and under-emphasized neglect (17%).

Users of the coil emphasized sexual incompatibility (15%), poverty (24%) and infidelity (32%) and under-emphasized neglect (22%).

Users of the pill under-emphasized poverty (22%).

Users of withdrawal emphasized conflicting personalities (17%) and neglect (37%) and under-emphasized infidelity (20%).

What do you think tends to make a happy marriage?
Users of the diaphragm emphasized give-and-take (39%) and under-emphasized love (14%), comradeship (24%) and children (7%).

Users of the coil emphasized financial security (10%) and under-emphasized give-and-take (22%), mutual trust (12%) and comradeship (24%).

Users of the pill did not emphasize or under-emphasize any factor.

Users of withdrawal emphasized discussing things together (36%) and comradeship (37%).

7 Fidelity and casual adultery

i

Immediately after the question about their views on the birth-control pill, our respondents were asked: 'Now that the pill provides absolute safety, do you think faithfulness is or is not as important as ever in a marriage?' Ninety-two per cent answered in the affirmative, 7 % of the men and 10 % of the women with very great emphasis: 'Faithfulness is what marriage is to me' (the 38-year-old wife of a machine operator, whose husband had just left her); 'The pill makes it safer to go with other people, but would still destroy the marriage' (a 32-year-old skilled engineer, whose wife uses the pill); 'You should stick to your marriage vows and the pill doesn't make any difference' (the 39-year-old wife of a railway foreman); 'It's my feeling that there must be faithfulness to have a real marriage' (the 26-year-old wife of a technologist).

Five per cent of our respondents, very evenly divided throughout the population, said that faithfulness was now not so important, and a further 1 % qualified their views on the importance of fidelity 'Yes, I suppose it is important to be faithful – yes, it is important,' in the typical words of the wife of a 23-year-old builder; and a further 1 % claimed that the pill would conduce to promiscuity. 'I think it does make a difference; you are not likely to conceive or give somebody an unwanted baby' (the 31-year-old wife of a maintenance electrician, with a three-week-old baby); 'Up to a point, Yes; if I went to a party and my husband went down the garden with somebody after a few drinks, it might be better if he got it out of his system; I wouldn't like it if he did, though' (the 33-year-old wife of a design draughtsman); 'Women tend not to be as faithful if they know they are safe' (the 44-year-old wife of a post-office worker*); 'I'm not sure I think faithfulness is the be-all and end-all of marriage anyway, but I don't think contraception enters into it at all; it's how you feel' (the 30-year-old wife of an insurance clerk, now at teacher-training college); 'I don't think it is, now there is no come-back; I have my own principles, but I think one has the freedom now; I don't see why a woman should not please herself the same as a man can' (the 37-year-old wife of a bakery supervisor); 'It is the same, but in practice women are more unfaithful' (a 35-year-old barber, born in Jamaica).

The reply of this last respondent merges into that small group who feel convinced that the pill promotes promiscuity: 'This is the thing – the pill is likely to lead to this. This was always so – a man could always use contraceptives. I don't see the pill makes any difference; faithfulness must be important, but you must try and understand if people sometimes fail' (the 42-year-old wife of the manager of a large factory); 'I think a lot of people take advantage of the pill for messing about, just for the sake of it, but I think faithfulness is still just as important' (the 32-year-old wife of a gardener); 'I think it's more important; well, I think the pill seems to be too easily available to young people and it encourages them because they can feel safe using it' (the 33-year-old wife of a sheet-metal worker): 'It is as important, but the pill provides the opportunity to be unfaithful now, where they might have thought twice about it before' (the 41-year-old wife of a tool-setter).

Asked outside the context of the birth-control pill whether a husband or a wife should be faithful for the rest of their married lives, 90% of our married respondents said that husbands should be and 93% that wives should be; 3% said they did not know, and 7% said that husbands need not be, and 4% that wives need not be.†

There is little that can distinguish this eccentric group who do not think spouses should be faithful; they are very evenly divided throughout the population by age and sex; by self-ascribed social class they are rather heavily concentrated among those who will not place themselves socially (11% in the case of husbands and 7% in the case of wives) and are fewest in those

---

* This informant admitted to one lover since her marriage.
† For the views of the unmarried on fidelity, see Chapter Ten, p. 214.

who consider themselves working class without modification (5 % in the case of husbands and 3 % in the case of wives); but the figures are so small that they are doubtfully significant.

As the figures show, 3 % of the population apply a double standard, allowing licence to husbands which they refuse to wives; and these would appear to be predominantly women.* Among those upholding the double standard are the 41-year-old wife of an engineering foreman; the 29-year-old wife of a motor mechanic; the 33-year-old wife of a company director, born in Eire; and the 41-year-old wife of a long-distance driver who said: 'As long as they do not let their wives find out I do not think it matters.'

In only a few cases are the people who said that faithfulness is not necessary at the beginning of the interview the same as those who admitted to adultery at the end of it; in most cases it would appear that the rejection of the importance of fidelity is an intellectual attitude rather than a justification of one's own infidelity; and most of those who admitted to being personally unfaithful paid lip-service to the importance of fidelity.

ii

To explore further the emotional importance of fidelity, we asked all our informants their views on two hypothetical situations: 'How do you feel about a married man [woman] who has an affair with a woman [man] he [she] does not really love?'; and 'If a husband [wife] finds his wife [her husband] having an affair with another man [woman] what should he [she] do?' It was hoped that this contrast would mirror the alternative between the choice offered in the case of the unmarried† of 'one person or persons he loves or just anyone he feels physically attracted to', and the great majority of our respondents interpreted them in this way; nearly all assumed that the 'affair' referred to in the second question was emotionally serious.

Table Twelve shows in summary form the responses of both sexes to the question about a married man or woman having a

* See also Chapter Two, p. 36.
† See Chapter Two, pp. 36–37.

Table twelve

How do you feel about a married man who has an affair with a woman he does not really love?

How do you feel about a married woman who has an affair with a man she does not really love?

	About a man Total percentage	Men	Women	About a woman Total percentage	Men	Women
Strong moral disapproval	22%	17%	27%	23%	18%	27%
Disapproval of character	20%	16%	24%	18%	16%	20%
Disapproval of intelligence	6%	8%	4%	7%	8%	6%
Oversexed, lustful	14%	12%	16%	11%	10%	12%
Bad for marriage	4%	6%	3%	5%	5%	5%
Something lacking in marriage	15%	15%	15%	19%	17%	20%
Justified if spouse cold or absent	1%	1%	1%	1%	1%	1%
Pity – sorry for him/her	1%	1%	1%	1%	1%	2%
Won't judge – live and let live	10%	15%	6%	8%	13%	4%
No attitude unless it affects me	5%	7%	3%	6%	8%	4%
It's natural – human nature	3%	4%	2%	1%	1%	0%
Worse than for men	—	—	—	2%	1%	2%
Not so bad as for men	—	—	—	2%	1%	2%
Same as for men	—	—	—	11%	19%	4%
No answer	4%	5%	3%	2%	3%	1%

casual affair. A few of the categories had several synonyms: Strong moral disapproval includes 'wrong, terrible, disgusting, unforgivable'; Disapproval of character 'cad, cheap, no good, poor character, rotten'; Disapproval of intelligence 'stupid, callow, a bit of an idiot'; Oversexed 'out for own enjoyment, trying to boost ego'; Shows something lacking in marriage 'boredom, frigid wife, unsatisfactory husband' and so on.

As the table demonstrates, women are much more severe in their disapproval of a casual affair for either spouse than are men; whereas men are more likely to adopt a neutral or permissive attitude. The only extenuating circumstance that women advance more frequently than men is that such conduct shows that there is something lacking in the marriage; and they advance this excuse more frequently for wives than they do for husbands. Once again,* nearly a fifth of the men state that the conduct of husbands and wives should be judged by the same standard, a view held by only one woman in twenty-five; the same proportion state explicitly that women should be judged by different standards, though they are evenly divided in their views as to whether a wife's casual affair is or is not more heinous than a husband's.

With a single exception, this gamut of attitudes is remarkably evenly distributed throughout the population; neither age nor self-ascribed social class modify significantly the proportions of the replies. The one exception is the claim that such conduct shows the erring spouse to be over-sexed, lustful and other synonyms implying that the optimum of sexuality is less than the maximum. This view is held much less by the younger respondents than by their elders: it is advanced by 9% of those aged between 16 and 20 for both sexes; 12% in the case of men and 8% in the case of women by those aged between 21 and 24; 14% in the case of men and 10% in the case of women by those aged between 25 and 34; and 16% in the case of men and 12% in the case of women by those aged between 35 and 45. Lustfulness is stressed by those calling themselves lower middle class and is relatively seldom mentioned by those calling themselves upper working class.

Rather unexpectedly, the answers to this pair of questions provided some of the most vivid illustrations of the attitudes of our population towards sexual rigidity and permissiveness, ranging from 'He wants shooting' (the 30-year-old wife of a driver, a pious Roman Catholic) to 'Doesn't matter – I do at

* See Chapter Two, p. 36.

the factory' (the 22-year-old wife of a labourer); from 'Disgusting – immoral – does not love his wife, does not respect his wife, and does not respect other women or himself' (a 28-year-old greengrocer, a Jehovah's Witness) to 'It is entirely up to him; good luck to him if he can get away with it!' (a 22-year-old lorry driver);* and it therefore seems worth while quoting the views of a considerable number of our informants.

Strong moral disapproval is illustrated by 'It is horrible in a man and it is vile in a woman' (the 32-year-old wife of a metallurgist); 'I think it very wrong myself; there are thousands who do it, though. [For women?] The same thing; I disapprove' (the 31-year-old wife of a long-distance driver); 'I feel badly about it; it is unfair and highly immoral' (the 35-year-old wife of a sculptor); and from men: 'I don't think it is right; it should not happen; it is silly' (a 35-year-old brewery worker); 'I don't think much of it' (a 45-year-old fitter welder, born in Guyana); 'I don't think it a very nice thing to do' (a 31-year-old postman).

Disapproval of the character or intelligence of the casual adulterer is exemplified by 'Not much – out for what he can get. [For women?] A bleeding good hiding would do her good!' (the 28-year-old wife of a chemical processor); 'There's no point in having an affair; I think he's rotten. [For women?] The same; if she's not in love there's no point in it' (the 30-year-old wife of a steel erector); 'I can't stick them; I have liked a person as a friend but if that happens I go right off them; it causes pain and suffering. [For women?] I don't like that either; they start off as a whim and then when it comes out they are sorry' (the 24-year-old wife of a filleter); 'I think it is just a waste of time. [For women?] I think she is just going out for what she can get' (the 45-year-old wife of a turner engineer). And from men: 'Do not think much of him; it tends to be the way of life nowadays with these modern ideas' (a 36-year-old wages clerk); 'He would not go down in my estimation, but I think he would be a fool, because it could not have a happy ending' (a 33-year-old schoolmaster); 'I disagree with this relationship because it can wreck a marriage' (a 45-year-old lorry driver).

* This informant admitted to three partners during the year that he had been married.

Examples of the reproach of being over-sexed or lustful are: 'I think it's animalish, really; just to satisfy their baser instincts; it's disgusting' (the 44-year-old wife of an accountant); 'To me that is just sexual; he will get it out of his system' (the 38-year-old wife of a wholesale clothing manager); 'I think it's horrible; if he just goes with her for sex, I don't agree with it' (the 22-year-old wife of a marine engineer, temporarily separated from her husband). Men's views can be illustrated by: 'This is just lust' (a 43-year-old slaughter-house manager); 'I feel he is satisfying a purely sexual urge and his moral standards are low' (a 45-year-old draughtsman, a pious Baptist); 'He is doing it just for sex, I would say. [For women?] Perhaps she is unhappy in bed with her husband' (a 43-year-old haulage contractor).

It was predominantly our male respondents who held that, far from casual extra-marital affairs showing that the man was lustful and over-sexed, such behaviour is both natural and enjoyable. 'This applies to most men; he's taking a chance; it's all right if he's not caught out. [For women?] If a chance is there, good luck to her!' (a 37-year-old holiday-camp attendant); 'It's all right if his wife doesn't know; and the same for women' (a 33-year-old miner); 'Nothing wrong with it under certain circumstances; the time and place could have a lot to do with it. [For women?] Again, I don't really think there is anything wrong; she can feel the necessity sometimes to give way there and then' (a 29-year-old free-lance cartoonist); 'It's a bit immoral but passes the time; probably doesn't want to become involved; a woman is probably bored' (a 35-year-old commercial designer); 'A joker – just for kicks on the spur of the moment; a good thing and I have nothing against it. [For women?] About the same' (a 35-year-old self-employed taxi-driver). 'I suppose if they are both enjoying the same thing it is all right. He mustn't bring trouble back home. [For women] If she and her husband aren't happy together and she wants the physical side, it is all right' (the 24-year-old wife of a long-distance lorry driver).

Considerably more men than women assumed an 'I'm all right, Jack' attitude; they say that they have no feelings about such behaviour unless it affects them personally. 'It wouldn't bother me as long as my family was not involved' (a 40-year-old

builder's agent); 'It's his business; nothing to do with anyone else. [For women?] As long as it's not my wife, I couldn't
care less' (a 20-year-old painter, very recently married); 'It's
up to the individual. Good luck to him! it's not a terrible thing
to do. [For women?] I wouldn't object, though I would if it
involved me' (a 25-year-old lift-erector's mate). This view was
also advanced by a few women: 'Men do these things; as long
as it's not my husband, it doesn't really worry me. [For women?]
The same. I don't think much of them, but people are different
now and some don't think anything of this sort of behaviour'
(the 41-year-old wife of a tool-setter).

The charitable refusal to pass any judgement without more
information was advanced considerably more frequently by
men than by women;* but nearly all the statements illustrating
this attitude which I marked for excerpting come from women,
presumably because they struck me as unusual during the analysis. Thus the 38-year-old wife of a bank clerk:

'I would think he doesn't care about making his marriage work.
Perhaps he doesn't love his wife. Depends on the person. [For
women?] I find it difficult to believe a woman would do this. I
couldn't say how I would feel unless I knew the people involved, and
why it would happen.'

'It all depends. There must be a reason why, so it's hard to judge
without knowing all the facts. [For women?] There's always a
reason for these things; it's hard to judge' (the 23-year-old wife of a
service craftsman).

'There can't be any point to it. If you don't love a person you
don't get any satisfaction out of it. Wouldn't know why he did it.
[For women?] The same. She can't enjoy it much. Don't know that
I feel anything about it; it's her business' (the 28-year-old wife of an
ink-maker).

'I think that is pretty ghastly. Perhaps he's been frustrated at home;
perhaps he is trying to prove something to himself or his wife, or
trying to impress the other girl with what a man of the world he is.
[For women?] I think again she must be frustrated sexually. Perhaps
her husband is so absorbed in his work she just wants amusement.
Perhaps she is getting a little older and wants to try and prove

* 15% of the men made this refusal in the case of men and 13% in the
case of women; the corresponding figures for women are 6% and 4%.

something to herself' (the 41-year-old wife of a lecturer in economics, an observant Anglican).

'I would feel contempt for such a man, but would want to know more about his home life before making any decision about this. [For women?] Even less than for a man because she often has a family to occupy her; but again her married life would have to be taken into consideration' (the 27-year-old wife of a municipal engineer).

This last reply fades into the one non-condemnatory explanation of casual adultery that women advance more frequently than men: that it must be interpreted as a symptom of something unsatisfactory in the marriage, and therefore the erring spouse is more to be pitied than condemned.

'I should think he is bored or has a cold wife and looks for things outside the home he can't find there. [For women?] Sorry for her; she must be unhappy' (the 24-year-old wife of a naval electrician).

'The wife – there is something wrong with the wife. Perhaps she is not interested in sex or something. [For women?] There'll be something lacking in her sex life as well, or she's beginning to feel a bit of a cabbage and wants to get out and have a bit of excitement' (the 26-year-old wife of an engineer).

'I'd look to myself to see why he'd gone; he must have been desperate. [For women?] There must be something wrong with the husband; she must be unhappy' (the 27-year-old wife of the owner of a grocery).

'Not enough love and affection at home. His wife should go out with him more often. [For women?] She must be bored; husband doesn't tell her often enough that he loves her' (the 27-year-old wife of a council caretaker).

'It just depends what is going on at home. If he is not having sexual intercourse with his wife he looks elsewhere; if this is the case he is entitled to. [For women?] If it is probably a younger man she might think more of him; her husband might be a lot older or away from home' (the 27-year-old wife of a deck-hand).

'I think any man would if it were offered him on a plate – the best of them. A man is a lot weaker than women in that way. [For women?] It is probably because her husband is not satisfying sexually and she's going elsewhere to get satisfaction' (the 37-year-old wife of a toolmaker).

'He's probably not getting enough at home. [For women?] Unless she's getting paid for it, I can't imagine; probably over-sexed herself' (the 33-year-old wife of a design draughtsman).

'Sorry for him; he's looking for comfort. [For women?] Sorry for her; she must not be content at home' (the 38-year-old wife of a welder).

'I feel very sorry for them, that they are not capable of controlling themselves; if there's no love I just can't understand it. [For women?] If a woman is happily married she won't want to go looking for another man. I know it's considered modern these days but I disapprove of it' (the 44-year-old wife of a dairy worker).

'He wants to have his cake and eat it; trying to hurl his marriage to one side and have a good time with someone else. If that is so there must be something lacking in his own marriage. [For women?] Could be because of husband neglecting her, or she could be a nymphomaniac; it depends on the situation' (a 31-year-old solicitor's clerk).

'Have a great sympathy with him; there must be something that is missing there' (a 45-year-old chief cashier).

Most of the respondents quoted so far have assumed, either implicitly or explicitly, that men and women are sufficiently similar in their innate characteristics and sexuality to be judged by the same standards. There is, however, a sizeable minority among the younger English who hold that men and women are naturally so different that different standards must be applied. The most usual statement is that sexual desire is stronger in men so that they can engage in intercourse casually, whereas women have to feel love as well as desire, but there are quite a number of variants of this belief. Such beliefs are held by members of both sexes, but are voiced more frequently by women. Such beliefs were, of course, much more widely held in this country a century ago.

A typical statement is that of a 29-year-old wife of a motor mechanic:

'I just think it's natural. They can still love their wife. Men are funny people! [For women?] I wouldn't think it is possible. Unless you have a strong feeling for a man you couldn't do it.'

'I think this is a thing that happens all the time. I think a man goes to a woman for his needs and not his love in a lot of cases. [For women?] I can't understand it personally, myself. I don't see how they can go off with another man' (the 24-year-old wife of a self-employed builder).

'There's something wrong with him; but a man has a drink and everything looks easy and that's how things start. [For women?] I can't see a woman having an affair with a man unless she really loves him; it is against a woman's nature to give herself without love' (the 33-year-old wife of a company director, born in Eire).

'Very typical, but not very honest – just sexual desire. [For women?] I do not think many women really do. I think women need more than just sexual satisfaction; they need to feel love and attraction for a man' (the 24-year-old wife of an assistant draughtsman).

'I think it is horrible, but I think sex to a man is different than a woman – they do not feel the same. [For women?] This is horrible, just coarse and horrible' (the 32-year-old wife of a caretaker).

'It's something a man might do, but I don't see it happening, except a man seems able to do these things. [For women?] I don't see how she could if there's no love' (the 29-year-old wife of a skilled gas-fitter).

'Not a lot; it's understandable as men are different from women· They say that men can go with women and not think anything of it. [For women?] Not a lot. I do not think I would do it. I am not exactly disgusted but I do not approve of it' (the 30-year-old wife of a carpenter).

'If his wife don't give it him, he can't help hisself. [For women?] She shouldn't do it; she's got the children' (the 31-year-old wife of a wood labourer).

'If his wife is cold, sometimes there's a reason. I think all life revolves around sex. If the man can't have his needs fulfilled at home, he'll look elsewhere. [For women?] Personally, myself I couldn't do it; I'd feel awfully guilty if I did something wrong like that' (the 26-year-old wife of a factory foreman).

A few of our male respondents voiced their beliefs in the different nature of the two sexes, even though this often was in conflict with the overriding male value of justice, as is illustrated by a 26-year-old postman who said:

'Either desperately unhappy at home, or else he's just doing it for variety. Usually either driven to it or doing it just for kicks. [For women?] Disgusting! I can't really say that though, because the same thing as for a married man must apply; although I can't see how a woman could make love to a man she doesn't love. Women like that are in a minority.'

'O.K. if his wife doesn't find out; if it goes too far it could wreck a marriage. [For women?] Don't think she should, because she can't break away, gets too involved' (a 32-year-old skilled engineer).

'If he's enjoying himself, good luck to him! [For women?] For a man it is quite a thing – but not for a woman. If a man gets a chance and thinks he can get away with it, he will; but a woman will not unless she is very loose or has got no feelings for her husband' (a 27-year-old painter and decorator).

A very few men advanced the belief that casual adultery was more permissible in women than in men, a view which has rather more female advocates.

'Don't really believe in it and it's not for me. [For women?] Slightly more permissible, but still don't like the idea of it; but since a woman needs a certain amount of flattery to maintain her ego, maybe not too bad' (a 23-year-old self-employed builder and decorator).

'Stupid and asking for trouble. [For women?] Very foolish, but will make allowances for solitary life, if kidded on' (a 45-year-old local government officer).

'I think he's awful; it's not fair on the girl. [For women?] She must be unhappy in her married life and I would feel sorry for her' (the 31-year-old wife of a fishmonger).

'I think that's pretty dirty – in the sense that it is unnecessary. [For women?] I think that might be permissible because she might be bored. I don't agree with it but boredom could be a very good reason for a woman going off the rails that way' (the 41-year-old wife of an engineering foreman).

'Don't think much of him. Distasteful. [For women?] Don't mind that so much; a woman doesn't get so involved as a man' (the 31-year-old wife of a photogravure retoucher).

'I think he's wrong and just out for what he can get. He leads her on and throws her off. It's a sexual affair and a woman has more to lose.

He's a cad really, and thinks he's a Don Juan. [For women?] There must be some reason, something lacking somewhere; perhaps not enough attention from her husband. It must be wrong if you are married, but not to be condemned. It is easy to sit in judgement on others; being married doesn't really stop you loving another member of the opposite sex' (the 32-year-old wife of a qualified surveyor).

'Selfish nature – lustful and bad. [For women?] Depends. Might be because she is lonely and neglected; I do not condone and do not condemn' (the 45-year-old wife of a postman).

'It's reprehensible. Perhaps he's infatuated; but if it is just cold-blooded sex it is not admirable. [For women?] I don't approve of it, but I couldn't pass judgement on her; she probably has her reasons' (the 30-year-old wife of an insurance clerk).

iii

These views on casual adultery were elicited relatively early in the interview; towards the end our informants were asked about their actual experiences; and frequently there was little consistency between their views and their admissions.

Twenty-two per cent of our married informants answered positively the question: 'Apart from kissing people in greeting or in fun (such as under the mistletoe) have you ever kissed anybody except your husband/wife since marriage?' More husbands than wives made this admission; they were predominantly over the age of 25, and there was some concentration among the early school-leavers, and in the lower middle and skilled working classes.

Eight per cent of our married informants said that they had made love to somebody besides their spouse since marriage; 5 % said they had gone 'all the way', 3 % that they had not. Twice as many husbands as wives made these admissions; again they were predominantly over the age of 25, most numerous in those who consider themselves skilled working class or who refuse to place themselves in a social class, and fewest among those who consider themselves upper working class. Three per cent, evenly divided between the two sexes, said they had had a love relationship with somebody since marriage without actually going 'all the way'.

Of the 5 % who had gone 'all the way' 2 % said they had only had one partner, and 1 % two, 1 % three and 1 % more than three. Slightly more wives than husbands admitted to only one partner, but the higher numbers are predominantly claimed by men.

I consider it a tribute to the interviewers' skill and to our informants' sincere collaboration that this number of admissions was secured in the course of single interviews; but with such small figures, very little more can be said about the social distribution of these candid informants.

Cross-correlations give somewhat more information. Extramarital flirtations and love-affairs would appear to be more general among the parents of large families; one might say that casualness in the two major aspects of marriage are correlated. Of those who said they had kissed somebody besides their spouse seriously (22 %), 26 % had five or more children, 26 % four, 24 % three, 23 % two, 20 % one and 19 % none. Of those who had 'made love' (8 %), 11 % were parents of four children, 9 % of three, 7 % of five or more, 6 % of two, 6 % of one and 3 % were childless. Of those who had gone 'all the way' (5 %), 8 % were parents of four children, 7 % of three, 5 % of five or more, 5 % of two, 5 % of one, and 3 % were childless. Of course, the parents of larger families are likely to be older than the parents of smaller ones; but those with more than three children are only 10 % of our total married population.*

Secondly, those who admit to adultery are likely to have had varied sexual experience before marriage also. This is not quite the same thing as saying that the promiscuous before marriage continue to be promiscuous after; a number of our respondents who had had more than one partner before marriage denied having strayed after marriage; but of those who did admit to flirting or love-making after marriage nearly all were sexually experienced beforehand.

Of those who said that they had seriously kissed someone besides their spouse after marriage (22 % of the total) there were 16 % of those who had not had intercourse before marriage, 21 % of those who had married their first partner, and 35 % of those who had married someone else. Of the total of 8 % who had 'made love' there were 2 % of those who had not had intercourse

* See Chapter One, page 20.

before marriage, 5% of those who had married their first partner and 15% of those who had married someone else. Of the 5% who had gone 'all the way', only 1% came from those who had had no intercourse before marriage, 5% from those who had married their first partner and 12% of those who had married someone else.

Correlating the number of partners admitted to after and before marriage, of those who had one post-marital partner, 4% had had one pre-marital partner, 8% two, 3% three and 4% more than three before marriage. Of those who had two post-marital partners, 1% had had only one partner before marriage, 4% had had three, and 7% more than three. Those who admitted to three or more partners after marriage had had, at the least, three partners before marriage.

The majority of those who admitted to their own extra-marital affairs were insistent on the importance of fidelity for the preservation of marriage and in many cases were very rigid in their views of how infidelity should be regarded; I only noted one informant who seemed conscious of the contradictions implicit in his different replies. This was a 28-year-old garage owner who had had two partners before marriage and one after; he replied to the question: 'Now that the pill provides absolute safety, do you think faithfulness is or is not as important as ever in marriage?' by saying: 'Yes – but I must seem like a hypocrite after my earlier answers!'

A 32-year-old skilled engineer replied to the same question: 'Just as important; the pill makes it safe to go with other people, but it would still destroy a marriage'; yet earlier he had admitted to two partners since marriage and was in favour of young men and women sleeping with anyone they were attracted to: 'One or two isn't enough; it's like he isn't getting a chance of picking his own partner; he must feel he is picking his own.'

Similarly, a 24-year-old taxi-driver thinks that despite the pill (which his wife takes) faithfulness is 'as important, indeed more so'; he had more than three partners before his marriage and two after.

Other respondents are very severe when they contemplate a husband or wife having a serious affair with another person:* 'Divorce her; divorce him' said a 22-year-old lorry driver, who

* See Chapter Eight.

admitted to three partners in his year of marriage. He was one of the fairly uncommon young men who maintained a double standard for pre-marital sexual behaviour; for young men 'Before you marry you should have your fling', but for young women: 'Most men would not like to marry a woman who had had intercourse with someone else!' He started intercourse when he was sixteen: he considers his three times a week average.

A 28-year-old postman said if he found his wife having an affair with another man 'I would tell her to go'; he has had two partners since marriage, though he had had none beforehand; he apparently regrets this, for in principle he is in favour of pre-marital experience: 'He won't be so incompetent when married if he has it before; so it broadens his mind and when he then falls in love he'll know what it is, and that it's not just sex.' Despite his varied experience, he does not believe women have orgasms.

Only a few of our informants were frankly hedonistic. Among these was a 44-year-old gas-board foreman who left school at 14, started intercourse at 16, had more than three partners before marriage and two since; he still has intercourse three times a week, which he considers average. When asked about a man or woman having an affair without loving the partner he replied: 'It doesn't make any difference, does it? It's just opportunity, more or less. [For women?] That happens regular; a woman's more made that way! It doesn't mean anything to me.'

A 43-year-old garage owner, a nominal Roman Catholic, started intercourse at the age of 14, had had more than three partners before he married at the age of 20 and has had several since; he volunteered the information that he had had between twenty-five and thirty women to date. To the question what a husband should do if he found his wife having an affair with another man he replied: 'I would play up hell, more for her allowing herself to be found out; I would make up then. Wives make better partners if they have an affair and make up.'

Another widely experienced man, both before and after marriage, is a 28-year-old electrical engineer, who answered the question about a casual affair: 'Good luck to him if he's well away from home and not likely to make his wife unhappy by her finding out. [For women?] If discreet, I guess one must accept it; but I like to think in my own case it wouldn't happen.' Rather inconsistently, he thinks a marriage can be wrecked by infidelity and no children.

The 31-year-old wife of a photogravure retoucher also thinks that a marriage will be wrecked by unfaithfulness, money problems or cruelty; she has had two partners since marriage.*

The 44-year-old wife of a postal clerical worker admitted to one partner after marriage; in reply to the question about the pill and fidelity she replied: 'Women tend not to be so faithful if they know they are safe.' She disapproved of pre-marital experience for either sex: 'You just like to think you're the first.'

The 25-year-old wife of a machinist thought that the pill made no difference to fidelity: 'Just the same'; on the pill itself she said: 'It takes the element of risk out of sex, but it is a good thing for limiting the family; it has made me less able to enjoy sex.'† She started intercourse at the age of 15, had three partners before her marriage at 16 and has had two since.

Another possible cousin of Molly Bloom is the 33-year-old wife of a partner in a building firm who had one partner before marriage and two after. She confided to the interviewer that her extra-marital relationships had helped her marriage, because she can achieve sexual satisfaction with other men but not with her husband.

* Her views on casual adultery are quoted above, p. 158.
† See footnote, p. 141.

Table 44

8 Serious adultery, separation and divorce

i

Almost without exception, our informants interpreted the questions 'If a husband finds his wife having an affair with another man, what should he do?' 'If a wife finds her husband having an affair with another woman, what should he do?' as referring to a serious love-affair in which, at least temporarily, affection and love are withdrawn from the spouse and transferred to another; and they answered these questions in quite different terms to the questions about a married man or woman having an affair without love analysed in the previous chapter.

These questions were also asked in *Exploring English Character**
but the sample was very different; in 1950 only married men
were asked about what action a husband should take and married
women about wives; in the present survey all respondents, whatever their sex or marital condition, were asked both questions.
Nevertheless, it seems worth while examining the similarities
and differences between the two surveys. Only very occasionally
did respondents advise that husbands and wives should take
different courses in a similar predicament.

Table Thirteen presents the results in tabular form. As can
be seen, it has been necessary to add two new categories: consultation with the Marriage Guidance Bureau, an institution
which had not been invented in 1950; and secondly analysing
the situation, a course advocated by a quarter of our population. I think there is more than a semantic difference between
'analysing the situation' and 'talking it over' with one's husband or wife, a course advocated by a quarter of the respondents
in both surveys; analysis implies making an intellectual effort
to understand and be articulate, at least to oneself, concerning

* *Op. cit.*, pp. 145–61 and Table 59.

Table thirteen

If a husband finds his wife having an affair with another man what should he do?

If a wife finds her husband having an affair with another woman what should she do?

Most of the answers in the present survey are almost, or completely identical for men or women; when there is a difference of 2% or over the figure for the action considered appropriate for women is given in parentheses.

Action advised	This survey				Exploring English Character		
	Total percentage	Married only	Men	Women	Total percentage	Men	Women
Talk it over with spouse	29%	26%	24% (26%)	31%	26%	24%	29%
Examine self/own faults	7%	8%	5%	10%	18%	20%	14%
Analyse situation	24%	25%	25%	24%	—	—	—
Try to reconcile	19%	18% (22%)	19%	19% (21%)	12%	10%	15%
Forgive – give one more chance	5%	6%	4%	6%	8%	8%	9%
Consult marriage guidance bureau	3%	4%	3%	3%	—	—	—
Ignore passing fancy	1%	1%	1%	1%	5%	3%	6%
Do nothing	1%	1%	1%	0%	4%	1%	9%
Preserve marriage for sake of children	4%	3%	4%	4%	7%	6%	7%
Make self more attractive	1%	1%	0%	1%	10%	1%	22%
Separation	15%	16%	17% (15%)	13%	14%	18%	9%

Table thirteen (*continued*)

Action advised	This survey				Exploring English character		
	Total percentage	Married only	Men	Women	Total percentage	Men	Women
Separation as last resort	5%	4%	4%	5%	12%	13%	10%
Divorce	7%	6%	10%	4%	9%	12%	5%
Divorce as last resort	5%	4%	8%	3%	12%	11%	12%
Physical violence on intervener	2%	2%	4% (1%)	1%	5%	9%	1%
Physical violence on spouse	5% (2%)	6% (2%)	6% (2%)	4% (1%)	5%	5%	0%
Upbraid spouse	2%	2%	2%	1%	6%	7%	6%
Upbraid intervener	2%	2%	3%	2%	5%	3%	8%

what has occurred, implicitly and, occasionally, explicitly, ex-
cluding the emotions of anger, jealousy or grief which might
cloud one's judgement. This attitude is consistent with the very
high value given to articulateness as a component of a happy
marriage which was analysed in Chapter Three.

This interpretation of 'analysing the situation' would appear
to be confirmed by the very marked diminution in the advocacy
of violent emotional responses: physical violence, such as
beating up the erring spouse or their paramour, the intervener,
or making scenes, upbraiding either. The few advocates of
such courses are almost entirely confined to those who consider
themselves working class or who refuse to classify themselves,
and particularly those living in the more traditional rural South-
West.

One course advocated by more than a fifth of the women in
1950 has practically disappeared today: this is the advice that a

wife can win back a straying husband by making herself physically more attractive. As I wrote then:*

Women tend to assume that the reason for their husband straying is that they have lost their physical attractions, and that they can win him back by smartening themselves up. It would be interesting to know whether this rather pathetic belief that an erring husband can be reclaimed by a new hair-do and smarter clothes has any foundation in fact or experience, or whether it be entirely the product of skilful advertisements and the women's magazines which carry them. Very few men indeed believe that improving their own appearance would be any help.

Analogous to the female belief that the husband had strayed because she had lost her physical attractions was the advice, proffered more by husbands than wives, that a man should examine himself and his own faults to see why the wife had strayed. This form of self-reproach, too, has considerably fewer advocates today; the interpretation of a husband's or wife's infidelity as a justified punishment for one's own sins of commission or omission seems to be quite markedly on the wane. This is, of course, congruent with the diminishment in religious belief and practice documented in the Introduction;† the belief that one's misfortunes in this world are due to one's misbehaviour in this world is a feature of many variants of Protestant ethics.

There is some increase (particularly from the husbands) in the advice that one should try to seek a reconciliation and quite a marked decrease in the envisaging of separation or divorce as a last resort, if the attempts at reconciliation or winning back the erring or straying spouse fail; but the percentages of those who consider that infidelity should automatically terminate a marriage remain remarkably constant. In 1950 12% of the husbands advocated immediate divorce and 18% separation; in 1969 the figures are 10% for divorce and 17% for separation. In 1950 5% of the wives advocated divorce and 9% separation; in 1969 the figures are 4% for divorce and 13% for separation. Although wives are less rigid than husbands, and presumably make some allowance for the believed differences in male and

* *Op. cit.*, pp. 145, 147.
† See pp. 10–12.

female sexuality, something like a sixth of the younger married women still believe that infidelity automatically ends a marriage, as do more than a quarter of the men. Many of these respondents are extremely rigid and unforgiving.

The choice between separation and divorce as a legal device for terminating a marriage, once infidelity has been discovered, is one of the most marked denotators of social class. The establishment of legal aid does not seem, yet, to have made any marked difference. Those who call themselves skilled working class or working class without modification have 19 % advocating separation to 8 % advocating divorce; the middle and lower middle classes have 11 % advocating separation and 5 % divorce.* Those calling themselves upper working class are somewhat anomalous; they are the only social group with more advocates for divorce than for separation.

As a generalization, one can say that as one goes down the socio-economic scale, the more rigid the unforgiving attitude towards infidelity. The middle class and the AB category advocate analysing the situation and talking it over; only 16 % think that the marriage should automatically be terminated. The picture is almost entirely reversed in the working class and the DE category; they are for action, not words, and the action envisaged is typically punitive. In a less marked degree, our older respondents, those aged over 35, are less forgiving than their juniors and less inclined to 'talk it over'; but the percentage differences are considerably smaller.

Typical advocates of a would-be rational approach to a wife's infidelity are: 'Not blow up; talk to her; not go off the deep end; and if they couldn't patch it up, let her go' (a 44-year-old butcher); 'Try to hold your temper and discuss the position first; otherwise just wait and see what happens. Losing my temper wouldn't do any good' (a 32-year-old skilled engineer†); 'If personal feelings and anger were controllable, I would like to be able to discuss the cause of it' (a 33-year-old driver).

Wives advancing similar views include the 35-year-old wife of a sculptor: 'Well, show understanding up to a point, and

---

* The contrast is even clearer on the Registrar General's categories. AB 2 % divorce, 6 % separation; C1 5 % divorce, 8 % separation; C2 8 % divorce, 18 % separation; DE 10 % divorce; 22 % separation.

† This informant admitted to two partners since his marriage.

state that you'd rather it was not so. It would be absurd to make dramatic demands'; 'Talk it over, and give him a second chance; if he still wanted the other woman I should let him go' (the 24-year-old wife of a filleter); 'Try and sort it all out and try to keep the marriage intact; I believe in the sanctity of marriage' (the 44-year-old wife of a dairy worker, an observant Anglican); 'It should not be secret; she should find out who is at fault; perhaps it is her fault' (the 41-year-old wife of a storekeeper, an ardent Spiritualist).

This last informant might perhaps have been included in that decreasing group who feel that their spouse's infidelity is their own fault. 'If it was me I'd ask why and where it was I'd failed. If you found this out, ask could he give her up? Try and keep the marriage and if there are children involved, I think a very special effort should be made' (the 28-year-old wife of a building sub-contractor, born in Eire and an observant Roman Catholic); 'She should have a long hard look at why he is having an affair; the first time she should hold her tongue and make herself more attractive; the first time it will probably peter out' (the 41-year-old wife of an engineering foreman).

Among self-reproaching husbands is a 38-year-old wages clerk: 'What was wrong with himself? Why could he not keep her happy and contented? He must make himself face the situation; if nothing comes of talking it over he would have to try and get a divorce.'

Nearly a fifth of our population advocated reconciliation or giving the erring spouse one more chance; but they were mostly very vague as to the means by which this should be achieved. 'Try and get him to give her up and start again together' (the 35-year-old wife of a painter and decorator); 'Ask him about it, if it's serious. If he's that sort of man, don't rush for a divorce; he'll probably get over it' (the 30-year-old wife of an insurance clerk); 'See if the marriage is worth saving; I'd rather not know' (the 23-year-old wife of a demolition worker); 'If it is the first time, they should try and talk things over and start again, but consider it a warning; if it happens again, it's no use continuing' (the 24-year-old wife of a clerical accountant, born in Corunna in Northern Spain); 'Forgive him and forget; wives can forget more easily. I am talking from experience' (the 41-year-old wife of an engineering maintenance surveyor); 'I always say I wouldn't have any second-hand goods, but I feel too much for him to give him up. My friend had a husband like that, and now it's all right again' (the 35-year-old wife of a service manager); 'If there are children they should sort it out and keep together for their sake, especially if there are young children; I wouldn't leave my children if it happened. If they are really unhappy and there are no children, they might as well leave each other, but when there are children I think they should put up with it' (the 33-year-old wife of a charge hand); 'Try to make things right. Personally I'd fight tooth and nail to keep my husband' (the 30-year-old wife of a systems-analyst programmer).

A 41-year-old plumber who had been divorced and re-married said: 'Depends on the affair – and on circumstances. It shouldn't be the end of everything. Stop the affair first and make sure that whatever caused it doesn't happen again. If this fails, then break up.' 'Try and get to the bottom of what made her step out on him. Be more attentive and understanding and try to make her forget all about it; but don't be too soft either' (a 28-year-old electrical engineer); 'Look at the qualities of the spouse and married life and if these are essential and rich in happiness the affair should be overlooked and efforts made to win him or her back' (a 43-year-old lecturer in economics); 'Try and save his marriage, by being understanding for what she has probably done and trying to reason with her as to why. I think if you go off the deep end you do not achieve anything' (a 36-year-old architectural assistant); 'Belt the wife and then the man first of all; I would then try to reason with the wife to stay for the children's sake. If one had not got children I would tell her to move out' (a 30-year-old school-teacher, a pious Pentecostal nonconformist); 'Give her a good hiding and talk her out of it' (a 35-year-old foreman electrician); 'He should not divorce his wife because of marriage vows; he should try to reason with her, point out to her the right course she should take and hope to win her back again' (a 45-year-old draughts-man, a pious Baptist).

Although recourse to the Marriage Guidance Council was recommended by 3 % of both sexes, by accident I only excerpted recommendations from women, and these are mostly middle-class, middle-aged and religious. Nevertheless, I think it worth giving their recommendations at some length, since this relatively new institution has valuable potentialities. The 39-year-old wife of a technical representative, an observant Roman Catholic, said:

'Depends, but the Marriage Guidance Council and that sort of thing is good because it is more impartial – it's hard to sort things out yourself when you're so involved. If he has a temper he could make a row – my husband would – I think he would. [For a wife?] The same sort of thing; but she should make a few more allowances because men are more swayed by their feelings. A woman feels she has more to lose – family and house; a man doesn't think like that.'

'First of all talk to her about it, if he can try and be rational, and find out why. It depends on the person, what he says, and the type of woman – whether she bursts into tears or has fits of temper. After he has talked to her, if they cannot solve it, go to a Marriage Guidance or a Minister for advice. [For a wife?] Examine herself; compare herself with the other woman. If she is a very young girl, see if she has let herself go' (the 32-year-old wife of a qualified surveyor).

'First of all he should talk to her very seriously, and if nothing comes of that, perhaps consult his Vicar or the local Marriage Guidance Council. If he consults his family there is a chance they will take sides. It all depends on the person. If he knows the other party he ought to approach him and see what can be done. [For a wife?] First of all try and have it out and put it on an open footing, then perhaps she should try to persuade him to go with her to the M.G.C. She probably won't manage this and find herself going on her own. I couldn't go to the other woman myself because I couldn't hold my temper. I'd follow the advice of the Marriage Guidance people and pray about it. I'd see how things went' (the 41-year-old wife of a lecturer in economics, an observant Anglican).

'Talk to the wife and find out what happened to their marriage. [For a wife?] Talk it over first – no good losing your head. If you cannot come to an agreement go and seek advice from the Marriage Guidance Bureau' (the 41-year-old wife of a plumber).

A small group advise doing nothing about it, or revenging themselves by taking a lover of their own. For a very few of our respondents different standards should be applied to the adultery of a husband than to that of a wife.

'Accept it, if it's only pure "sex" reasons, if the husband still

loves his wife' advises the 25-year-old wife of a machinist;*
'Ignore it as much as you can; man isn't sexually monogamous.
You must expect him to notice other people besides you' (the
33-year-old wife of a design draughtsman); 'Let it pass over if
he really loves her; no reason to break up the family if she
really loves him' (the 44-year-old wife of a clerical worker in the
G.P.O.);† 'Pay her back at her own game; do the same; I
would anyway' (the 26-year-old wife of a boat-builder); 'Do
nothing – I don't; go and do it yourself' (the 22-year-old wife of
a labourer.

Among men who advocate a double standard are a 36-year-
old chartered accountant:

'I'd probably blow my top, but initially, I'd try and talk about it,
find out why – there's probably something wrong with me to have
brought it on. [For a wife?] Women are more emotional than men
and their affairs are different. A man's affairs don't go very deep,
but when a woman is a nyphomaniac she must have affairs.'

'Talk to her; discuss it; but I don't think I'd stick it; not divorce,
but go my own way. [For a wife?] I don't know; there's not a lot
she could do. If they have children, nag at him, I would think, or go
home to her mother' (a 20-year-old painter, very recently married).

'Beat her. [For a wife?] Sleep on the sofa' (a 35-year-old commercial
designer).

'Shoot her. [For a wife?] Try and understand the reason for it'
(a 41-year-old holiday-camp entertainer).‡

'Beat her. [For a wife?] It's natural for a man to do it' (a 35-year-old
barber, born in Jamaica).

'I would give the bloke a bleeding good hiding. I would take custody
of the children and there would be no coming back for her. [For a
wife?] Best thing for her would be to go to the Marriage Guidance
and let them advise her' (a 34-year-old window cleaner).

'One of two things: clobber the missus or clobber the bloke. [For a
wife?] Find out what went wrong in order to rectify this' (a 28-year-
old tyre-fitter).

* This informant had three affairs before marriage and two since, but
considers that she has never been in love.
† This informant has had one lover since marriage.
‡ This informant has had numerous affairs since his marriage.

Several of our women informants also applied a double standard; as was shown in Chapters Two and Seven* in most situations women are more liable than men to apply a double standard, but this does not seem to be the case with serious adultery.

'Thump her round the nose. My husband would; he told me so. Look at it in perspective and discuss it. There must be a reason for her unfaithfulness, unless she is promiscuous, and not all that many women are. They are usually more stable than men are. Unless they are completely incompatible to start with I think there is usually a remedy. [For a wife?] I think the majority of men's affairs are not as serious; find out why he has to have an affair with someone else. Age enters into it of course. If possible, try to make it up and start afresh' (the 24-year-old wife of an assistant draughtsman).

'Give her a darned good hiding. [For a wife?] I'd rather sit down to talk and find out how it started, and sort it out' (the 24-year-old wife of a long-distance lorry driver).

'Tell her to go. [For a wife?] Depends how deep; if my husband really loved another woman, I would give him a divorce; I would be more offended if it was a light affair' (the 25-year-old wife of a toolmaker).

'Leave her if it's her fault; but if he hasn't been looking after his wife then it's his fault, and he'll have to put up with it. [For a wife?] If he can provide for you, you should put up with it; if not, leave him' (the 38-year-old wife of a labourer, born in Jamaica, who has been in England eleven years).

'Leave her. Just leave her. She wouldn't be a good wife. Leave her. [For a wife?] See why it happened; see who was wrong. The wife might have been wrong, not being a good wife to him; talk it over' (the 28-year-old wife of an ink-maker).

'He should have self-control and not beat her; talk about it and if she continues to do it, then he must leave her. [For a wife?] It is not as bad as when a woman does it. If he treats his wife bad, she must leave him; but if he still treats her good she must ignore it, and then he'll come home again for certain' (the 40-year-old wife of a driver, who was born in Jamaica and has been six years in England).

'I think he should try and give her another chance. [For a wife?] I

* pp. 43, 151.

think I would be ruthless; I can't forgive easily' (the 31-year-old
wife of a planning clerk).

'That's very difficult; I couldn't sit in judgement. He could try to
patch it up, but I don't think the wife's always to blame. [For a
wife?] If she's got children and he still loves her, to turn a blind eye
and keep one's fingers crossed is best. Every woman senses and knows
when her husband is interested in another woman; it is often best to
let it take its course' (the 35-year-old wife of a company director,
born in Eire).

A few of the informants last quoted would be unforgiving for
one of the straying spouses; but apart from these, I have so far
been quoting from the two-thirds (approximately) of our respondents who do not consider that discovered adultery should
automatically end a marriage. The remaining third are rigid
and unforgiving and, typically, very terse: 'Divorce him'; 'Turn
her out'; 'That would be the end' and the like. A few expatiated:

'He shouldn't forgive her; that's the end. I don't agree with that
caper; I'd always bring it up in an argument. He wouldn't really
ever forgive. [For a wife?] I couldn't forgive him. She should pack
her bags and go; she'd have to be a cabbage to stay' (the 35-year-old
wife of a self-employed building contractor).

'That would be the end. He would have nothing to do with it.
Some could forgive, but those that do I think have a guilty conscience
too. [For a wife?] As far as I'm concerned, the same – finish – done
with it' (the 39-year-old wife of a poultry farmer).

'Put her out when that happens; it's never the same. [For a wife?]
Let him out of the door and that's final; don't let him back again'
(the 31-year-old wife of a fish salesman).

'Once they start that way it's pretty hopeless; and probably it is better
to finish than to try to patch it up. It doesn't usually work anyway.
[For a wife?] Leave him; nothing else would work. If he's that way
he'd be doing it all the time and it's not worth trying to keep two
people together when they don't love one another' (the 24-year-old
wife of a steel fixer).*

'He should not have any blows or bother; he should just turn her
out, put her suitcases through the door. [For a wife?] I should never

* This is this informant's second marriage; her first marriage was terminated by a divorce.

want to have anything to do with him again; just leave' (the 44-year-old wife of a worker in the Midlands who was not sure what her husband's job was'.*)

'I think he should kick her out. If there's any children it's not as easy. I do not think he could ever trust her again. [For a wife?] Kick him out. If I found my husband was having an affair with another woman I would never trust him any more and I would never be happy any more' (the 45-year-old wife of a bricklayer).

'Mine says he would kill me; I think he would throw me out; I think this is how most men would act. [For a wife?] Turn him out or leave him; I would leave mine' (the 41-year-old wife of a foreman builder).

'Not have anything else to do with her; have her as a housekeeper and just be like a lodger, if he couldn't turn her out, especially if there are children. [For a wife?] I think if the wife is independent she should pack up and go; but it might be wiser to turn the other cheek and try and forgive him, if he'll give up and start afresh' (the 37-year-old wife of a herdsman, a very observant member of the Church of England).

'Leave her. That sort of woman wouldn't be a good wife or mother. I should think he would leave her unless he was a very forgiving sort of man. It would depend on them both – what they were like. [For a wife?] If it was me, I would finish the marriage. I have sisters who have been through this, and what they've been through is dreadful. I would say leave him straight away' (the 39-year-old wife of a railway foreman).

'He should sling her out. [For a wife?] I would forgive but never forget; I did this' (the 28-year-old wife of a chemical processor).

'My husband told me once he would shoot me and the other man as well. I think he would tell me not to come into the house again. I think he should tell her to clear off and not take it lying down. I do not think he should tolerate to live with her. [For a wife?] Give her husband to know that if he wants to carry on with it, she would separate. It is easier for a man to have an affair and get away with it' (the 30-year-old wife of a carpenter).

'I can't say "Forgive and forget" because I was brought up in an unhappy home. I would always doubt him. Looking at it from a man's point of view, he would feel the same. Once the seed of distrust is sowed, it is a lot to get over. Stay together if possible;

* See Chapter Four, p. 92.

but if they are going to brood, it is better to part. [For a wife?] Forgive and forget if possible; but rather than brood over it, it is better to part; it is much worse for the children to be brought up in an unhappy home' (the 36-year-old wife of a businessman).

'Get a divorce straight away; there can be no deep love there to want something else or somebody else. [For a wife?] Leave him. I've got very strong views on that point' (the 29-year-old wife of a gas-fitter).

'She deserves a good hiding; and I think they'd have to separate because it would always be on his mind and he wouldn't ever forget. [For a wife?] I'd never forgive my husband but I'd have to stick it out because of the children and my religion' (the 34-year-old wife of a power-press operator, a very observant Roman Catholic born in Eire).

'Throw her out; I'm a bit funny about anything like that' (the 45-year-old wife of an engineer).

'I think it better if they part right away rather than try a reconciliation. I think if they are looking for someone else, there must be something wrong with the marriage in the first place. [For a wife?] Again I think it's better for them to part. I don't think much good comes of trying to patch things up between them' (the 23-year-old wife of a plumber).

'It would depend on circumstances. In my case we'd probably part. I don't think it would be any use trying to patch it up if you get into the state of wanting to go out with someone else. [For a wife?] I think a man tends to have an affair more easily; but otherwise I think the same; once this sort of thing starts I think it is the beginning of the end' (the 24-year-old wife of a self-employed builder).

Unforgiving men tend to be less wordy. 'Let her go to her fancy man' (a 43-year-old haulage contractor); 'Finish the marriage as so few relationships are ever built anew' (a 45-year-old lorry driver); 'Could not carry on with the marriage; would not be able to take back the wife' (a 41-year-old lorry driver born in Ceylon, a Buddhist); 'Send his wife packing, that's all' (a 38-year-old local government employee); 'I would give my wife a good hiding; if it were serious enough, if there was not a chance of patching it up, then divorce' (a 31-year-old fitter); 'My pride would be hurt more than anything else; the only answer would be separation' (a 45-year-old chief cashier).

ii

We prepared a number of questions to be asked of those whose marriages had broken down; but they were only asked of sixteen divorced and twenty-four separated or deserted people* (2 % of our total population); and consequently the analysis of these answers into percentages seems to me to be of dubious significance. When one individual represents $2\frac{1}{2}$ % of a total, precise percentages appear, to me, to give a misleading impression of exactitude.

Infidelity and adultery accounted for about a third of the marriage break-downs; other causes which had more than single examples were lack of communication, neglect and social incompatibility. Of these broken marriages a quarter had lasted under three years and another quarter between four and six years. The longest marriage which was finally dissolved had lasted sixteen years. A third of these broken marriages had been childless; in a few cases this was the cause of the break-down.

Compared with the marriages which have endured, there was a tendency for marriages which did not endure to be entered into after fairly short acquaintance; precisely half had known the future spouse a year or less before getting married, a fifth less than six months. Betrothals, if any, were short; a third did not have any formal betrothal. Several of the marriages were 'forced' by the future wife's pregnancy; in quite a few cases the husband had had no sexual experience before his unfortunate marriage.

Half of those with broken marriages expected to marry again, a quarter did not, and a quarter were uncertain; a third had a second legal partner in view. Half of the informants had been 'physically intimate' with another man or woman since the break-up of their marriage; the great majority had only had one other partner.

In their views of what makes for a happy marriage the divorced and separated emphasize (in contrast with those whose marriage has endured) give-and-take and financial security; they under-emphasize discussing things together, comradeship

* There were a few informants in these categories to whom the interviewers omitted to pose the appropriate questions; but they did not reach two figures.

and children. In their views of what tends to wreck a marriage they emphasize poverty, conflicting personalities, sexual incompatibility and in-laws; they under-emphasize selfishness, neglect, bad temper and lack of affection. The ideal of a symmetrical marriage, discussed in Chapter Two, does not seem to be operative in the minds of those whose marriages have failed. The emphasis on financial security and poverty would seem to arise, at least in part, from the dire financial straits of some of the abandoned wives. A 23-year-old separated woman who had to get married because she was pregnant, at the age of 16, and who had had a second child was meant to receive £9 3s. 0d. a week 'but I haven't had anything from him for some weeks'; another in a similar case, the 30-year-old wife of a city merchant said: 'He allows me £6 a week to keep the children and lets me live here without paying anything.' A woman living on social security (she too had had to get married for a baby) was questionably worse off.

The two questions whose answers gave the most information were: 'What went wrong with your marriage?' and 'Have you any advice you would like to give to young people so that they might avoid the unhappiness you have been through?';* and it is predominantly from these answers that I shall quote. Where it seems relevant, I shall also quote their answers to the question discussed above on what a husband or wife should do if they find their spouse having an affair with another man or woman. For the sake of convenience I will first quote separated men, secondly separated women, thirdly divorced men and finally divorced women.

A 45-year-old boilerman separated from his wife:

'Because there weren't any children and she wouldn't have any. Her brother was living with us and she would feed him and not give me any food.'

A 39-year-old injection moulder said:

'Another man took her away. [Any advice?] The man who took her away was a workmate of mine and I used to bring him home for meals, etc. My advice would be not to bring friends home too often.'

* Indicated in the quotations by [any advice?].

The 22-year-old former wife of a chief engineer on a trawler separated from her husband:

'The main reason was that my husband wanted sex without my consent, and his dislike of the twins because they weren't his. I have a baby girl by him. General lack of respect.'

Despite the obvious side-step before her marriage, this informant's views on adultery are severe. On the question about casual adultery she answered:

'I think it's horrible; if he just goes with her for sex I don't agree with it. [For women?] Horrible; I don't agree with casual affairs.'

And on a serious affair:

'It all depends how far the affair has gone. They should talk about it; and if there is a chance of giving the other woman up, they should forget about it and start again. [For a wife?] Talk it over, and then, if there's no hope, they would be better separated.'

What she considered could wreck a marriage were:

'Various things; in-law trouble; mothers interfering. When they start to go out with unmarried friends, and you don't know where they are going. If you *have* to get married, they don't let you forget it.'

The only advice she had to give was: 'to get to know the man as long as possible before you think of marriage.'

A rather pathetic case was a 22-year-old woman, deserted by her husband after only seven months of marriage, and left to bring up her child on social security payments only:

'He ran off – I don't know what else. He is living with another woman with two kids. Left after a week's rows. I heard he fancied someone else.'

She had met her husband through a friend of his in the Army:

'He used to write to me while I was going out with the friend. [Any advice?] Be careful, and speak to the parents about boys. I was scared to ask my parents in case they bit my head off. I didn't know the facts of life; I still don't know a lot.'

She was in favour of pre-marital sexual experience for young men, but not for young women. In the case of young men:

'They know about how to do it – men don't ever get tired of it! [For young women?] You can get fed up with it; you've had it all before. There's nothing to look forward to.'

Her idea of a good husband is a man who is 'Able to stand up to anything; able to keep a job; able to decorate the house'; and she sees as the cause of a marriage being wrecked:

'Rows; disagreements about money matters. If you have to get married for a baby, that often doesn't work out.'

In the case of serious adultery, she advised:

'If there are children concerned, they should try and patch it up for the child's sake; [For a wife?] Give him one more chance, a warning; and if he does it again, think again. Again, if children are involved, sort it out.

A 23-year-old woman met her husband at a dance in a pub and married him when she was 16; she has two children:

'Looking back, I don't think he could ever have loved me; of course he had to marry me, so you don't know, do you? We had to get married when the first was on the way. [Any advice?] Get to know the man well before, so that you really know what he's like.'

An unfortunately timed interview was with the 38-year-old wife of a machine operator; when asked the question about serious adultery she replied:

'I don't know. I really don't know. I honestly don't know. I might forgive him for the children's sake. My husband has just left me and I don't know what to do.'

One can almost hear the tears in her voice. She was clearly full of self-reproaches; when asked about the faults wives tend to have, she replied: 'Wives tend to nag; I went to work too much; too house-proud.' Her views on casual adultery were severe:

'He is no husband to have; it must be awful for the wife. Don't think a lot of him at all. [For women?] I don't understand how she could; it's not natural if you have a husband and children.'

What went wrong with the marriage of a 30-year-old woman to a prosperous city merchant was:

'Lack of communication. Lack of understanding. I couldn't get over to him what was important. I had mother-in-law trouble and never got his support and he was always on her side. Now he is saying he'll sue for divorce because of my adultery. [Any advice?] To sort out any differences beforehand. I knew I had this mother-in-law trouble, but I thought he would be more for me. He let me down, I shall always say that. I wanted us to make our own little world and everything and everybody else to come after that. He didn't see it that way. I wish he would change his mind and have me back.'

She named, as the qualities a husband should have:

'Loyalty, over moral issues. Kindness, in respect to your relationships with other people, to back you up. Generosity, as far as finances go.

On casual adultery, as far as men are concerned:

'I think it's natural. It's the basic instincts of a man which come to the fore, much more than in the case of a woman. [For women?] I don't think much of them; it isn't quite so natural; sex doesn't usually interest a woman as much.'

On serious adultery:

'He should be prepared to discuss it and find out what went wrong. He should find out what makes her go to other men. If she's been unfaithful there's nothing else he can do. [For a wife?] The same – it's just the same.'

A 30-year-old dress machinist was married at the age of 17 and has five children; she is a very observant Seventh Day Adventist, born in the West Indies. She had known her husband all her life:

'We grew up together. We came over from the West Indies together; and then he wanted to go back and I preferred to stay here. If he had stayed in England we would still be together. Three of the children are with me here, the two younger ones are with my mother in the West Indies.'

The 25-year-old separated wife of a carpenter, a fairly observant Roman Catholic, said in reply to the question about what went wrong with her marriage:

'I don't really know. I think my husband got attracted to another woman; he didn't like being tied down. He's living with her now. [Any advice?] Do things together as much as you can without being possessive, but yet keep an eye on each other. People shouldn't marry too young. I don't think I was as sexually mature as my husband, he was nine years older.'

On serious adultery, her advice was:

'I think first of all discuss it, and then it is individual; it depends on the woman; one wouldn't want her back, another would forgive. I think she should have a second chance. [For a wife?] I think she should ask her husband to give this other woman up. I think it is easier for men; their make-up is different. If he's unwilling, there's nothing to be done; but she should have him back if she can.'

She named, as desirable qualities in a husband:

'I think he should be honest – I mean truthful. I think he should enjoy the family life. I think he should put his wife and family before anyone else.'

Among divorced men was a 29-year-old electrical engineer, who entered marriage without any sexual experience:

'She went off with another man. Reasons were that I thought more of my car and my work than of her. [Any advice?] I'd never trust another woman with any man other than the husband, leaving them together for any length of time.'

A 34-year-old remarried tool-fitter said:

'The wife was put in the family way by a stranger to me. I gave my first wife all the money I earned, and this left me without any at all to take her out; she wanted to have the cake and eat it.'

A 42-year-old man with his own car-hire business:

'Did not agree sexually. [Any advice?] Before engagement you should know the person at least two years; should go on holiday together.'

A 43-year-old warehouseman, whose marriage had lasted eighteen years and produced two children, who were living with him, said that what went wrong with his marriage was:

'The culmination of two or three things, but in the main, I could not satisfy my wife sexually. [Any advice?] I can't really. It happens in life. I mean you can't teach how to act in sex life.'

A 35-year-old representative said with refreshing candour 'My fault – another woman'; he had no advice to give. When questioned about casual adultery, he replied:

'It's happened to me; I think it's wrong; probably happens when least expected. [For a woman?] I can't understand it.'

But his views on serious adultery were surprisingly severe:

'Thump her – then the man – try to patch it up with the wife, find out why she went astray; if this fails, divorce. [For a wife?] Have it out with the husband and try to straighten it out; but if there are children and talk fails, I do not know what should be done; it depends on the woman.'

This obviously honest and honourable respondent gives one of the best illustrations I know of the self-punishing strict conscience.

A 43-year-old long-distance driver approached marriage without any sexual experience, and his marriage was childless. He considered this latter cause the main reason for his marriage break-down:

'No children; and my being away at night on long-distance driving. [Any advice?] Start a family early in marriage, because children keep the marriage together.'

He was still opposed to sexual experience before marriage: 'It is not right to have intercourse with anybody unless you're in love.'

Another driver, aged 37, had had no sexual experience before his marriage at the age of 30. 'I was neglected – food point of view'; he had no advice to give.

A 39-year-old chemical-process worker had six children in his nineteen years of marriage; the cause of his marriage break-down was:

'In-law trouble. She would not leave them and I wanted us to live on our own. [Any advice?] I would say tolerance and give-and-take.'

A 40-year-old headmaster said of his former marriage:

'We were totally unsuited both temperamentally and physically; it was a big mistake. [Any advice?] Make sure they have some cultural and common principles in life.'

On casual adultery he said:

'Asking for trouble, for an unhappy home life. He is thinking about sex, rather than doing his best for his wife and family.'

A 41-year-old plumber was first married at the age of $17\frac{1}{2}$, and has since re-married; of his first marriage he said:

'We hated the sight of one another. We were completely different people and intolerant of one another. Sexual life practically non-existent for the last seven or eight years of marriage. [Any advice?] The chief thing is to get to know your partner well enough before marriage. Act as one unit when married; no secrets; all property in common.

A 45-year-old electrician did not have intercourse before his marriage at the age of 21, and still disapproves of pre-marital experience: 'There are too many complications if a pregnancy results and it is morally wrong'; what happened to his marriage was:

'She was a bad money manager, which led ultimately to loss of love between us. [Any advice?] No, it's all a matter of circumstances.'

Among the divorced women was a very inarticulate 40-year-old wife of a porter. This was her third marriage and she had twice been divorced for adultery; her first marriage lasted ten weeks, the second two years.

A rather sad story is that of a 45-year-old woman who had moved with her factory-worker husband from Wales to a town in the Midlands:

'My husband became involved with a woman who wouldn't leave him alone. She threatened suicide several times; police were involved. He was all right in Wales; this was in L— [Any advice?] No. Everything was all right until we came to L—; you can't know what lies ahead; I wouldn't have thought it could happen.'

The 32-year-old wife of a scrap-metal merchant was first married at the age of 17; with this marriage 'almost everything' went wrong 'including the fact that he had another woman'. She would give no advice: 'You learn only by your own mistakes.' Her second marriage appeared very happy; she has intercourse nearly every night.

A woman who was 24 at the time of the interview had led a very active sexual life. She had had more than three partners between the age of 17 and meeting her former husband, a laminator, at the age of 21; they met at a dance and got married after two months' acquaintance. While she was married they had intercourse fourteen times a week, which she considers average; she complained: 'My husband was very underdeveloped physically and mentally.'* Despite her own history, her views on casual adultery are strict:

'Not much: if he's like that he can't be a good husband. [For women?] Disgusting, I think; really, it's worse than when a man does it.'

The 45-year-old wife of a printer had a first marriage which only lasted two years; she did not get engaged to her first husband, just 'knew him for a few months':

'We just didn't get on at all, and he drank a lot. [Any advice?] Know someone for quite a while and get to know his habits and family background.'

The 33-year-old wife of a machine-setter operator said:

'We lived together for four years. I had to have an operation and my husband didn't understand me. [Any advice?] From the woman's point of view, I think she should have a complete check-up before she marries; that is because of my trouble; but probably it is not necessary in most cases. I should say never have secrets from each other: complete trust.'

A 37-year-old woman, now working as an executive secretary, said of her marriage:

'Mental cruelty. My husband had a Jekyll and Hyde nature; he was lazy and would not work. [Any advice?] In my case it was a question of mental health. It is hard to give advice; but I would like to say to avoid a lengthy period of suffering. As soon as you feel something is wrong, and you have had medical advice, make the break as soon as possible.'

This woman took a fairly lenient view of casual adultery:

'Would not condemn him; could be sexual attraction. [For women?] Would not condemn her; you don't have to be in love to have an affair.'

On serious adultery:

* This is what the interviewer wrote down; I think it possible that the informant said: 'My husband was very overdeveloped physically and underdeveloped mentally.'

'Find out first how deep the feeling is for the other woman; ignore it if it's a mere flirtation; if it's a lot more than this she should leave him.'

The 39-year-old wife of a works manager said of her first marriage:

'We just drifted apart. We took a public house and didn't have enough time for each other. We were always working and often had to have our meals at different times. [Any advice?] Not to get married too young. Go out and enjoy themselves before they settle down to marriage. It's a long time; and they wouldn't regret it if they had enjoyed themselves before marriage.'

Although the numbers of the divorced and separated in the sample are too few for any valid generalizations, I think it worth while calling attention to the relatively minor role played by infidelity in the break-up of these marriages, and the relatively major role played by ignorance: ignorance of the spouse's character when marriage is based on very short acquaintance; ignorance of birth-control techniques when marriage is forced by an unwanted pregnancy;* and in some cases, one cannot help suspecting, ignorance of the technique of heterosexual intercourse.

Figures of distribution

If a husband/wife finds his wife/her husband having an affair with another man/woman, what should he/she do?

Differences of 3 % are treated as possibly significant.

By age Those aged 16–20 emphasize divorce (13 % in the case of the husband, 12 % in the case of the wife); divorce as last resort (10 % in the case of the husband and 9 % in the case of the wife); talking it over (37 % for both spouses); try to reconcile (23 % in case of the husband); verbal reproaches to the intervener (5 % in the case of the wife). They under-emphasize separation (11 % in the case of the husband, 10 % in the case of the wife); for the husband they also under-emphasize physical violence on the wife (2 %), analysing the situation (21 %) and

* The lack of birth-control precautions among the unmarried is documented in more detail in Chapter Ten, p. 216.

considering the effect on the children (1 %); in the case of the wife they under-emphasize examining oneself (5 %).

Those aged 21–24 under-emphasize separation in the case of the wife (11 %)

Those aged 24–34 are on the average.

Those aged 35–45 emphasize separation (17 %) and under-emphasize talking it over (25 %).

By self-ascribed social class. The middle class emphasize for both spouses talking it over (33 %), and analysing the situation (28 % and 29 %); they also emphasize that a husband should examine himself (10 %). They under-emphasize separation (11 % for both spouses).

The lower middle class emphasize for husbands examining himself (11 %) and for wives trying to reconcile (23 %) and ignoring the passing fancy (3 %). For both spouses they under-emphasize separation (12 % for husbands, 10 % for wives); for wives they also under-emphasize divorce (4 %) and separation as a last resort (2 %).

The skilled working class emphasize separation (18 % for husbands, 17 % for wives) and divorce in the case of a wife (10 %); they under-emphasize divorce as a last resort (2 % for both spouses).

The upper working class emphasize divorce for both spouses (15 % in the case of the husband, 14 % in the case of the wife) and trying to reconcile (25 % in the case of the husband and 24 % in the case of the wife); in the case of the husband they emphasize separation (18 %); in the case of wives considering the effect on the children (7 %). They under-emphasize husbands' talking it over (25 %) and wives analysing the situation (20 %) and separation (7 %). This social class has the largest group (7 %) who say they do not know what should be done.

The working class emphasize separation (19 % in the case of husbands, 20 % in the case of wives); for husbands they also emphasize trying to reconcile (16 %) and violence on the intervener (4 %). For both spouses they under-emphasize talking it over (23 %) and analysing the situation (21 % in the case of husbands, 22 % in the case of wives). In the case of wives they also under-emphasize examining herself (5 %).

Those who refuse to place themselves in a social class emphasize in the case of the husband physical violence on the erring spouse (8%) and giving one more chance (8%); they under-emphasize analysing the situation (19%). In the case of the wife they emphasize separation (17%) and considering the effect on the children (8%); they under-emphasize analysing the situation (19%) and examining oneself (5%).

The Registrar General's categories AB emphasize talking it over (37% for a husband, 35% for a wife) analysing the situation (31% for a husband, 30% for a wife) and examining one's own faults (10% for a husband, 13% for a wife). In the case of a husband 7% say they don't know. They under-emphasize separation (6% for either spouse) and divorce (2% for either spouse). In the case of a husband they under-emphasize physical violence on the wife (2%), divorce as a last resort (2%) and separation as a last resort (1%). In the case of wives they under-emphasize trying to reconcile (16%).

C1 emphasize for both spouses examining oneself (11% and 12%) and under-emphasize separation (8% and 9%).

C2 heavily emphasize separation (18% in the case of a husband and 17% in the case of a wife).

DE emphasize separation even more strongly (22% in the case of a husband and 20% in the case of a wife) and divorce in the case of a husband (10%). They under-emphasize talking it over for both spouses (23% in the case of a husband, 25% in the case of a wife); and for wives they under-emphasize analysing the situation (20%) and examining oneself (4%).

The regions The North-East and North under-emphasize talking it over (24% in the case of the husband, 25% in the case of the wife) and separation as a last resort (2% for both spouses).

The Midlands have a high proportion of those saying they do not know (8% in the case of a husband, 7% in the case of a wife). In the case of a wife they under-emphasize talking it over (25%), analysing the situation (22%) and giving one more chance (3%).

The South-East heavily emphasize talking it over (31% in the case of a husband, 33% in the case of a wife).

The South-West is in many ways the most anomalous region. In the case of a husband they emphasize physical violence on the wife (8%) and physical violence on the intervener (7%); they also emphasize trying to reconcile (28%) and separation as a last resort (8%). In the case of a wife they emphasize separation (17%) and divorce as a last resort (8%); but they also emphasize trying to reconcile (32%) and considering the effect on the children (7%). For both spouses they under-emphasize talking it over (21% in the case of a husband, 20% in the case of a wife).

The North-West emphasize talking it over (31%) in the case of a husband and analysing the situation (32%) and giving one more chance (10%) in the case of a wife. For both spouses they under-emphasize trying to reconcile (13%), examining oneself (3% in the case of a husband, 4% in the case of a wife) and divorce as a last resort (2%).

9 *Homosexuality and the gamut of attitudes*

i

The final topic on which the whole sample was asked its views was homosexuality. To the best of my knowledge, a scientifically selected sample has never been simultaneously asked its views on homosexuality and the various aspects of extra-marital heterosexuality in any country; I thought it might be possible to establish whether the distaste for or disgust at homosexuality was of a different nature to the distaste for or disgust at pre-marital or extra-marital heterosexuality.

The question asked was 'How do you feel about people who fall in love with members of their own sex?' This form of words was chosen intentionally to imply emotional involvement, analogous to the questions about sexual experience before or after marriage; in this context I was not interested in investigating adolescent experimentation or the improvisations of sexually segregated groups. I wanted our informants to consider emotional commitments, not physical expedients.

Some people did, indeed, express revulsion, 23 % of the men and 25 % of the women, and they were not questioned further; the remainder were asked: 'Have you yourself ever felt any sort of attraction towards a person of your own sex? What did you do about it?' The 2 % of the men and 3 % of the women who answered this question positively will be considered later in this chapter.

I established the following categories on the basis of a 10 % sample; I am giving first the key word, and then the synonyms I supplied, in some cases, to assist the coders.

Revulsion; disgusting behaviour, turns my stomach, makes me curl up inside: voiced by 23 % of the men and 25 % of the women.

Moral disapproval; completely wrong, awful: voiced by 5% of the men and 4% of the women.

Dislike; don't like it, don't agree with it, against it, no patience with it: voiced by 10% of the men and 6% of the women.

Not understandable; odd, abnormal, strange, queer, kinky: voiced by 14% of the men and 12% of the women.

Ridiculous: voiced by 4% of the men and 2% of the women.

Mentally ill; sick: voiced by 10% of the men and 13% of the women.

Can't help it; need help: voiced by 5% of the men and 9% of the women.

Need psychiatric or medical help: voiced by 3% of the men and 2% of the women.

Pity; sorry for them, thankful I'm not: voiced by 16% of the men and 28% of the women.

Tolerance; their own business, live and let live, it's natural for them, doesn't bother me, could happen to anyone: voiced by 16% of the men and 8% of the women.

Five per cent of our respondents had no decided views (some said so in as many words; some just did not answer); and a very few said it was unkind to make fun of homosexuals. Although I provided a special category for this view, I am omitting it in the following analysis.

These categories can be amalgamated into three major groups: the hostile (revulsion, moral disapproval, dislike); the neutral (not understandable, ridiculous, mentally ill, need psychiatric help, can't help it); and the tolerant (pity and tolerance). These three groups are of almost identical size.

The chief difference between the sexes is in the expressing of tolerance; twice as many men as women phrased this directly, whereas nearly twice as many women as men indicated their pity. The only other categories with a marked percentage difference were dislike voiced by 4% more men than women, and can't help it, voiced by 4% more women than men.

Toleration decreases and hostility increases quite markedly with age, though the young, between 16 and 20, have a high proportion (8%) with no decided views. Tolerant views were advanced by 30% of those aged between 16 and 20, 40% of those aged between 21 and 24, 39% of those aged between 25 and 34, and 28% of those aged between 35 and 45; hostile views were advanced by 27% of those aged between 16 and 20, 38% of those aged between 21 and 24, 34% of those aged between 25 and 34, and 43% of those aged between 35 and 45. The proportion of neutral views changes very little with age, apart from a slight drop over the age of 35. These figures suggest that there is a marked increase in the toleration of homosexuality in those under the age of 35.

With the exception of the rather anomalous group who call themselves upper working class, toleration decreases and hostility increases as one goes down the scale of self-ascribed social class or the Registrar General's categories. Regionally, the greatest amount of hostility is found in the North-West, followed by the Midlands; the greatest amount of toleration is found in the South-East, followed by the North-East. Possibly these contrasts could be correlated with increasing sophistication and education, or the increasing rejection of even nominal religion; but unfortunately these calculations were not made.

Some of our informants expressed their hostility in very violent terms, but so did others on the topic of casual adultery. 'I can't put words strong enough; utter contempt; would drown the lot of them' (a 38-year-old cemetery foreman); 'Terrible; shocking; degrading' (a 37-year-old painter and decorator); 'It's revolting; disgusting; can't see what's in it; there must be something wrong with them' (a 37-year-old holiday-camp assistant); 'Pity, no, disgust, I think it is an incurable hereditable disease brought about by the fault of the mother' (a 41-year-old shop-manager); 'I don't agree, and would not allow any excuse for this practice' (a 36-year-old butchery manager); 'Disgusting; not only going against God's laws but also defiling their bodies; using their organs for things they were never intended for, and reaping disease from it, which they do' (a 28-year-old greengrocer, a very observant Jehovah's Witness); 'I dislike the practice; I believe it is due to lack of early sex with girls' (a 43-year-old garage owner); 'Do not like them – have nothing to do with them – but they cannot help it; they are just perverted' (a 19-year-old unmarried* charge-hand fitter, a very observant Roman Catholic); 'Disgusted, but sorry for them; however I do not think such conduct is acceptable, or that it should be tolerated' (a 45-year-old draughtsman, an observant Baptist); 'I accept it – I can understand women, they seem harmless, but not male homosexuals; I'm always wary of them, find them off-putting' (a 31-year-old solicitor's clerk).

Female hostility can be illustrated by: 'Personally, I think it's awful. I don't like it. It's repulsive to me to think of women going together. I'd rather a married woman having an affair with another man than that. I think it must be something they are born with' (the 24-year-old wife of a self-employed builder); 'Disgusting; they want shooting' (the 41-year-old wife of an electrical engineer); 'Horrifies me; I hate to see it' (the 38-year-old wife of an inn-keeper); 'Terrible that is; it makes me feel sick' (the 24-year-old divorced and remarried wife of a steel-fixer); 'Revolting – not so bad in a man but unforgivable in a woman' (the 24-year-old wife of an industrial engineer, who was born in India); 'Terrible: not right having "bread and bread"' (the 45-year-old wife of a taxi-driver.)

Neutrality can be illustrated by: 'Must be crackers – just not natural – hard up for sex' (a 38-year-old accountant); 'They are hypocrites; they are probably idiots; they just annoy me and I have no time for them' (a 26-year-old unmarried medical orderly); 'It is a little bit unnatural, due to some hormone im-balance; they are unhealthy people who need treatment' (a 33-year-old anaesthetist, born in Pakistan); 'Until a few years ago I was disgusted, but as I get older I think they need special help' (a 32-year-old skilled engineer); 'They are like a music-hall joke; they need medical treatment' (a 37-year-old car-penter).

Among the neutral are the 33-year-old wife of a factory charge-hand: 'It seems silly to me; quite honestly, I can't see what fun or enjoyment there is or anything in it really.'† 'I don't think they can; they only think they do' (a 27-year-old

---

* In this chapter, for the first time, I am quoting some unmarried in-formants; the reason, I think, is obvious.

† In reply to the question whether she had ever felt any sort of attraction herself, this informant said: 'No; I do not think women can agree; I think they are like cats and dogs.'

unmarried woman, working as an upholsterer); 'I don't know very much about it, but I feel they need help. It's probably something medical, or perhaps frustration, or perhaps something happened to them as children to put them off the opposite sex. I don't understand it, but I don't condemn; there but for the grace of God . . .' (the 41-year-old wife of a lecturer in economics, an observant Anglican); 'I don't think it's their fault; there must be something wrong with them' (the 23-year-old wife of a self-employed builder); 'Not much; but then I do not think they can always help it. They do what they like; you only have one life and you can do what you like with it as long as they do not involve anyone else' (the 30-year-old wife of a carpenter); 'I think it's natural really. It may be their nature; some people can't help it. I feel I can understand the men, perhaps, but not the women' (the 35-year-old wife of a service manager); 'Just one's make-up; one can't help it' (the 27-year-old wife of a machine manager).

Pity is predominantly a feminine response; it was very succinctly phrased by a 16-year-old schoolgirl: 'I pity them; not at all disgusted, but glad I am normal'; 'I think it's just very sad for them; I don't think they can help it; it's born in them; I don't condemn them' (the 26-year-old wife of an overseas service engineer); 'Sorry for them actually; I think it's sex off balance. Although it's legal now, it's still looked down on. You can't blame people' (the 32-year-old wife of a technical representative, an observant Roman Catholic); 'I don't quite know. I was never one of those to have crushes on female school-teachers. I think this is a general problem; I feel sorry for them' (the 32-year-old wife of a surveyor, an observant Methodist); 'With men I feel sorry for them; but with women it disgusts me' (the 23-year-old wife of an R.E.M.E. craftsman); 'I feel sorry for them; I feel they are missing a lot in life. When a relationship between a man and a woman works out all right that is how it is meant to be' (the 36-year-old wife of a businessman).

Among the men who express pity is the 40-year-old divorced and remarried schoolmaster, who was quoted in the last chapter:* 'Revolted; but sorry for the disease they have; one could almost say "There but for the grace of God go I"; it is a disease'; 'Seems silly, but I appreciate there may be something

* See p. 183.

wrong with them; and they should be treated with some sympathy in this respect and helped where possible; they should
not be condemned out of hand' (a 26-year-old bank clerk); 'I
am at a loss with this one; it is some form of illness and more to
be pitied than anything else' (a 44-year-old heating engineer).

Many of the married men and women who express tolerance
or indifference have a very active heterosexual life, whether in
the number of partners or frequency of intercourse; the first
two quoted have intercourse nightly. 'Nothing wrong with it as
long as they keep it to themselves' (a 22-year-old electrician's
mate); 'I think it is up to them; it doesn't appeal to me but I
don't condemn other people for it' (a 20-year-old painter, very
recently married). Many of the others had admitted to numerous heterosexual adventures: 'It doesn't worry me so long as it
doesn't interfere with me' (a 35-year-old divorced and remarried representative); 'I've an open mind; it doesn't bother
me' (a 40-year-old holiday-camp assistant); 'I understand it;
it's fair enough; everybody to their own liking' (a 28-year-old
postman); 'They are entitled to it; it happens in a big way, a
lot, and they have the right to do it' (a 41-year-old divorced and
remarried plumber); 'That goes on a lot more than people
think; up to a point I can understand it and I can agree with it'
(a 44-year-old gas-board foreman); 'They are perfectly entitled
to it, as long as it is kept private and not flaunted' (a 39-year-
old chauffeur courier); 'Live and let live' (a 32-year-old self-
employed taxi-driver, and several others).

A smaller group of women answered in much the same terms:
'This is up to them; I feel that it is up to people to live their own
lives in the way they wish' (the 26-year old wife of a factory
foreman); 'Doesn't matter; let them if they like it' (the 22-year-
old wife of a labourer); 'I think it is quite natural for some
people; some people have not the right balance of hormones'
(the 22-year-old wife of a computer engineer).

A few of our informants instanced their personal experiences
as the reason for their feelings, predominantly hostile but occasionally tolerant, about homosexuals. 'Terrible; shocking;
I saw it happen too much when I was in the Navy' (a 40-year-
old fitter); 'Where I work I come into contact with quite a few
of them and I find them quite obnoxious, especially when they
start taking a fancy to me' (a 29-year-old male nurse); 'No

particular feelings; it just doesn't interest me. Actually I have a very good friend who is a bit 'that way' and he's a bloody good bloke and I feel a bit sorry for him; he can't help it' (a 28-year-old electrical engineer); 'I know several homosexual men; they are friends of mine and I accept them. The actual physical side of it I prefer not to think about, but I appreciate that that is how they are' (a 39-year-old bank official, an observant Roman Catholic); 'It's queer, rather repulsive; I've had advances made but I don't like that sort of thing' (a 41-year-old small-holder).

'I understand them; I have met quite a few lesbians at work' (the 29-year-old wife of a press operator); 'Unhealthy; I find women become attracted to me but I never feel anything like that for them' (the 33-year-old wife of a design draughtsman); 'I feel desperately sorry for them; I was a nurse so I understand it and feel sick inside; but I think it's the way they are made' (the 41-year-old wife of an engineering foreman); 'Terrible; it's an illness really. . . . I have seen it; two women at work – they had to be separated – they messed about with each other. One of them had a rubber thing she used to strap around herself; she showed it to us at a Christmas party; I thought it was horrible' (the 32-year-old wife of a gardener).

ii

Among our unmarried male respondents there were a few, without any heterosexual experience, who expressed their interest in homosexuality fairly unequivocally: 'Intrigued – not revolted, just curious' (a 27-year-old civil servant); 'Fairly sympathetic – probably men who can't get on with women' (a 28-year-old joiner); 'Why not? No reason why not if consenting adults' (a 31-year-old writer); but they all denied any overt activity.

Probably more significant are the male virgins who express their hostility to the idea of homosexuality with excessive verbal violence; in some of these instances, it is difficult not to suspect a classic psychoanalytic defence against repressed homosexual desires. Thus a 37-year-old bachelor, working in a professional capacity in a large hospital, who has never had heterosexual intercourse and does not expect to marry, said about those who fall in love with their own sex:

'It's unnatural. A feeling of disgust. The more homosexuality is sanctified, this weakens the strength of the rest; this happened to a number of empires before. Must stop it spreading!'

In a similar case is a 36-year-old labourer who is 'disgusted' at the idea of people falling in love with members of their own sex, but has no interest in women; and a 24-year-old maintenance worker who said of homosexuals 'They should be done away with'; he too has had no heterosexual experience, and does not expect to marry.

As has been stated, 2 % of the men and 3 % of the women said they had felt some sort of attraction for a member of their own sex, though a considerable number of them said they had done nothing to give physical expression to these feelings. As with the admissions of casual adultery, I think it remarkable that the interviewers were able to get so many admissions on a single interview; but obviously these figures cannot be interpreted as a measure of the percentage of homosexuals in the younger English population; there was almost certainly a good deal of individual reticence. At the same time, my impression – it cannot be justified by any data at my disposal – is that these low figures for emotional involvement are probably nearer to reality than the inflated figures given by Kinsey* and some books of propaganda which have used his material. I have tried to examine emotional commitment, not casual, uninvolved homosexual activity.

Most of the unmarried who admitted to having felt some sort of attraction for their own sex said they had done nothing about it; the one exception was a 38-year-old welder, without schooling or any heterosexual experience, who replied tersely: 'Yes; that's my business.' Much more typical is a 32-year-old army officer, without any heterosexual experience, who said that he sympathized with those who fall in love with their own sex and had himself felt some attraction but 'I did my best to ignore it and the situation cleared itself'. A professional entertainer aged 37 said: 'I agree: it is entirely up to the persons themselves; I don't see anything wrong with it'; he had felt some attraction and 'shared a flat with him for six months'; he also has quite an active heterosexual life. Similarly, a 29-year-old electrical

---

* *Op. cit.* pp. 361–66.

engineer: 'I don't see anything wrong with it; I experimented, but found I didn't like it.' A 22-year-old skilled worker said he had felt 'deep friendship only; not physical attraction'. A 28-year-old joiner, without heterosexual experience, and who doesn't expect to get married, feels about homosexuality: 'Fairly sympathetic; probably men who can't get on with women'; but denies that he has ever felt any attraction himself.

A rather interesting comment was made by a 23-year-old draughtsman:

'With mixed feelings. The homosexual act in itself revolts, but reason behind it now invokes my sympathy. I was approached in Brussels when a kid and was terrified; but I understand now I'm older that much of it is a passing phase, and of no lasting significance.'

Unmarried women have rather similar replies. A 23-year-old virgin, the daughter of a railway worker, considers that those who fall in love with their own sex are 'in need of medical help'; she had felt attraction for another woman but 'ignored it, when I was much younger'. A 19-year-old girl, studying to be a teacher said: 'I feel sorry for them because so many people mock them'; she had only felt attraction 'inasmuch as I have noticed other girls who are pretty'. A 24-year-old nurse had felt some attraction but 'we did nothing; it was just a very good friendship; we worked together'.

Some of the successfully married admitted that they had been attracted by members of their own sex, but had either not given their feelings physical expression or else the episodes were brief. Among those who said they had done nothing was a 45-year-old representative, who considered homosexuality 'very wrong' and had been attracted by another man 'but not completely; it was very deep friendship.' In similar case was a 41-year-old civil servant: 'I waited until the attraction wore off.' A 35-year-old commercial engineer, with a very active heterosexual life said of homosexuality: 'I think the relationship would be more intimate'; but he had never given expression to the attraction he had felt. A 32-year-old estate agent, an observant Roman Catholic, said of homosexuals: 'I feel sorry for them because they cannot help it; but they should not be social outcasts'; as a schoolboy he had felt some attraction and 'we engaged in a certain amount of play and finally both went our separate ways from school'. A 29-year-old cartoonist with an active heterosexual life, said:

'Nothing wrong with it; it is a question of personal preference. Some of my best friends are queer. Once I did go through a stage; we indulged in sex play; we didn't enter one another. It only lasted three or four months; I was only 16 at the time.'

The 35-year-old wife of an artist said: 'I feel it's sad. It can't be satisfactory although one knows of many cases where it compensates fairly well.' She had been conscious of some attraction and 'as a schoolgirl, the nearest thing to making love'. The 44-year old wife of an ex-serviceman, now training to be a teacher said: 'I had a crush on the geography mistress, but that soon passed. We didn't do anything in any sexual way; it was just a school-girl crush.' The 35-year-old wife of a worker in a hospital finds homosexuals 'just unfortunate'; she had felt some attraction but grew out of it. The 35-year-old wife of a skilled worker, born in Scotland, had similarly felt some attraction 'when I was still at school; but apart from that, no'. The 27-year-old wife of a docker:

'It doesn't bother me. I feel it is all right. When I was single I palled up with a girl and felt a lot for her. We went around together until my future husband came along and he split us up. My husband split us up, but she stood for me at the wedding. She got married and I haven't seen her since.'

iii

The question about homosexuality came almost at the end of the questionnaire; and, after I had analysed several hundred, it seemed to me that I could forecast what a respondent's attitude to this topic would be, on the basis of his or her attitudes towards extra-marital heterosexuality (pre-marital, discussed in Chapter Two, casual adultery, discussed in Chapter Seven, and serious adultery, discussed in Chapter Eight) and towards female sexuality (discussed in Chapter Five). We therefore had the appropriate cross-correlations made, to check whether there was any substance in my hunch that the rigidity or permissiveness of people's attitudes towards unlicensed sexuality was not much influenced by the sex of the hypothesized illicit partner.

Because the answers to the questions about homosexuality and casual or serious adultery were so numerous, I have only transcribed the polar categories in the accompanying tables: the components of toleration or hostility towards homosexuality; the most marked disapproval and the most marked indifference towards casual adultery; and either the choice or the rejection of drastic action in the event of the discovery of a spouse's infidelity.

Table fourteen

Correlations between attitudes towards homosexuality and sexual experience before marriage

Attitudes to homosexuality	Toler- ance 12%	Pity 22%	Revul- sion 24%	Moral dis- approval 4%	Dislike 8%
Do you think young men should have some sexual experience before marriage?					
No (37%)	16%	42%	38%	42%	33%
Yes (52%)	67%	49%	50%	46%	59%
If Yes, one person or persons only (30%)	33%	30%	32%	24%	38%
Just anyone (19%)	32%	15%	16%	19%	18%
Do you think young women should have some sexual experience before marriage?					
No (54%)	29%	60%	63%	56%	49%
Yes (35%)	59%	33%	29%	35%	45%
If Yes, one person or persons only (25%)	38%	23%	21%	22%	36%
Just anyone (8%)	19%	7%	6%	13%	4%

Table fifteen

Correlations between attitudes towards homosexuality and casual adultery

Attitudes to *homosexuality*	*Toler-* *ance* *12%*	*Pity* *22%*	*Revul-* *sion* *24%*	*Moral* *dis-* *approval* *4%*	*Dislike* *8%*
A married man having an affair with a woman he does not love					
Strong moral disapproval (22%)	14%	21%	29%	29%	17%
Disapproval of character (22%)	15%	23%	20%	18%	22%
Won't judge (10%)	19%	11%	6%	13%	13%
No attitude unless it affects me (5%)	8%	5%	4%	2%	5%
It's natural (3%)	5%	2%	2%	6%	3%
A married woman having an affair with a man she does not love					
Strong moral disapproval (23%)	13%	23%	30%	29%	20%
Disapproval of character (18%)	15%	19%	19%	19%	22%
Won't judge (8%)	17%	10%	5%	10%	10%
No attitude unless it affects me (6%)	10%	5%	4%	6%	6%

So few people thought such behaviour natural in women that this line has been omitted.

Table sixteen

Correlations between attitudes towards homosexuality and serious adultery

Attitudes to homosexuality	Tolerance 12%	Pity 22%	Revulsion 24%	Moral disapproval 4%	Dislike 8%
If husband finds wife having affair with another man					
Divorce (7%)	6%	4%	9%	7%	8%
Separation (15%)	12%	9%	18%	21%	17%
Analyse situation (24%)	27%	27%	25%	25%	21%
Try to reconcile (19%)	19%	22%	16%	24%	23%
Talk it over with wife (28%)	28%	33%	25%	25%	28%
If wife finds husband having affair					
Divorce (7%)	7%	4%	9%	6%	8%
Separation (14%)	10%	8%	17%	20%	17%
Analyse situation (25%)	27%	28%	27%	23%	19%
Try to reconcile (20%)	20%	24%	17%	24%	23%
Talk it over with husband (29%)	25%	34%	25%	18%	29%

Table seventeen
Correlations between attitudes towards homosexuality and female sexuality

Attitudes to homosexuality	Toler- ance 12%	Pity 22%	Reval- sion 24%	Moral dis- approval 4%	Dislike 8%
Do you think women have a real physical climax					
Yes (69%)	79%	72%	66%	62%	68%
No (21%)	13%	19%	21%	25%	19%
If Yes,					
All women (7%)	12%	7%	6%	8%	10%
Most women (38%)	43%	38%	39%	27%	37%
Some women (24%)	24%	26%	21%	28%	20%

As can be seen, there is quite a marked tendency for people to be reasonably consistent in their views. Those who disapprove of pre-marital heterosexual experience have low tolerance and high hostility towards homosexuality, and conversely. Those who think the unmarried should sleep with just anyone by whom they are attracted are particularly high in tolerance. Similarly, those who voice strong disapproval of the morals or character of a married man or woman having an affair with someone they do not love are markedly disapproving of and revolted by homosexuality; those who would not pronounce a judgement without more information, or said they had no attitude unless they were personally affected, were high on tolerance and low on revulsion. Those who would respond with automatic divorce or separation to the discovery of a spouse's infidelity have little tolerance or pity for homosexuals; those who would analyse the situation, try to reconcile and talk it over with their spouse are particularly likely to express pity for homosexuals.

To my mind, the most revealing correlation was that with the belief in female orgasm. It will be recalled* that far more

* See Chapter Five, p. 125.

women than men denied the existence of female orgasms; and those who do not believe in female orgasms are markedly hostile to homosexuality; those who believe that all or most women do have orgasms are markedly tolerant.

It would seem plausible to suggest that those who, whether from belief or experience, think of sex as enjoyable, as fun, are likely to be tolerant of the idea of homosexuality, or sorry for the pleasure homosexuals are losing; whereas those who think of sex as a 'sacred' duty, to be treated solemnly and not necessarily enjoyed, are hostile and disapproving. I think these tables suggest that the attitudes towards homosexuality are congruent with the attitudes towards heterosexuality and that the implication of general loathing of such 'unnatural' behaviour, advanced without evidence by the advocates of punitive legal punishment for detected homosexuality, has little justification in the views of the majority of the younger English people.

iv

There would appear to be a gamut of attitudes towards extra-marital sexuality (whatever the sex of the partner) among the younger English from extreme censoriousness ('He wants shooting', 'They should be done away with') often violently expressed, to extreme licentiousness ('If it comes along you don't turn it down', 'It's a bit immoral but it passes the time', 'Good luck to him if he can get away with it', 'Everybody to their own liking') where even the idea of sexual pleasure is welcomed with the equivalent of winks, nudges and leers. Between these two extremes is the majority who do not get over-excited about the idea of sex in either direction and who accept the fact that sexuality is an important and interesting subject which can be discussed without heat or embarrassment, to which the very low rate of refusal to answer the most intimate questions bears witness.

Is it possible with the data at our disposal to determine the size of the censorious and licentious groups? The answer can obviously only be an approximation; it would need more information than can be gathered in a single interview to state unequivocally that a man or woman was licentious, though censoriousness does appear to be manifested very convincingly.

The problem is complicated by the present state of mass communications. It sometimes seems as if the licentious were almost completely dominant in the popular newspapers, in the production of paperback books (or, at any rate, their jackets), in the theatre, cinema and television, and in what is implied in all the talk about our 'permissive' society, 'swinging' London or Liverpool, and the like; and it sometimes seems as if the vocal portion of the audiences for these mass media were almost entirely composed of the censorious.

A possible guide to the size of these two groups can be found in the answer to the question: 'Do you think a man and a woman can have a real friendship without sex playing any part?'; for it can be surmised that neither the censorious nor the licentious, though for very different reasons, would consider such a relationship possible. Twenty-nine per cent of the men and 27% of the women answered No; a further 3% of the men and 5% of the women said they did not know. The age-distribution of these replies is suggestive. Of those aged between 16 and 20 17% said No and 7% Don't know; of those aged between 21 and 24 23% said No and 4% Don't Know; of those aged 25 and 35 28% said No and 4% Don't Know; and of those aged between 35 and 45 32% said No and 4% Don't Know. Those who accept the possibility of a comradely relationship between a man and a woman, without sex playing any overt part, are markedly more numerous in the younger groups. About 70% of the total population would appear to be reasonable, cool and unexcited about the relationships between the sexes: the remaining 30% comprise the censorious and the licentious, but in what proportions?

Clues can be found in the answers to the questions about casual adultery* and fidelity;† about pre-marital experience both in theory and practice‡ (those who consider that a young man should sleep with just anyone they are attracted to and those who admit to numerous partners can be considered to be among the licentious) and in the differing views on female sexuality§ (those who hold that 'most women don't care much

* See Table Twelve, p. 156.
† See Chapter Seven, pp. 147-9.
‡ See Chapter Two, pp. 31-7.
§ See Table Ten, p. 123.

about the physical side of sex' must surely be counted among the censorious) and in some of the attitudes towards the birth-control pill.*

Putting all these figures together, I would hazard, as a rough approximation, that the licentious represent about 10 % of our sample of the English aged between 16 and 45, with about four times as many men as women; and the censorious represent about 20 %, with twice as many women as men. Licentiousness decreases slightly, and censoriousness increases markedly with age; a sizeable minority of men under the age of 25 are likely to be licentious; about a third of the women over thirty-five will be censorious. Since these groups feel so intensely about sex, it is understandable that their voices are heard much more frequently than those of the majority whose imaginations are less heated.

Figures of distribution

How do you feel about people who fall in love with members of their own sex?

Differences of 3 % are treated as of possible significance.

By self-ascribed social class Middle class emphasize pity (26 %)

Lower middle class emphasize not understandable (16 %) and under-emphasize tolerance (9 %).

Skilled working class emphasize not understandable (17 %) and under-emphasize pity (19 %) and can't help it (3 %).

Upper working class emphasize pity (28 %) and can't help it (11 %) and under-emphasize moral disapproval (1 %), dislike (4 %) and not understandable (8 %).

Working class under-emphasize pity (15 %)

Those who will not place themselves in a social class emphasize tolerance (16 %), mentally sick (14 %) and ridiculous (6 %); they under-emphasize revulsion (14 %).

The Registrar General's categories AB strongly emphasize pity (33 %) and less strongly not understandable (16 %); they

* See Table Eleven, p. 138.

strongly under-emphasize revulsion (18%) and less strongly mentally ill (7%); none in this category think such behaviour ridiculous.

C1 emphasize tolerance (15%), pity (28%) and can't help it (10%); they under-emphasize revulsion (20%).

C2 emphasize revulsion (23%) and under-emphasize pity (19%).

DE emphasize moral disapproval (7%) and under-emphasize tolerance (8%) and pity (15%).

The regions The North-East and North under-emphasize revulsion (18%).

The Midlands emphasize revulsion (28%) and not understandable (16%) and under-emphasize pity (16%) and can't help it (4%).

The South-East emphasize tolerance (15%) and pity (28%).

The South-West emphasize pity (26%), moral disapproval (7%) and can't help it (11%); they under-emphasize mentally ill (8%).

The North-West emphasize revulsion (29%) and mentally ill (20%); they under-emphasize tolerance (4%), pity (15%) and not understandable (10%).

Do you think a man and woman can have a real friendship without sex playing any part?

By self-ascribed social class Middle class: Yes 71%; No 25%; don't know 3%.

Lower middle class: Yes 64%; No 30%; Don't know 5%.

Skilled working class: Yes 63%; No 31%; Don't know 4%.

Upper working class: Yes 75%; No 19%: Don't know 5%.

Working class: Yes 63%; No 32%; Don't know 4%.

Those who will not place themselves: Yes 61%; No 27%; Don't know 8%.

PART TWO

10 *The Unmarried*

i

Because the sample was based on electoral registers, the unmarried and those under the age of 21 (who are, of course, to a
great extent the same people) were seriously under-represented.
The 18-year-olds were not on the electoral registers in May
1969; and many of their elders, who are not living at home,
tend to be somewhat mobile, living in shared flats or lodgings,
and frequently fail to get on electoral registers. Most of our
younger informants were the children of older informants; but
there were not enough of them, or not enough were questioned,
to reach the correct proportion (based on census data) of 30%
of the total population. The unmarried are only 19% of our
sample – 274 men (representing 28% of all men) and 107 women (representing 11% of all women); the figures for the sexes,
based on the census, should be 41% of all men aged between 16
and 45, and 19% of all women.

As far as the tables are concerned, this defect can be taken
into account by statistical 'weighting'; and this has been done
for several of the more significant tables;* the difference is
usually 1 or 2 per cent. But this correction of the percentages
still leaves me with only 281 interviews. Compared to the data
on which all the preceding chapters have been based, that
available for analysing the behaviour and attitudes of the unmarried is rather sketchy.

Besides being asked their views on most of the same topics as
the married, nine extra questions were asked of the unmarried
only. These will be dealt with first.

* Appendix Three. Weighted tables are so indicated.

ii

The unmarried represent 89 % of those aged between 16 and 20, 39 % of those aged between 21 and 24, 11 % of those aged 25–34, and 5 % of those aged between 35 and 45,* There is a marked concentration of the unmarried in those considering themselves upper working class, with 41 %; there are 30 % to 31 % in the lower middle and working classes, and 25 % to 26 % in the middle and skilled working classes.

Eighty-six per cent of these bachelors and spinsters expect to get married some day, 6 % do not and 8 % are uncertain. For 27 % the date of marriage is fixed, with the highest proportion in the lower middle and upper working classes; the remaining 59 % have no date in mind.

At the time of the interview, 44 % said that they had a special girl- or boy-friend (this, of course, includes the 27 % of those who have a date for their wedding fixed and 17 % who have not immediate marriage in mind); 52 % said they had not, and 4 % did not answer.

As with the married, the most likely place for girl and boy to meet one another is at a dance (particularly favoured by the upper working class); other meeting places were school and college (particularly in the middle and lower middle classes) and parties or through mutual friends; the lower middle and working classes are somewhat likely to meet their friends at work; and some also met in pubs or cafés and through pick-ups. With such small numbers, the percentages are not very meaningful.

Precisely half of those with a current girl- or boy-friend said they were on terms of 'real physical intimacy' with their partner, but a quarter of these said that this intimacy did not go as far as complete intercourse, and several of these can, I think, be considered chaste out of principle and not from timidity. Among these is the 16-year-old son of a foreman in an engineering factory who met his girl-friend at a dance but has never had intercourse: 'I think any unmarried man should not just have sex with anyone he has no feelings for'; the 17-year-old son of a turf accountant, who has just left school, does not expect to

---

* When the figures are 'weighted', the percentages are 90 % of those aged 16–20, 47 % of those aged 21–24, 12 % of those aged 25–35, and 7 % of those aged 35–45.

get married before he is out of his apprenticeship and dis-approves of sexual experience outside marriage 'on principle'; a 27-year-old civil servant who has a girl-friend who lives in another flat in the same house but has never had intercourse because he disapproves of intercourse outside marriage 'for religious reasons'.*

A 19-year-old girl at teachers' training college (she expects to graduate when she is 21) has a steady boy-friend with whom she is on terms of 'real physical intimacy, but I have not had full intercourse'. She said sensibly:

'If you are going with someone you love for a long time, while saving to get married, you will get so used to going so far and no further that finally when you get married there may be difficulties, due to the restraint you have used for so long.'

The 21-year-old daughter of a railway worker, a virgin without a steady boy-friend, said:

'I have been brought up to believe that you should wait until you are married; and I think if you love someone enough you can be prepared to wait until marriage.'

The 34-year-old daughter of a retired shop-owner has never gone 'all the way'; she said rather hesitatingly that she expects to get married.† This woman takes the birth-control pill for menstrual trouble.

A 40-year-old nurse has a boy-friend whom she met at a dance, introduced by a friend, but is not on terms of physical intimacy. She is a Roman Catholic, a weekly communicant, and 'Religion states it is wrong before marriage'.

Of the 16% whose 'real physical intimacy' with their boy- or girl-friend includes intercourse, 3% had only had one sexual partner; 2% two; 2% three and 9% more than three. Some men, of course, have intercourse without friendship. Of those whose partner is a steady, 10% think they need not be faithful

---

* This informant is a member of the Church of England and goes to services once or twice a year.
† The interviewer noted: 'She was very hesitant about giving a "Yes" here. She obviously does not know when her boy-friend will be free to marry her; for she had mentioned previously that he had already had one unhappy marriage and she was hoping to marry him one day.'

P

to their partner but 8 % are in practice (particularly among the upper working class); 7 % do not expect their partner to be faithful.*

Among those with one steady partner is a 22-year-old electrical fitter, an observant Roman Catholic, who does not expect to marry his present girl-friend. He practises withdrawal. He is in favour of pre-marital intercourse for young men because 'they get frustrated with a woman if they don't; something lacking in their life if they have no sex'; for young women it will be 'a little outlet for themselves and prevent them getting married too soon'. The 21-year-old son of a coal merchant met his girl friend at a Church Youth Club; they started intercourse when he was 19 years old and engage in it once or twice a week; he uses a sheath.

A 17-year-old girl, still at school, met her boy-friend at a public library; she expects to marry him and thinks she should be faithful. A 23-year-old factory worker, born in St Lucia in the West Indies, who has been in London for three years, had one lover whom she wanted to marry; she is a very observant Jehovah's Witness. The 20-year-old daughter of a postman, still at college, met her boy-friend at a college dance; she says she does not sleep with him but volunteered: 'Most of the girls at college are on the pill; they all sleep with boys and think it is a good prevention.' This girl follows a fairly common practice in imputing promiscuity to others and denying it for herself.

Eleven per cent of our unmarried population can be considered relatively promiscuous, since they have had three or more partners. This 11 % is overwhelmingly male, and predominantly young – more than half under 20, and nearly half between 21 and 24. They occur almost equally in all social classes; there are a few more in the skilled working class, and a few less in the working class without qualification; but with such small numbers the figures of distribution cannot be very significant. Many of these partners would appear to be one-night stands. These people would appear to be the only group to

* Eight per cent of the unmarried did not think a husband should necessarily be faithful and 5 % did not think a wife should be. These percentages are slightly higher than the views of the married. See Chapter Seven, p. 148.

whom the journalistic term 'permissive society' can be applied with any justification.

Typical of these promiscuous people is a 19-year-old lorry driver: he got interested in girls at 13, started intercourse at the age of 15, and met his present girl-friend, the last of a considerable number, in a pub. 'If it comes along you don't turn it down'; but he thinks a couple should be faithful to each other for the duration of the affair. He expects to marry some day.

The 18-year-old son of a transport manager started intercourse just after his seventeenth birthday: he has it 'when I can get it, I suppose once a fortnight or so'; he too expects to marry some day. A 22-year-old skilled worker feels that 'If the partners are having it on the basic understanding that they are having an affair just for sex, that is all right': he practises withdrawal with his numerous partners. A 25-year-old engineer met his present girl, the most recent of a long series, at a dance; this man was rather inconsistent in his views on pre-marital experience. For young men:

'It is good for your ego; it is a natural thing to lead to lovemaking if your feelings are mutual; one has not got to be in love to make love; physical attraction is all that is wanted.'

But for young women:

'I may be old-fashioned, but the woman I marry must be a virgin, not necessarily at the wedding, but as far as I'm concerned.'

A 29-year-old electrical engineer started intercourse at the age of 17; he now has it 'irregularly – about once a month'. His present girl was picked up in a pub. A 26-year-old medical orderly in the Merchant Navy became interested in girls at the age of 18 and first had intercourse when he was about 19; his sexual life was always very irregular and is 'almost none at present' because he is expecting to get married.

A 22-year-old woman, an observant Baptist, came to this country from the West Indies when she was 13; she met her present boy-friend, her second lover, at a dance; she had a baby by the first. She considers it is not right to make love to more than one person at a time.

Among our informants was a representative of one of the potent mythological figures of our time: an 18-year-old schoolgirl (she knows her father is a skilled worker, but seems unclear as to his occupation, and has no notion of his income) who is on the pill and has had a series of lovers.* She started intercourse when she was 16; she met her present lover in college. She has intercourse 'twice a week, if she likes the boy; this depends on exams'. She expects to get married, but not for five years: 'I want to go to university; but if the "man of my dreams" comes along . . .'

Her rate of intercourse is high for the unmarried. Table Eighteen shows the frequencies they reported; as can be seen, only 11% have intercourse more than once a week, whereas 18% have it less often than once a month. A third of the unmarried population, whose earlier answers had established that they were virgins, were not asked this question; and 8% of the unmarried refused to answer.

If one works out the absolute numbers, 115 of our bachelors and 55 of our spinsters have steady girl- or boy-friends; and of these, 52 of the men and 11 of the girls have experienced heterosexual intercourse.†

What does seem to me disturbing is that the majority of the unmarried who are having intercourse do not regularly use any form of birth control. Of the 44% who have experienced intercourse at least once, 25% say they do not use any; of the remainder the vast majority use the sheath; 2% practise withdrawal: 4% of the unmarried women use the pill.‡ The risk of unwanted pregnancies is still run much too frequently; and as previous chapters have shown, a marriage forced by an unwanted pregnancy has a very poor prognosis.

The unmarried are much more likely to engage in intercourse if they live in the South-East and Midlands than in the other parts of the country. Predictably, there is quite a concentration of the promiscuous, those having three or more partners, in London and the South-East.

---

* This informant is so outstandingly articulate that most of her answers to the questionnaire will be quoted in full at the end of this chapter.

† These figures and percentages are closely comparable to those given by Michael Schofield in his *Sexual Behaviour of Young People* (Pelican Books, 1968); see especially pages 109 and 136.

‡ This works out as four unmarried women in our sample; and one of these was taking the pill for menstrual disturbances.

Table eighteen

Rates of intercourse of the unmarried

The total percentages in column one are the same as those in Table Seven, Chapter Five, p. 114. The 33 % who were not asked this question again had indicated earlier in the interview that they had never had intercourse; the interviewers were not consistent in their marking of this second question on the same topic.

Rates of intercourse	Total percentage	Percentage unmarried respondents	Absolute numbers
Daily or more often	1%	—	—
6 times a week	—	—	—
5–6 times a week	—	—	—
5 times a week	1%	—	5
4–5 times a week	1%	1%	4
4 times a week	2%	1%	5
3–4 times a week	5%	2%	11
3 times a week	7%	—	—
2–3 times a week	6%	1%	5
Twice a week	14%	3%	18
Once or twice a week	6%	3%	18
Once a week	14%	4%	24
2 or 3 times a month	5%	3%	15
Less often	8%	9%	54
Not consistent	5%	9%	54
Never	9%	24%	109
Refused	5%	8%	48
Not asked	11%	33%	—

iii

In this section I propose to describe the views of the unmarried on those topics on which the views of the married have been discussed in the previous chapters; I will follow the same order. As will become clear, there is a tendency for the unmarried (like those under 20) to take rather extreme positions, compared with their elders and their married contemporaries; they are either more restrictive and severe or more easy-going.

Thus, on pre-marital experience, a 17-year-old apprentice draughtsman said: 'It should only be done after marriage'; and a 22-year-old bus driver, a virgin: 'I think sex makes a marriage and if there is sex beforehand there is no point in getting married'. In contrast, a 34-year-old gypsy, who can only read numbers:

'Best to get around when you're young and free (I know I did). If not, it will only worry you later on. It's better if you're around with more than one when you are young, best not to get too involved.'

A 29-year-old skilled engineer, who refused to say anything about marriage ('I am not married, so I cannot say') advised for unmarried men and women:

'If a person is attracted to someone he should have sex; and I feel that having sex before marriage helps him to get adjusted to the sexual side of marriage.'

A 23-year-old draughtsman, an observant Roman Catholic:

'Reservations (strong); but on balance I think that the experience may have real advantages later on in the selection of the right girl for a wife. I don't like the idea of sex without real love – too animal. [For young women?] Again serious reservations and my instincts suggest No; but when one thinks it through it is only fair a girl should experiment a bit too; then it is more likely for her to select the right partner for marriage. She must think anyway she loves the man she goes with; goodness knows where those "animal instincts" would lead to.'

A 27-year-old civil servant who goes to Church of England services once or twice a year, allows men pre-marital experience 'because he would enjoy it', though he himself denies having had any heterosexual experience; but he is against it for young women:

'For religious reasons, because of my beliefs; but if they had experience, I would not hold it against them; I could not be offended if my fiancée was not a virgin.'

A 30-year-old sales representative:

'A man should be satisfied that he has knocked around enough before he gets married, so that when married he accepts the moral obligation of marriage without thinking he has missed anything – just anyone, because man is physically polygamous by nature and the emotional side of sex is less important to a man than a woman. [For young women?] One person or persons, providing she has chosen according to her conscience someone she loves; because girls who sleep around are just searching for something they can't find, and end up by making men more interested in her body than in herself.'

A 20-year-old secretary, a virgin girl:

'It will help the marriage, rather than going about it awkwardly. If he has no experience, the first time could be a let-down, and turn her off for life. [For young women?] If she marries as a virgin, she might start wondering what the other fellow's like in bed. She can make a choice better and know he's right for her.'

A 17-year-old lad who has just left school, and works for a turf-accountant, has had no sexual experience yet but feels that:

'It helps to have some sexual experience at the time of marriage. [For young women?] Yes, if they want to; but not just for the sake of it.'

A 31-year-old bank clerk said for men: 'It would promote a good marriage; it is mostly wrong'; and for young women: 'It is mostly wrong, but it could promote a good marriage.'

A 17-year-old hairdresser's apprentice considers that a young man 'should not go with a girl for one night; they should be attracted to each other, or in love'; but of his own sexual experience, he said: 'Only had it once - not now.'

Quite a few of our unmarried respondents refused to discuss marriage: 'I just haven't given the matter any thought at all – I am sorry, I cannot help you' (a 23-year-old master printer); 'I have not given the matter any thought because I intend to stay single at least until after my mother is dead' (a 38-year-old wool porter); 'I have never had a lot of interest in the opposite sex' (a 31-year-old road worker).

When they do give their views on what makes for a happy marriage, they put more emphasis than do the married on discussing things together (26%), love (26%) and financial security (8%); they put less emphasis on give-and-take (22%) and mutual trust (17%).

No less than 14% of the unmarried said they did not know the answer to the question about the most important qualities a husband or wife should have. In contrast to the married, they put more emphasis on faithfulness (15%), intelligence (8%), tolerance (10%), moral qualities such as sincerity and integrity (12%), personal qualities, such as attractiveness and cleanliness (25%), being a good mother (21%) and a good cook (10%). They under-emphasize understanding and consideration (28%), love and affection (26%), sense of humour (11%), patience (11%), equanimity or good temper (9%), generosity (4%), fairness (3%), economical (4%), love of home (4%) and being a good father (3%).

Unmarried women with strong religious convictions are rather exigent in the qualities they desire in a husband. 'Understanding your way of living; used to same way of life; must be a Christian as I enjoy Church life' (a 27-year-old upholsterer, Church of England); 'Love his wife; living up to his marriage vows; living up to the principles of the Bible' (a 23-year-old factory worker, born in St Lucia, Jehovah's Witness); 'Smartly dressed; understanding of her and her views; personality good and strong' (a 40-year-old nurse, Roman Catholic).

Unmarried men seem to have given the matter less thought; and their views tend to be conventional: 'Good personality; good cook; well dressed' (a 28-year-old joiner). The 17-year-old son of a master butcher hopes for 'Good personality; attractive; a person as good as my Mum'.

Compared with their married contemporaries, the unmarried emphasize as the causes of the breakdown of a marriage infidelity (28%) and conflicting personalities (19%); they under-emphasize neglect (27%), selfishness (22%), poverty (12%) and sexual incompatibility (7%). Five per cent say they don't know.

The greater realism with which girls envisage marriage can perhaps be illustrated by the fact that they have only 18% who say they do not know the answer to the question: 'What are the three chief faults husbands tend to have?'; whereas no less than 27% of the bachelors were unable to answer the parallel question about the faults of wives. Compared with their married sisters, spinsters emphasize drinking and infidelity (29%) and taking the wife for granted (25%); they considerably under-emphasize selfishness (32%), meanness with money (8%), bad temper (4%), untidyness (3%) and nagging (2%). Bachelors put more emphasis than married men on the fears that the wife will let herself go and become slovenly (14%), that she will take her husband for granted (11%) and be jealous (9%); they have fewer fears than the married that wives will nag and moan (32%), be extravagant (19%), selfish (13%), bad housekeepers (8%) or bad tempered (6%). It would appear that the appre-hensions of both men and women centre round the sexual aspects, including the fading of love, when they consider what could go wrong with their projected marriage; they do not en-visage the character defects which can make for married un-happiness nearly as much as do the experienced.

Illustrative of the fears of the unmarried are a 17-year-old son of a master butcher: 'Nagging; far too curious; too posses-sive'; the 17-year-old son of a turf-accountant:* 'Nag too much; want too much money'; a 23-year-old draughtsman, an obser-vant Catholic: 'Possessiveness; slovenly in regard to housekeep-ing; intolerance'; a 23-year-old school-caretaker: 'Some wives are domineering in their nature; tend to be too independent these days; I don't think young wives have enough interest in their home life'; a 28-year-old joiner: 'Worry about small un-important things; too much make-up'; a 29-year-old post-office engineer: 'Lack of interest in themselves, not taking a pride in their appearance; but could be the other extreme, spending too much time and money on themselves; bad managers with money; nagging their husband'; a 20-year-old secretary, the daughter of a divorced mother: 'Selfish; woman is there for their convenience; don't help in the home enough.'

The unmarried give slightly more approval than the married to the birth-control pill and they put more emphasis on its relevance to the population explosion; they have less fear of vague medical side-effects (8% compared with 12% of the

---

* This informant's prescription for a happy marriage was: 'When both partners do a share of the housework, etc., and help each other in little ways. The husband should take the wife out often.'

married), though some of them seem to confuse it with thali-domide: 'A bad thing because I have heard that it makes babies deformed' were the words of an 18-year-old baker and a 24-year-old assistant caretaker.

The extreme censoriousness of some of the young men can be illustrated by a 17-year-old market porter who considers the pill a bad thing: 'It proves they only have intercourse because they like it';* and a virgin 22-year-old bus-driver: 'Single girls are taking the pill, and sex before marriage, with which I disagree.'

Its relevance to population control was stressed by a 29-year-old post-office engineer: 'A good thing if it will control the world population and relieve the women of worry if they already have a large family'; and a 19-year-old charge-hand fitter, a very observant Roman Catholic: 'A good thing for the world as a whole – you know, the population increase. In underdeveloped countries they do not know how to use it, but it helps keep population down in civilized countries.'

A 22-year-old printer, who normally uses withdrawal in his quite active sex life, approved of the pill: 'A lot of marriages are unhappy because of the withdrawal method; the pill results in a much happier marriage, and of course it is safer'; a 35-year-old painter and decorator, born in Jamaica said: 'Good; effective; people freer sexually'†; and a 16-year-old apprentice in a gent's hairdresser commented ruefully: 'A good thing, but not for our business; we don't sell nearly as many rubbers now.'

The views of the unmarried about casual adultery, their answers to the questions about a married man or woman having an affair with someone he does not really love, were not analysed separately. This is a topic on which men were much the most eloquent and, if they were virgins, extremely condemnatory. 'Wrong; he is ruining the lives of two people – his wife and the other woman' (a 22-year-old bus-driver); 'He is out for one

* This informant denied having any religion; he said he had had inter-course twice.
† In answer to the question whether the pill made any difference to the importance of fidelity in marriage, this informant replied: 'It is the same; but in practice women are more unfaithful.'

thing – sex; she is the same' (a 38-year-old wool porter); 'I would have thought that if he had to have an affair he would have it with someone he loved; otherwise he could go down to the West End and pay for it' (a 22-year-old unskilled labourer).

A 30-year-old sales representative was very analytical:

'He's trying to give a kick to his life through tasting the forbidden fruits – probably caused by dissatisfaction with his own wife. Or he got married for the sake of it; he's still in his mind a single man. [For women?] Probably trying to find some love and affection. Not very satisfied with her husband, or is the sort of person who needs continual reassurance from other people. One person is not enough to convince her she is what she thinks she is.'

The most common attitudes were less analytical or condemnatory. 'It would not worry me, as it would not be any of my concern' (a 29-year-old post-office engineer); 'I sympathize with him; he is satisfying his baser instincts, but I pity that he hasn't more self-control. It could quite easily happen to me' (a 27-year-old civil servant); 'I approve, except where there are children to be considered. [For women?] As long as there are no children I don't disapprove; sometimes it cannot be avoided' (a 38-year-old professional entertainer); 'If the partners are having it on the basic understanding that they are having an affair just for sex, it is all right' (a 22-year-old unskilled worker); 'It's really up to him; I'm inclined to say good luck to him! [For women?] She shouldn't do it if they have children of the marriage' (the 16-year-old apprentice to a gent's hairdresser, quoted at the end of the last section); 'Doesn't matter. [For women?] This is bad; wives should toe the line' (a 35-year-old painter and decorator, born in Jamaica); and, as the height of cynicism, the 17-year-old virgin son of a master butcher: 'A change is as good as a rest.'

On the question of serious adultery – a husband finding his wife having an affair with another man, and conversely – the views of the unmarried were analysed separately. Compared with the married, they put much more emphasis on talking the matter over with the husband or wife (34% compared with 26% or 27%), and somewhat more on trying to reconcile (22% as compared with 18% and 19%) and divorce as a last resort (9%

and 7 % as compared with 4 %). In the case of a husband finding his wife having an affair with another man the unmarried put a little more emphasis (2 % in each case) on divorce (8 %), attacking or reproaching the intervener (4 % each) than do the married. The unmarried envisage separation much less frequently than do the married (10 % and 9 % in contrast to 16 %), and, by small percentages, mention less frequently examining oneself and one's own faults (5 % and 6 %), giving one more chance (3 % and 4 %), and considering the effect on the children (1 % and 2 %). They have fewer advocates for beating up the wife (4 %). Seven per cent said they did not know the answer to this question in the case of the husband, and 8 % in the case of the wife.

The views of the young tend to be rather extreme. On the one hand: 'Go to the police about it' (a 17-year-old market porter) or 'Well – um – try to get his own back, go out with another woman' (the 17-year-old hairdresser's apprentice); on the other hand, the 17-year-old apprentice to a turf accountant said:

'If the wife really loves the other man, the husband should let her go – i.e. give her a divorce. If there is no real love, the husband should forgive his wife. [For a wife?] The wife should not take hasty action, but try and discover if the same thing has happened before and divorce him if so; but definite arrangements should be made for the children.'

A 19-year-old charge-hand fitter, a very observant Roman Catholic:

'Tell her he knows about it, and ask her what she wants to do about the romance; also tell the other bloke to leave his wife alone. Find out whether she still wants to live with him, or why she wants a divorce – or separation, I should put, being a Roman Catholic.'

The views of older unmarried men and women cover much the same gamut as their married contemporaries do:

'Face up to this problem. Try to find out why the wife wants this affair, and try to right marriage and give marriage a second chance. Divorce as a last resort, if there are no young children involved' (a 25-year-old school-keeper).

'The husband should make sure his wife is happy, then she wouldn't bother with anyone else. [For a wife?] She should find out why he isn't happy and do something about it' (a 40-year-old nurse, an observant Roman Catholic).

'Remain calm and collected initially. Ask himself why it happened. Am I providing adequate? Try to find a way of making marriage work. If she's really promiscuous, then repeated affairs are intolerable and will lead to the breakdown of marriage and divorce' (a 22-year-old draughtsman, another observant Roman Catholic).

'Call it a day. I shouldn't bend at all. I should seek a divorce' (a 29-year-old post-office engineer).

Addendum

Some excerpts from the answers to the questionnaire given by an 18-year-old girl student working for her 'A' levels and hoping to go on to university; her father is a skilled worker but she has no idea of his income.

What are the three chief faults wives tend to have? Become involved in petty things – home too important. Tend to put children before husband. Don't take enough interest in husband's work.

What are the three chief faults husbands tend to have? Don't allow wives to go out to work. Too dominating – not fifty-fifty. Selfishness; unfair comparisons to Mum.

What do you think tends to wreck a marriage? Not telling each other all their troubles; they lose contact with each other, getting too involved in other things. They 'let themselves go' after marriage; not glamorous for each other.

And what do you think tends to make a happy marriage? Helping each other in their work; a man should overcome his embarrassment when necessary and talk to his wife. A sense of humour is necessary.

If a husband finds his wife having an affair with another man, what should he do? Review the situation; decide whose fault it is. If his, they should become reconciled; if wife's fault, he must decide if it's likely to be repeated or not and separate if he feels she's going to be often unfaithful and he couldn't live with her.

If a wife finds her husband having an affair with another woman, what do you think she should do? Her thinking will be complicated if she has children. She should talk it out with her husband, because often husbands are only trying to get lost youth back by having an affair.

How do you feel about a married man who has an affair with a woman he does not really love? Man's natural inclination; I accept it regretfully.

How do you feel about a married woman who has an affair with a man she does not really love? Sorry for her; obviously something lacking in her married life, if she's not a nymphomaniac.

Should a young man's sexual experience before marriage be restricted to one person or person he loves, or just anyone he feels attracted to? A young man doesn't want to be emotionally involved with many girls, only physically; he won't feel 'in love' very often.

Should a young woman's sexual experience before marriage be restricted to one person or person she loves, or just anyone she feels attracted to? She will most probably convince herself she *is* in love at the time.

How old were you when you first had full intercourse? Sixteen.

About how often do you have intercourse? Twice a week if I like the boy. It depends on exams!

Do you think this is about average for people like yourself? Average for steady unmarried couple.

On balance, do you think the invention of the pill for birth control a good or bad thing? A good thing; much safer; compared to Durex much more aesthetic.

Now that the pill provides absolute safety, do you think faithfulness is or is not as important as ever in marriage? Just as important; it makes no difference; it means that often people who were faithful before were only faithful out of fear of pregnancy.

Which birth-control method do you use? The pill.

Do you expect to get married some day? Have you any idea when this will be? Yes; but not for five years. I want to go to university. But if the 'man of my dreams' comes along . . .

Have you any special boy friend at present? Yes.

Where did you meet him? College.

Are you on terms of real physical intimacy with him? Yes.

With about how many other people have you been on terms of physical intimacy? More than three.

APPENDIXES

Technical aspects of the sampling and interviewing

By Humphrey Taylor (Managing Director of Opinion Research Centre)

1 The pilot survey

The purpose of the pilot survey was to find out if it was possible to obtain reliable information in response to the intimate and embarrassing questions included in the survey, and if so, what was the best way of carrying out the research.

The pilot survey comprised three experiments in which different ways of obtaining the information were tested.

Experiment A

With one sample, the interviewers tried to complete both Part 1 of the questionnaire (the less embarrassing questions) and Part 2 (the more embarrassing questions) in the personal interview.

Experiment B

With the second sample the interviewers asked Part 1 of the interview in the normal way, and then left Part 2 to be completed by the informant and collected later that day or the following day.

Experiment C

With the third sample the interviewers left Part 2 of the questionnaire and asked informants to complete it and return it to ORC in a stamped addressed envelope.

In each of the three experiments men interviewed men and women interviewed women. The interviewers used a form of introduction in all cases explaining the reasons for the survey, reassuring informants of the completely confidential use of the information.

The experiments were carried out in five Parliamentary Constituencies, with pre-selected samples of electors taken from each constituency for each of the three experiments (i.e. there were 15 sub-samples).

The results of the experiments were analysed in two ways:

(a) The response rate (the number of refusals and numbers of incomplete questionnaires).
(b) The extent to which people were prepared to admit to relatively 'immoral' activities.

The results of the three experiments are shown in the following tables: (figures are actual numbers not percentages).

	A		B		C	
	Men	*Women*	*Men*	*Women*	*Men*	*Women*
Named persons contacted	19	28	19	30	19	30
Refusals/no reply/incomplete	—	3	13	10	16	18
'Admit' intercourse before marriage with wife/husband	—	3	3	1	2	1
'Admit' intercourse before marriage with someone else	4	2	2	1	1	2
'Admit' intercourse since marriage with someone not wife/husband	2	—	—	—	—	1
'Faithful'	14	22	2	18	1	9

The main conclusions were:
(a) Surprisingly few people would refuse to be interviewed if approached by a capable and sympathetic interviewer.
(b) Methods B and C were completely unsuccessful.
(c) Method A was therefore used in the main survey.

2.1 The main survey
First Stage: Constituencies

The sample was designed to be representative of the adult population aged 16 to 45 in England.

The 511 Parliamentary Constituencies in England were stratified by
(a) The Registrar General's Standard regions.
(b) Conurbation and size of town.

(c) Political complexion (ratio of Conservative to Labour votes in 1966 General Election).

The 100 constituencies were selected with probability of selection proportionate to the size of electorate. Alternative constituencies were designated 'male' and 'female' constituencies, so that there were 50 of each.

Second Stage: Polling Districts

In each constituency selected, a random number was generated and the electoral register for the polling district in which this fell was obtained. Where this polling district included less than 800 names, the register for the subsequent polling district was also obtained.

Third Stage: Electors

In each polling district (or districts) selected, every fifth elector was underlined if and only if he (or she) was of the correct sex for the 'male' and 'female' constituencies until eighty named electors had been underlined.

Thus in every 'male' constituency eighty men were underlined, and in each of the fifty 'female' constituencies eighty women were underlined. In all 8,000 named electors were marked in this way.

2.2 Sampling procedure

(a) Using male investigators to interview males, and female investigators to interview females, the persons whose names were underlined were called on, and an interview attempted with electors aged under 45. Those aged 45 or more were eliminated from the sample.

(b) When each call was made interviewers were required to ask whether there was a non-elector in the household aged 16 or more, and if so, they attempted to interview him/her.

In the event of there being more than one non-elector of the same sex as the interviewer, a random selection procedure was adopted, whereby the interviewer was to attempt to interview the person whose Christian name initial was nearest to his/her own.

2.3 Success rate

65·6% of the electors eligible were interviewed. While this is lower than for some other random samples, it is much higher than might have been expected for a survey on this subject.

		%
Total named electors	8,000	100
Not traced	62	0·8
Dead	95	1·2
Moved	630	7·9
Over 45	4,422	55·2
Total ineligible	5,209	65·1
Interviews attempted with electors	2,791	34·9

		%
Total electors eligible	2,791	100
Not interviewed because:		
On holiday	48	1·7
Too ill/in hospital	43	1·5
Out after four calls	291	10·4
Refused	495	17·8
Other reasons/incomplete questionnaire	83	3·0
	960	34·4
Electors interviewed	1,831	65·6
Non-electors interviewed	156	—
Total interviews obtained	1,987	

The Fieldwork

Interviewing was carried out between 14th April 1969 and 12th May 1969, by Opinion Research Centre's investigators. In every case males interviewed male respondents, and females interviewed females.

Fieldwork was under the control of Opinion Research Centre's Field Manager and Area Supervisors.

Every interviewers' work was subject to a 25% postal back-check, and physical back-checking was also done to ensure a high standard of interviewing and honesty.

Any interviews which were considered unsatisfactory in the backchecking were eliminated from the final sample.

Analysis

All questionnaires were coded and edited at Opinion Research Centre and the data was transferred to I.B.M. punch cards. Analysis was done on an I.B.M. 1130 computer.

Weighting

Because of the method of sampling, and in particular the use of electoral registers, the sample as selected under-represented those in the youngest age groups. The reasons for this are:

(a) The electoral register is notoriously deficient in the youngest age groups. Young people have a tendency not to get on the register.

(b) The method of selecting non-electors under-represents those in families where there are more than one non-elector.

The effect of these deficiencies meant that the sample as selected under-represented not only those in the youngest age groups but also single adults. The sample was therefore weighted using a simple, eight cell, series of weights. For the great majority of tables the effect of this weighting was very slight, altering the figures by no more than one or two per cent.

The Questionnaire

Occupation of head of household

Sex	Class	Age	Region
Male	AB	16–20	North
Female	Cl	21–24	Yorkshire (E. and W. Ridings)
	C2	25–34	East Midlands
	DE	35–45	East Anglia
			South-East (except Greater London)
Elector			Greater London
Non-elector			South-West
			West Midlands
			North-West

Good morning/good afternoon. I am from the Opinion Research Centre. We have been asked to carry out a survey which it is expected will be of great value to doctors, psychologists, and to social workers who try to prevent marriages breaking down.

Some of the questions are rather personal but the information will be treated with the strictest confidence.

Ask all

Q.1 (a) Marital status

Single   Married   Divorced   Separated
Widowed

(b) Is this your first marriage?
Yes   No

(c) If re-married ask: Why did your first marriage end?
Death of partner   Divorce   Separation

Q.2 Did you grow up in this neighbourhood?
Yes No

If no ask:
Q.3 Where did you grow up? (precise answers, please)

Q.4 (a) Do you think it is natural for young people to be shy?
Yes No Don't know
(b) Do you think when you left school that you were exceptionally shy?
Yes No Don't know
(c) Are you less shy now than you used to be?
Yes No Don't know
(d) Do you think shyness is a good thing?
Yes No Don't know

Q.5 (a) Would you say you have any religion?
Yes No

If yes ask:
(b) Which?

Q.6 (a) Did you go to church/chapel/synagogue last Sunday/Saturday?
Yes No
(b) About how many times a year do you attend your place of worship?

Show card
More than once a week
Once a week
Less than once a week but more than once a month
Once a month, less than once a month
Once or twice a year
Only for weddings and funerals etc.
Never

Ask all marrieds (*Singles go to Q.12*)

Q.7 (a) How many years have you been married?

(b) How old were you when you married?

(c) How many children have you?

(d) How long had you known your husband/wife before you became engaged?

(e) Where did you meet him/her?

(f) Before you became engaged to your husband/ wife did you ever seriously consider marrying another man/woman?

Yes   No

Q.8 (a) Which one of the following statements applies to you?

Show card

My husband/wife and I always go out together

We usually go out together

We go out separately and together equally

We usually go out separately

We always go out separately

(b) Which one of the following statements applies to you?

Show card

We always take our holidays together

We usually take our holidays together

We take our holidays both separately and together equally

We usually take our holidays separately

We always take our holidays separately

Married men

Q.9 What do you do about housekeeping for your wife?

Read out

Give her the whole pay packet (and get some back)

Give her a housekeeping allowance

Let her cash cheques on a joint account

Other (write in)

Married women

Q.10 How do you get housekeeping money?

Read out
Get whole pay packet from husband (and give him
some back)
Husband give me housekeeping money
Cash cheques on joint account
Other (write in)

Ask all married

Q.11 Do you and your wife/husband have single beds or
do you share a double bed?
Single beds   Double bed

Ask all women about husbands

Q.12 (a) What do you think are the three most important
qualities a husband should have?

Ask all men about wives

Q.12 (b) What do you think are the three most important
qualities a wife should have?

Ask all

Q.13 (a) What are the three chief faults wives tend to have?
(b) What are the three chief faults husbands tend to
have?

Q.14 What do you think tends to wreck a marriage?

Q.15 And what do you think tends to make a happy
marriage?

Q.16 (a) Do you think that when you get married, a
husband should be faithful for the rest of his
married life?
Yes   No   Don't know
(b) Do you think a wife should be faithful for the rest
of her married life?
Yes   No   Don't know

Q.17 (a) If a husband finds his wife having an affair with another man, what should he do?

(b) If a wife finds her husband having an affair with another woman, what should she do?

Q.18 (a) How old were you when you first started getting really interested in girls/boys?

(b) How soon after this did you have full sexual intercourse?

(c) Did you *later* marry the person with whom you first had intercourse or did you marry somebody else?

Married person later with whom first had intercourse
Married somebody else
Did not have full intercourse before marriage

(d) With how many partners did you have intercourse before marriage?

1   2   3   More than three

Q.19 (a) Would you say that you had ever been really in love?

Yes   No

If yes

(b) Has that happened to you more than once?
Yes   No

(c) Do you think most people really fall in love?
yes   No   D/K

If yes

(d) Do you think this happens to most people more than once?
Yes   No   D/K

(e) Do you think it is possible for a man to be in love with more than one person at the same time?
Yes   No   D/K

Q.19 (f) Do you think it is possible for a woman to be in love with more than one person at the same time? Yes No D/K

Q.20 How do you feel about a married man who has an affair with a woman he does not really love?

Q.21 How do you feel about a married woman who has an affair with a man she does not really love?

Ask all women
Q.22 (a) At what age did you become physically a woman?

Ask all men
(b) At what age did you become sexually a man?

Ask all
Q.23 (a) Which *one* of these statements do you most agree with (*Code one*)
(b) Which *one* of these statements do you most disagree with (*Code one only*)

Show card
Most agree with   Most disagree with
(a) Most women don't care much about the physical side of sex
(b) Most women don't have such an animal nature as men
(c) Most women enjoy the physical side of sex as much as men
(d) Most women enjoy sex more than men

Q.24 When a man and a woman are making love do you think that women have a real physical climax to the act of lovemaking in the same way as men?
Yes No Don't know

If yes ask:
Would you say:
Read out
All women   Most women   Some women

Q.25 (a) Do you think that young men should have some sexual experience before marriage?

Yes   No   Don't know

If yes

(b) Should it be restricted to one person or persons he loves, or with just anyone he feels physically attracted to?

One person, or persons.
Just anyone
Don't know

(c) Why?

Q.26 (a) Do you think young women should have some sexual experience before marriage?

Yes   No   Don't know

If yes

(b) Should it be restricted to one person or persons she loves, or with just anyone she feels physically attracted to?

One person, or persons
Just anyone
Don't know

(c) Why?

Q.27 Do you think a man and a woman can have a real friendship without sex playing any part?

Yes   No   Don't know

Q.28 How important do you think sexual love is in marriage?

Very important
Fairly important
Not very important
Not at all important

Q.29 (a) How old were you when you first (if ever) had full intercourse?

(b) About how often do you have intercourse?

Q.29 (c) Do you think this is about average for people like yourself?

Average
Less than average
More than average

Ask all marrieds

Q.30 Apart from kissing people in greeting or in fun (such as under the mistletoe) have you ever kissed anybody except your husband/wife since marriage?

Yes   No   D/K/Can't remember

Q.31 (a) Have you ever made love to anybody except your wife/husband since marriage?

Yes   No

If yes
(b) Did you go all the way in making love or not?
Yes   No

If yes
(c) How many partners, one two, three, more than three?
One   Two   Three   More than three

Q.32 Have you had a love relationship with anybody since marriage without ever actually going all the way?

Yes   No

Ask Q.33 of all marrieds and those answering 'Yes' at Q.29(a). *Others go to Q34.*

Q.33 (a) When you first had full intercourse was it with the man/woman you married or planned to marry or was it with some other person?
(b) With how many partners did you have full intercourse?

Ask all

Q.34 (a) How do you feel about people who fall in love with members of their own sex?

Q.34 Ask all except those who express disgust about Q.34(a)

(b) Have you yourself ever felt any sort of attraction towards a person of your own sex?

If yes

(c) What did you do about it?

Ask all

Q.35 On balance do you think that the invention of the pill for birth control is a good or a bad thing?

Q.36 Now that the pill provides absolute safety, do you think faithfulness is or is not as important as ever in a marriage?

Ask all except those answering 'No' at Q.29(a)

Q.37 (a) Do you regularly use any birth control methods?

Yes   No

If yes

(b) Which? (Sheath, diaphragm, the pill, withdrawal, other)

(c) Who normally takes responsibility for birth control precaution?
Self   Partner   Both   Sometimes one and sometimes other   Neither

Ask all single people only

Q.38 (a) Do you expect to get married some day?

Yes   No   Don't know

If yes

(b) Have you any idea when this will be?

Yes   No

Q.39 (a) Have you any special girl friend/boy friend at present?

Yes   No

(b) Where did you meet him/her?

Q.39 (c) Are you on terms of real physical intimacy with
her/him?
Yes   No

If yes
(d) With about how many other people have you been
on terms of physical intimacy?
None   One   Two   Three   More than three

Q.40 Do you feel you should be absolutely faithful to your
present special girl/boy friend?
Yes   No   Don't know

Q.41 Are you faithful?
Yes   No

Q.42 Do you think that he/she should be physically
absolutely faithful to you?
Yes   No   Don't know

Ask only divorced or separated Q.43–Q.50
Q.43 What went wrong with your marriage?

Q.44 (a) How many years were you married in your first
marriage?
(b) Did you have any children?

If yes
(c) With whom do they live?

Q.45 (a) How long had you known your former husband/
wife before engagement?
(b) Where did you meet him/her?
(c) How long was your engagement?

Q.46 If a third party was involved in the breakup (See
Q.43). Did you know the other man/woman or not?
Yes   No

R

Q.47 Have you any advice you would like to give to young people so that they might avoid the unhappiness you have been through?

Ask if applicable
Q.48 Do you think you will marry again?

Yes   No   Don't know

Q.49 Have you anybody in view?

Yes   No

Q.50 (a) Have you been physically intimate with another partner since your marriage broke up?

Yes   No

If yes
(b) How many partners?

Ask all
Q.51 Age at which full-time education was finished.

Q.52 Approximate income (Men). Income of head of household (Women)

Q.53 If you were asked to say what social class you were, how would you describe yourself?
Upper class
Upper middle class
Middle class
Lower middle class
Skilled working class
Upper working class
Working class

Q.54 Age

Note

The tabulations of the answers to the following questions are not printed in Appendix Three.

Question 11

Ninety-eight per cent of our married respondents had double beds; so the distribution of single beds is not significant.

Questions 25(c), 26 (c)

Owing to any ambiguity in the instructions to the interviewers (see footnote, p. 38) over a third of our informants were not asked these questions.

Questions 29(a), 33(a), 33(b)

Repeated questions 18(b), (c), (d) in slightly different words, as a check on whether our respondents were being consistent; the answers were so consistent (see footnote, p. 31) that it did not seem worthwhile reproducing these confirmations.

Questions 34 (b), (c)

Since only between 2 % and 3 % answered these questions affirmatively, the distribution does not appear significant.

Question 37(c)

This question was badly phrased, and the interpretation of the answers is ambiguous.

Questions 43-50

Only 40 divorced or separated informants answered these questions (see Chapter Eight, p. 177); therefore the figures of distribution are not meaningful.

Tables 1-50

List of tables in appendix three

The following Tables are 'weighted' to compensate for the under-representation of the unmarried and the under-21 in the sample (see Appendix One, p. 235): 1, 8, 18, 19, 20, 21, 22, 34, 35, 36, 47, 48, 49, 50. Question 1 is also reproduced in unweighted form. Question 35 is reproduced both weighted and unweighted, to demonstrate the (relatively insignificant) effect of 'weighting' on the percentages.

Table

15 Before you became engaged to your husband/wife did you ever seriously consider marrying another man/woman?

16 Questions about shyness.

17 How old were you when you first started getting really interested in girls/boys?

18 Questions about being 'really in love'.

To Chapter Two

19 Did you later marry the person with whom you first had intercourse or did you marry somebody else?

20 How old were you when you first (if ever) had full intercourse?

21 Do you think that young men should have some sexual experience before marriage?

22 Do you think that young women should have some sexual experience before marriage?

To chapter three

23 Questions about outings and holidays.

24 What do you think tends to make a happy marriage?

25 What do you think are the three most important qualities a husband/wife should have?

To chapter four

26 What do you think tends to wreck a marriage?

27 Questions about the distribution of money in the family.

28 What do you think are the three chief faults husbands tend to have?

29 What do you think are the three chief faults wives tend to have?

To chapter five

30 About how often do you have intercourse?

31 Do you think this is about average for people like yourself?

32 At what age did you become physically a woman? sexually a man?

33 How important do you think sexual love is in marriage?

Table

34 Choice of statements about the nature of 'most women'.

35 When a man and a woman are making love do you think women have a real physical climax to the act of lovemaking in the same way as men?

35a The same question unweighted.

To chapter six

36 Do you regularly use any birth control methods? Which?

37 On balance do you think the invention of the pill for birth control a good or a bad thing?

To chapter seven

38 Now that the pill provides absolute safety, do you think faithfulness is or is not as important as ever in marriage?

39 Do you think that when you get married, a husband/wife should be faithful for the rest of his/her married life?

40 How do you feel about a married man who has an affair with a woman he does not really love?

41 How do you feel about a married woman who has an affair with a man she does not really love?

42 Have you ever kissed anybody except your husband/wife since marriage?

43 Have you ever made love to anybody except your husband/wife since marriage? Did you go all the way?

To chapter eight

44 If a husband finds his wife having an affair with another man what should he do? If a wife finds her husband having an affair with another woman what should she do?

To chapter nine

45 How do you feel about people who fall in love with members of their own sex?

46 Do you think that a man and a woman can have a real friendship without sex playing any part?

Table

To chapter ten

47 Do you expect to get married some day? When? Do you have any special girl/boy friend at present?

48 Where did you meet him/her?

49 Are you on terms of real physical intimacy with her/him?

50 Do you feel you should be absolutely faithful to your present girl/boy friend? Are you faithful?

Table 1

Question 1 (a) Unweighted Form

What is your Marital Status?

	Single	Marr.	Div.	Sep.	Wid.
Age					
16–20	89	11	—	1	—
21–24	39	60	—	2	—
25–34	11	86	—	2	—
35–45	5	91	1	1	1
Sex					
Male	28	70	1	1	—
Female	11	86	1	1	1
Social class					
Middle	16	81	1	1	1
Lower Middle	20	78	1	1	1
Skilled Working	16	81	1	1	1
Upper Working	26	73	1	—	—
Working	21	76	1	2	—
'Blank'	22	77	—	1	1
All	19	78	1	1	1

Questions 1 (b) and (c)

Is this your first marriage? If not, why did your first marriage end?

	Yes	No	Death	Divorce
Age				
16–20	11	—	—	—
21–24	59	1	—	1
25–34	85	3	1	2
35–45	88	6	1	4
Sex				
Male	67	3	1	3
Female	85	4	1	3
Social class				
Middle	77	5	1	4
Lower Middle	78	3	1	2
Skilled Working	80	3	—	3
Upper Working	71	2	1	1
Working	75	3	1	2
'Blank'	75	3	2	2
All	76	4	1	3

Table 1a

Question 1 (a) Weighted

What is your marital status?

	Single	Marr.	Div.	Sep.	Wid.
Age					
16–20	90	9	—	1	—
21–24	47	52	—	1	—
25–34	12	86	—	2	—
35–45	7	89	1	1	1
Sex					
Male	41	58	1	1	—
Female	19	79	1	1	1
Social class					
Middle	26	72	1	1	1
Lower Middle	30	68	1	1	1
Skilled Working	25	73	1	1	—
Upper Working	41	58	1	—	—
Working	31	66	1	2	—
'Blank'	22	77	—	1	1
All	30	68	1	1	1

Questions 1(b) and (c)

Is this your first marriage? If not, why did your first marriage end?

	Yes	No	Death	Divorce
Age				
16–20	10	—	—	—
21–24	51	1	—	1
25–34	85	3	1	2
35–45	86	6	1	4
Sex				
Male	56	3	1	2
Female	77	3	1	3
Social class				
Middle	68	4	1	3
Lower Middle	67	3	1	2
Skilled Working	72	2	—	2
Upper Working	57	2	1	1
Working	65	3	1	2
'Blank'	75	3	2	2
All	67	3	1	3

Table 2

Analysis of Registrar General's classes by other categories.

	AB	C1	C2	DE
Age				
16–20	11	23	34	32
21–24	7	19	50	22
25–34	11	24	45	19
34–45	13	24	43	19
Sex				
Male	39	49	47	51
Female	61	50	52	48
Social class				
Upper	2	—	—	—
Upper Middle	17	5	1	—
Middle	57	48	26	22
Lower Middle	9	15	7	6
Skilled Working	2	6	19	7
Upper Working	1	5	6	5
Working	5	13	34	55
'Blank'	8	8	6	6
All	11	23	44	21

Table 3

Question 53

If you were asked to say what social class you were, how would you describe yourself?

	Upper Class	Upper Middle Class	Middle Class	Lower Middle Class	Skilled Working Class	Upper Working Class	Working Class	No Class, Don't Know, or Don't Believe in Class
Age								
16–20	1	3	27	7	8	9	35	9
21–24	—	4	31	9	9	6	34	7
25–34	—	3	36	7	13	5	29	8
35–45	—	4	33	11	13	4	30	6
Sex								
Male	—	4	26	9	15	6	32	9
Female	1	3	40	9	8	4	30	5
Class								
AB	2	17	57	9	2	1	5	8
C1	—	5	48	15	6	5	13	8
C2	—	1	26	7	19	6	34	6
DE	—	—	22	6	7	5	55	6
Area								
South-East	1	3	36	10	11	6	26	7
South-West	1	1	27	12	7	3	48	2
Midlands	—	4	35	7	15	5	29	3
North-West	—	4	34	8	13	6	34	1
North & Yorks	—	4	27	6	9	4	32	17
All	—	3	34	9	12	5	31	7

N.B.–The Upper and Upper Middle Classes have been included on this Table for the sake of completeness.

Table 4

Question 51

At what age did full-time education finish?

	14 or under	15	16	17	18	19	20	21	22 and Over	Still Continuing	No Answer
Area											
South-East	23	38	19	9	3	1	1	1	2	3	—
South-West	30	51	10	4	1	1	—	1	3	—	—
Midlands	29	40	17	4	3	—	—	1	1	3	—
North-West	30	44	11	5	2	2	—	1	2	2	—
North & Yorks	25	43	15	6	3	1	2	1	3	1	—
Age											
16–20	3	40	22	7	2	—	—	—	—	23	1
21–24	2	51	21	5	3	2	1	1	2	2	—
25–34	5	59	18	8	3	1	1	1	2	—	—
35–45	58	18	11	5	2	1	—	1	2	—	—
Sex											
Male	28	39	17	6	2	1	1	1	3	2	—
Female	25	43	16	7	3	1	1	1	1	2	—
Class											
AB	9	21	21	16	9	3	1	4	10	5	—
C1	21	28	24	10	5	2	2	2	4	4	—
C2	30	48	14	4	1	—	—	—	—	1	—
DE	34	51	9	2	1	—	—	—	—	2	—
Social class											
Middle	22	37	18	8	4	2	1	1	3	3	—
Lower Middle	25	31	22	10	3	1	1	1	2	3	1
Skilled Working	35	45	13	3	—	1	—	1	—	1	—
Upper Working	22	41	25	6	2	—	1	—	1	3	—
Working	31	50	12	3	—	—	—	—	—	1	—
'Blank'	27	39	12	10	5	—	2	1	4	1	—
All	26	41	16	6	3	1	1	1	2	2	—

Table 5

Question 52

Ask men. What is your approximate income?
Ask women. What is the approximate income of the head of the household?

	Less than £6 p.w.	£6–£8 p.w.	£8–£10 p.w.	£10–£13 p.w.	£13–£17 p.w.	£17–£20 p.w.	£20–£25 p.w.	£25–£35 p.w.	£35–£50 p.w.	Over £50 p.w.	Don't know	Refused to answer
Age												
16–20	1	5	6	7	21	12	10	5	1	1	27	2
21–24	1	—	2	4	17	20	24	14	3	1	12	2
25–34	1	1	—	2	9	15	22	28	8	3	7	3
35–45	—	—	1	2	11	12	24	21	10	6	9	3
Sex												
Male	1	1	1	3	14	16	24	24	8	4	2	2
Female	—	1	1	2	10	13	22	18	7	3	17	4
Social class												
Middle	1	1	1	2	8	10	21	24	11	7	11	3
Lower Middle	1	2	1	2	10	13	20	28	8	2	11	2
Skilled Working	—	1	—	—	11	19	27	27	5	—	5	3
Upper Working	—	—	—	4	10	19	31	20	4	1	8	4
Working	1	1	2	4	19	17	24	15	3	1	11	2
'Blank'	—	—	3	3	11	17	20	23	5	1	11	4
All	1	1	1	3	12	14	23	21	8	4	10	3

Table 6

Question 5(a) and (b)

(a) Would you say you have any religion?
(b) If so, which?

	Have a religion	Have no religion	Church of England	Roman Catholic	Methodist	Baptist	Spiritualist, Christian Scientist, etc.	Other Non-conformist	Congregational, Presbyterian	Anglo-Catholic	Jewish	No answer
Area												
South-East	72	26	52	10	2	2	1	1	1	—	—	2
South-West	74	22	63	6	4	2	1	1	1	—	—	2
Midlands	81	17	57	9	8	2	2	—	2	—	—	2
North-West	80	20	49	21	4	—	2	—	1	—	—	2
North & Yorks	73	25	43	9	13	1	4	—	1	1	—	1
Age												
16–20	64	35	37	12	8	1	2	—	2	—	—	3
21–24	70	28	49	10	4	2	2	1	1	1	—	3
25–34	73	25	53	10	4	1	2	—	1	1	—	3
35–45	81	18	56	10	7	2	2	1	1	—	—	3
Sex												
Male	73	25	51	11	4	1	2	1	1	—	—	2
Female	78	21	54	10	7	2	2	—	1	—	—	3
Class												
AB	76	23	50	6	6	2	4	1	3	1	—	3
C1	78	21	51	12	5	2	2	1	2	1	—	2
C2	76	22	54	11	6	2	2	—	1	—	—	2
DE	71	27	50	11	5	1	1	—	—	—	—	3
Social class												
Middle	79	20	55	9	6	2	3	—	2	1	—	2
Lower Middle	81	17	56	9	5	2	3	2	1	—	—	2
Skilled Working	77	21	54	12	6	1	1	—	1	—	—	3
Upper Working	72	26	47	12	9	1	4	1	—	—	—	1
Working	72	26	51	11	4	1	3	—	1	—	—	2
'Blank'	65	32	39	11	8	2	2	—	—	1	—	4
All	75	23	52	10	6	2	2	1	1	—	—	3

Table 7

Question 6

(a) Did you go to church/chapel/synagogue last Sunday/Saturday?
(b) About how many times a year do you attend your place of worship?

	Yes	*No*	*More than once a week*	*Once a week*	*Less than once a week but more than once a month*	*Once a month or less*	*Once or twice a year*	*Weddings, funerals, etc.*	*Never*
Area									
South-East	11	55	4	6	4	7	21	29	8
South-West	7	63	1	7	7	10	26	26	10
Midlands	13	64	4	6	8	12	19	31	6
North-West	14	61	5	11	7	10	18	26	6
North & Yorks	11	58	2	7	7	11	14	37	6
Age									
16–20	14	50	5	11	9	9	13	21	11
21–24	11	57	2	7	4	9	14	35	7
25–34	10	58	4	6	5	8	22	31	7
35–45	12	62	5	7	7	12	20	30	6
Sex									
Male	10	60	3	7	5	9	18	32	6
Female	13	58	5	7	7	10	20	28	7
Class									
AB	17	57	6	10	11	13	22	17	7
C1	16	57	5	10	7	10	22	25	5
C2	8	62	3	5	5	9	19	34	9
DE	12	56	3	7	5	8	16	35	6
Social class									
Middle	12	61	4	6	7	10	21	28	6
Lower Middle	20	56	7	11	5	11	18	25	8
Skilled Working	9	63	3	7	5	9	22	31	7
Upper Working	11	58	3	7	8	6	14	37	6
Working	9	58	3	5	5	8	18	33	7
'Blank'	9	52	2	8	6	8	14	33	8
All	12	59	4	7	6	10	19	30	7

Table 8

Questions 2 and 3

Did you grow up in this neighbourhood? If No, where did you grow up?

	Grew up in this neighbourhood	Did NOT grow up in this neighbourhood	Same district (rural)	Same district (urban)	Other district (rural)	Other district (urban)	Scotland/Wales/Northern Ireland	Ireland (Eire)	Europe	West Indies	Overseas (other)
Age											
16–20	82	19	1	5	4	7	2	—	—	1	—
21–24	60	40	4	12	6	17	1	2	1	1	1
25–34	48	51	5	11	6	23	4	4	—	1	1
35–45	48	51	3	13	7	24	3	4	—	1	2
Sex											
Male	63	37	2	9	6	16	3	3	—	—	1
Female	49	51	5	12	6	23	2	3	—	2	1
Social class											
Middle	52	48	4	11	6	23	3	3	1	—	—
Lower Middle	58	41	4	10	7	20	3	3	—	—	—
Skilled Working	64	36	4	10	4	16	2	2	—	—	—
Upper Working	60	40	1	12	6	21	1	2	1	—	—
Working	59	42	4	11	6	16	3	3	1	—	—
'Blank'	52	48	2	11	5	19	2	5	—	2	8
All	56	44	4	11	6	20	3	3	—	1	1

Table 9

Analysis by region basis

	Greater London	South-East except Greater London	South-West	East Anglia	East Midlands	West Midlands	North-West	Yorkshire and Humberside	North
Sex									
Male	45	49	43	39	43	50	56	42	54
Female	55	51	57	61	57	50	44	57	46
Class									
AB	10	13	7	3	15	11	6	15	18
C1	28	26	16	18	22	19	23	18	31
C2	41	43	45	58	40	50	46	46	30
DE	19	16	29	21	24	19	24	21	21
Social class									
Middle	19	21	7	3	6	16	13	9	5
Lower Middle	16	27	11	3	6	13	11	9	3
Skilled Working	10	23	5	5	11	18	14	9	5
Upper Working	14	26	5	3	14	8	16	7	8
Working	15	13	13	5	7	14	15	12	7
'Blank'	31	11	2	—	5	6	3	40	3
All	17	19	8	4	8	14	13	11	6

s

Table 10

Question 7(a)

How many years have you been married?

	Less than a year	1–3 years	4–6 years	7–9 years	10–12 years	13–15 years	16–20 years	More than 20 years
Age								
16–20	3	7	1	—	—	—	—	—
21–24	8	30	17	3	—	1	—	—
25–34	2	10	21	24	20	8	1	—
35–45	—	1	3	5	9	19	34	21
Sex								
Male	2	10	9	10	9	10	12	8
Female	3	9	14	12	13	11	16	9
Social class								
Middle	2	11	11	13	13	10	13	8
Lower Middle	2	9	7	13	11	11	17	10
Skilled Working	3	7	13	13	9	10	17	11
Upper Working	1	10	14	12	9	10	12	6
Working	2	9	12	9	10	11	14	9
'Blank'	5	11	12	8	11	10	12	6
All	2	10	12	11	11	11	14	8

Table 11

Question 7(b)

How old were you when you married?

	Less than 17	17–17.11	18–18.11	19–19.11	20–20.11	21–21.11	22–23.11	24–25.11	26–29.11	Over 30
Age										
16–20	3	3	4	1	2	—	—	—	—	—
21–24	2	5	8	11	14	12	10	1	—	—
25–34	1	3	7	9	11	16	22	13	7	1
35–45	—	1	5	7	8	11	21	17	15	10
Sex										
Male	—	1	2	4	5	9	17	13	12	7
Female	1	4	10	12	13	15	18	10	6	2
Social class										
Middle	1	2	6	9	10	13	18	11	10	5
Lower Middle	1	2	5	7	10	11	18	11	11	7
Skilled Working	—	2	7	11	7	13	18	14	7	4
Upper Working	—	2	4	8	11	10	12	12	9	6
Working	1	3	8	8	9	12	16	12	7	3
'Blank'	—	5	5	6	8	9	23	11	11	6
All	1	3	6	8	9	12	18	12	9	4

Table 12

Question 7(c)

How many children have you?

	0	1	2	3	4	5+	Step.		Adopt.	
							1	1+	1	1+
Age										
16–20	5	6	—	1	—	—	—	—	—	—
21–24	20	20	14	4	1	—	—	—	—	—
25–34	13	18	32	15	4	3	1	—	—	—
35–45	9	18	34	17	8	7	—	—	—	1
Sex										
Male	11	16	22	11	5	3	—	—	—	1
Female	12	18	32	14	5	4	—	—	—	—
Social class										
Middle	13	20	28	13	4	4	—	—	—	—
Lower Middle	10	17	34	13	3	1	1	1	—	1
Skilled Working	14	16	29	12	6	5	—	—	—	—
Upper Working	8	17	29	15	2	—	2	—	1	—
Working	9	15	25	15	7	4	—	—	—	1
'Blank'	20	19	17	8	5	3	1	—	—	—
All	12	17	27	13	5	4	—	—	—	—

Table 13

Question 7(e)

Where did you first meet your husband/wife?

	Dance	*At work*	*Social gatherings*	*Mutual friends/relations*	*Pick-up, street/public place*	*Public amusement place*	*Friends/neighbours since children*	*Public house*	*School/College*	*Meeting/outing (church/chapel)*	*Holiday/leave*	*Other*
Age												
16–20	3	2	1	1	—	1	1	1	1	—	—	1
21–24	13	11	9	6	4	5	2	4	2	1	2	2
25–34	21	11	13	10	5	8	7	5	4	2	1	3
35–45	20	15	10	11	9	7	5	4	4	2	3	4
Sex												
Male	17	11	11	7	6	4	3	4	3	2	1	3
Female	20	13	9	11	6	8	6	4	4	2	3	3
Social class												
Middle	18	13	10	11	6	6	5	3	4	3	2	3
Lower Middle	18	12	10	7	11	4	5	2	5	2	3	2
Skilled Working	23	11	12	9	6	5	6	3	1	1	3	1
Upper Working	18	11	11	8	4	7	—	4	2	—	4	5
Working	17	12	8	9	6	8	4	6	2	2	1	3
'Blank'	20	10	8	8	5	5	7	7	7	—	—	4
Age at which education finished												
14 or under	21	15	9	11	9	8	7	4	3	1	2	3
15	20	12	9	9	5	7	5	6	2	2	2	3
16	16	9	10	10	4	6	3	3	3	2	2	2
17	16	17	16	5	5	2	4	3	4	1	2	4
18	16	20	12	4	—	4	2	—	12	2	2	2
All	18	12	10	9	6	6	5	4	3	2	2	3

Table 14

Question 7(d)

How long had you known your husband/wife before you became engaged?

	No engagement	Under 6 months	6–11 months	A year	1–2 years	2–3 years	3–4 years	4–10 years	10–20 years	All of life/since school
Age										
16–20	1	3	2	1	1	1	1	1	—	—
21–24	2	7	8	11	16	8	7	3	1	1
25–34	3	7	13	11	25	10	11	6	1	1
35–45	3	7	10	14	25	12	11	8	2	3
Sex										
Male	3	5	8	11	18	9	9	6	1	2
Female	3	8	12	13	25	11	10	6	1	2
Social class										
Middle	2	7	10	11	22	11	11	7	1	2
Lower Middle	3	3	11	11	24	10	8	8	1	2
Skilled Working	3	5	10	18	22	9	6	6	1	2
Upper Working	2	6	13	12	18	8	14	1	—	—
Working	4	6	10	12	20	11	8	5	1	1
'Blank'	4	8	10	8	23	5	14	5	2	5
All	3	6	10	12	22	10	9	6	1	2

Table 15

Question 7(f)

Before you became engaged to your husband/wife did you ever seriously consider marrying another man/woman?

	Yes	*No*
Area		
South-East	20	59
South-West	21	61
Midlands	19	56
North-West	18	61
North & Yorks	24	60
Age		
16–20	6	9
21–24	14	45
25–34	22	65
35–45	25	68
Sex		
Male	15	55
Female	15	63
Class		
AB	27	55
C1	22	57
C2	19	63
DE	17	55
Social class		
Middle	25	58
Lower Middle	21	60
Skilled Working	15	65
Upper Working	22	50
Working	18	60
'Blank'	16	63
All	20	59

Table 16

Questions 4(a), (b), (c) and (d)

(a) Do you think it is natural for young people to be shy?
(b) Do you think when you left school you were exceptionally shy?
(c) Are you less shy now than you used to be?
(d) Do you think shyness is a good thing?

	(a)			(b)			(c)			(d)		
	Yes	*No*	*D/K*	*Yes*	*No*	*D/K*	*Yes*	*No*	*D/K*	*Yes*	*No*	*D/K*
Age												
16–20	58	34	8	41	52	2	69	26	3	31	51	17
21–24	55	36	8	47	51	1	74	23	2	32	57	11
25–34	59	35	6	54	45	1	77	21	2	32	57	11
35–45	61	29	9	59	40	1	76	21	2	30	60	9
Sex												
Male	57	35	8	47	52	1	73	23	3	30	57	13
Female	61	31	8	60	38	1	78	20	1	32	59	8
Social class												
Middle	61	31	8	54	44	1	76	21	1	31	58	10
Lower Middle	60	30	10	49	49	1	75	23	2	28	59	13
Skilled Working	56	34	9	50	49	1	76	21	3	34	56	9
Upper Working	63	32	5	53	44	2	76	24	—	27	62	11
Working	56	36	7	58	41	1	74	23	2	30	60	10
'Blank'	57	35	8	52	47	2	73	20	3	39	50	10
All	59	33	8	54	45	1	75	22	2	31	58	10

Table 17

Question 18(a)

How old were you when you first started getting really interested in girls/boys?

	Under 11	*11–12*	*12–13*	*13–14*	*14–15*	*15–16*	*16–17*	*17–18*	*18–19*	*Over 19*	*Don't know/No answer*
Age											
16–20	7	4	11	16	22	23	9	1	1	2	4
21–24	1	2	8	14	23	21	17	7	4	1	2
25–34	3	3	5	10	22	20	17	10	8	5	—
35–45	2	2	6	6	16	16	20	12	11	8	2
Sex											
Male	3	3	6	9	18	18	18	9	9	7	—
Female	2	2	7	10	21	19	18	10	7	3	1
Social class											
Middle	3	2	8	11	19	18	15	10	8	5	—
Lower Middle	2	2	8	10	20	17	22	7	6	5	—
Skilled Working	4	4	5	9	21	17	19	9	7	4	—
Upper Working	2	3	7	12	18	19	18	11	10	2	—
Working	2	3	5	8	22	20	20	10	6	5	—
'Blank'	4	2	5	10	17	17	16	8	10	8	3
Age at which education finished											
14 or under	2	3	6	7	19	15	20	11	9	8	1
15	3	3	6	9	22	20	17	10	7	3	1
16	3	2	6	12	17	17	22	11	6	2	2
17	2	1	9	13	21	20	11	9	5	8	1
18	2	2	6	6	10	33	20	6	10	10	—
All	3	3	6	10	20	19	18	10	8	5	1

Table 18

Question 19 Weighted

(a) Would you say that you had ever really been in love?
   If Yes
(b) Has this happened to you more than once?
(c) Do you think most people really fall in love?
(d) Do you think this happens to most people more than once?

| | (a) | | (b) | | | (c) | |
	Yes	No	Yes	No	Yes	No	D/K
Age							
16–20	43	48	10	36	62	17	13
21–24	79	19	23	56	67	23	8
25–34	89	10	29	59	70	20	8
35–45	91	8	26	65	70	19	10
Sex							
Male	74	23	23	51	65	21	10
Female	86	11	25	62	71	18	8
Social class							
Middle	82	15	27	56	68	20	8
Lower Middle	84	16	23	61	67	24	9
Skilled Working	85	13	27	58	72	17	10
Upper Working	75	22	17	60	68	14	13
Working	77	19	22	56	66	20	9
'Blank'	84	19	30	54	64	20	14
All	80	17	24	57	68	20	9

If Yes

(e) Do you think it is possible for a man to be in love with more than one person at the same time?

(f) Do you think it is possible for a woman to be in love with more than one person at the same time?

Yes	(d) No	D/K	Yes	(e) No	D/K	Yes	(f) No	D/K
40	16	9	40	52	9	41	47	10
42	22	11	40	52	8	36	55	8
45	21	9	41	53	5	36	59	4
40	25	13	39	56	5	37	57	5
39	21	11	39	55	5	40	53	7
44	22	10	40	53	7	34	62	4
42	21	11	43	51	5	40	55	5
35	28	10	38	56	6	33	61	5
42	22	15	38	56	7	35	59	6
43	25	12	42	53	4	38	58	4
41	21	9	38	56	6	35	58	7
44	17	3	42	49	8	39	53	8
42	22	11	40	54	6	37	57	6

Table 19

Questions 18(c) and (d)

(a) Did you:
- (a) Later marry the person with whom you first had intercourse?
- (b) Later marry someone else?
- (c) Not have full intercourse until after marriage?

(b) With how many partners did you have intercourse before marriage?

	18(c)			*No. of Partners*			
	(a)	*(b)*	*(c)*	*1*	*2*	*3*	*More than 3*
Area							
South-East	14	20	35	19	4	3	9
South-West	19	21	38	23	6	2	7
Midlands	13	16	35	17	7	1	7
North-West	23	19	26	21	4	4	10
North & Yorks	19	22	32	18	4	2	12
Age							
16–20	5	2	3	10	2	1	4
21–24	19	14	19	21	3	2	8
25–34	21	24	42	23	5	3	10
35–45	16	26	49	19	6	3	10
Sex							
Male	12	31	16	16	6	4	17
Female	20	7	51	22	2	1	1
Class							
AB	10	13	44	9	4	2	6
C1	14	19	35	16	5	3	7
C2	18	21	35	21	4	2	10
DE	18	20	24	22	5	2	11
Social class							
Middle	16	15	40	16	5	3	6
Lower Middle	17	16	36	25	3	1	2
Skilled Working	16	29	30	22	5	3	14
Upper Working	13	15	31	15	1	3	8
Working	18	20	31	21	5	2	11
'Blank'	17	30	29	21	4	4	18

Table 19 (continued)

(a) Did you:
- (a) Later marry the person with whom you first had intercourse?
- (b) Later marry someone else?
- (c) Not have full intercourse until after marriage?

(b) With how many partners did you have intercourse before marriage?

	18(c)			No. of Partners			
	(a)	*(b)*	*(c)*	*1*	*2*	*3*	*More than 3*
Age at which							
Education finished							
14 or under	17	28	46	20	5	4	11
15	20	19	31	23	5	2	10
16	13	15	30	16	4	1	7
17	11	17	40	14	4	2	8
18	12	14	39	10	3	2	7
All	16	19	34	19	4	2	9

Table 20

Question 18(b) Weighted

How old were you when you first (if ever) had intercourse?

	Under 17	17–18	18–19	19–20	20–21
Area					
South-East	11	8	11	8	9
South-West	8	10	12	12	11
Midlands	11	6	10	11	7
North-West	10	8	11	7	9
North & Yorks	11	7	10	10	9
Age					
16–20	18	8	8	4	1
21–24	17	12	11	9	10
25–34	8	8	11	12	11
35–45	6	5	11	10	10
Sex					
Male	16	9	12	9	6
Female	5	6	10	10	11
Class					
AB	4	3	6	10	8
C1	8	6	10	9	9
C2	11	8	13	10	10
DE	15	10	10	8	8
Social class					
Middle	8	5	10	10	10
Lower Middle	7	3	12	12	12
Skilled Working	14	11	11	8	9
Upper Working	6	9	8	9	5
Working	13	9	12	10	9
'Blank'	13	11	11	6	5
Age at which education finished					
14 or under	7	7	12	10	12
15	12	10	12	12	11
16	8	8	11	8	10
17	8	4	10	13	9
18	4	2	6	8	4
All	10	8	11	9	9

21–22	22–23	23–24	Over 24	Not yet	Not until married	Refused
0	6	5	11	14	28	3
8	6	3	12	11	29	3
9	5	5	10	20	26	3
7	6	5	11	18	22	4
8	6	4	12	13	27	3
1	—	1	—	55	3	3
8	5	—	1	19	15	4
12	7	7	10	4	30	2
11	8	7	23	4	41	3
6	4	3	11	17	14	4
2	7	6	12	14	39	2
3	10	4	18	17	38	2
8	7	6	14	16	28	3
9	5	5	10	13	27	3
8	4	4	8	20	19	3
0	7	6	12	13	33	4
8	6	6	14	16	22	3
0	6	5	10	12	24	3
5	5	5	11	35	24	1
9	5	3	8	16	23	3
6	6	5	17	8	24	3
9	8	7	21	3	39	2
1	6	5	7	8	26	2
2	6	3	11	17	32	3
9	9	7	20	7	36	5
2	12	6	25	8	35	6
9	6	5	11	15	27	3

Table 21

Questions 25(a), (b) and (c)

(Weighted run for area and class only)

(a) Do you think that young men should have some sexual experience before marriage?

(b) If Yes: Should it be restricted to one person or persons he loves, or with just anyone he feels physically attracted to?

	A			B		
	Yes	*No*	*D/K*	*One person or persons*	*Just anyone*	*D/K*
Area						
South-East	55	35	8	30	22	2
South-West	51	29	13	30	19 ˚	5
Midlands	47	39	12	29	15	3
North-West	50	44	6	34	13	2
North & Yorks	54	36	10	30	21	2
Age						
16–20	58	25	12	33	24	2
21–24	64	25	8	37	25	3
25–34	55	36	.8	30	20	3
35–45	40	49	9	26	13	2
Sex						
Male	63	27	8	32	27	3
Female	39	49	10	28	9	2
Class						
AB	42	47	6	29	13	—
C1	46	41	11	24	18	3
C2	53	36	9	32	18	3
DE	61	30	9	35	24	3
Social class						
Middle	48	40	10	30	15	3
Lower Middle	44	44	9	26	14	4
Skilled Working	56	34	7	34	19	3
Upper Working	45	41	13	29	14	4
Working	54	35	9	30	21	2
'Blank'	58	38	5	30	24	2
All	51	39	9	30	18	3

Table 22

Questions 26(a), (b) and (c)
(Weighted run for Area and Class only)

(a) Do you think young women should have some sexual experience before marriage?
(b) If yes: Should it be restricted to one person or persons she loves, or with just anyone she feels physically attracted to?

	A			B		
	Yes	*No*	*D/K*	*One person or persons*	*Just anyone*	*D/K*
Area						
South-East	35	55	9	24	9	1
South-West	36	50	12	24	12	1
Midlands	36	53	10	28	5	3
North-West	34	58	8	28	4	3
North & Yorks	36	54	10	23	10	2
Age						
16–20	41	45	13	29	9	3
21–24	43	45	11	32	8	3
25–34	37	53	9	27	8	2
35–45	27	66	7	19	6	1
Sex						
Male	46	43	9	31	13	3
Female	23	68	8	19	3	1
Class						
AB	28	64	7	21	6	—
C1	34	57	9	23	9	2
C2	36	53	10	26	8	3
DE	39	49	11	28	9	2
Social class						
Middle	32	58	9	25	6	2
Lower Middle	29	62	9	20	6	2
Skilled Working	43	48	8	32	8	3
Upper Working	25	62	11	17	5	3
Working	36	53	10	25	9	2
'Blank'	35	61	5	23	12	—
All	34	56	9	25	7	2

T

Table 23

Question 8(a)

Which one of the following statements applies to you?
(1) My husband/wife and I always go out together.
(2) We usually go out together
(3) We go out separately and together equally
(4) We usually go out separately
(5) We always go out separately

	1	*2*	*3*	*4*	*5*
Area					
South-East	25	32	19	3	1
South-West	20	29	26	4	2
Midlands	23	27	19	6	1
North-West	21	35	18	3	—
North & Yorks	25	32	19	6	1
Age					
16–20	6	3	2	—	1
21–24	21	23	13	3	1
25–34	24	35	21	5	1
35–45	27	36	23	5	1
Sex					
Male	18	30	18	4	1
Female	29	32	20	5	1
Class					
AB	22	35	22	3	—
C1	24	31	19	4	—
C2	25	33	19	4	1
DE	20	25	19	6	2
Social class					
Middle	29	31	17	4	1
Lower Middle	19	32	24	5	—
Skilled Working	21	34	23	3	1
Upper Working	28	22	19	3	1
Working	19	32	19	6	1
'Blank'	28	30	14	5	2
All	24	31	19	4	1

Table 23 (*continued*)

Question 8(b)

Which one of the following statements applies to you?
(1) We always take our holidays together
(2) We usually take our holidays together
(3) We take our holidays separately and together equally
(4) We usually take our holidays separately
(5) We always take our holidays separately

	1	2	3	4	5
Area					
South-East	72	3	1	—	—
South-West	68	5	1	—	—
Midlands	65	3	—	—	—
North-West	72	2	1	—	—
North & Yorks	66	9	2	2	—
Age					
16–20	7	1	—	—	—
21–24	52	3	1	—	—
25–34	76	4	1	—	1
35–45	81	5	1	1	1
Sex					
Male	62	3	1	—	1
Female	76	5	1	1	—
Class					
AB	74	5	1	—	—
C1	71	4	1	1	—
C2	74	4	1	—	—
DE	54	4	1	1	—
Social class					
Middle	73	3	1	—	1
Lower Middle	74	3	1	—	1
Skilled Working	73	3	1	—	1
Upper Working	66	4	—	—	—
Working	64	5	1	—	—
'Blank'	64	6	1	3	1
All	69	4	1	1	1

Table 24

Question 15

What do you think tends to make a happy marriage?

	Comradeship	Discussing things together/ understanding	Give and take/Consideration	Mutual trust	Love and affection
Area					
South-East	27	31	31	19	20
South-West	32	23	33	26	21
Midlands	31	23	28	17	19
North-West	28	34	18	22	20
North & Yorks	29	27	26	20	14
Age					
16–20	25	30	21	20	27
21–24	26	31	24	17	26
25–34	30	29	27	20	17
35–45	30	27	31	21	16
Sex					
Male	27	26	24	21	20
Female	30	30	31	19	18
Class					
AB	28	31	28	20	17
C1	26	31	30	22	19
C2	31	28	28	19	17
DE	28	25	25	19	22
Social class					
Middle	28	31	28	18	19
Lower Middle	28	27	32	22	15
Skilled Working	31	29	24	18	22
Upper Working	22	31	32	23	16
Working	30	24	28	21	20
'Blank'	36	26	27	22	13
All	29	28	28	20	19

Children	Shared interests	No money problems	Happy home life	Sexual compatibility	Good temper	Home of one's own	Don't know
14	15	6	6	8	5	1	1
18	21	7	7	5	4	1	1
14	12	5	4	3	4	—	1
13	14	3	3	1	—	—	—
13	8	7	6	3	3	1	1
14	11	5	5	3	3	1	3
16	11	7	5	4	3	1	3
14	14	6	4	7	3	1	—
13	14	5	6	5	4	6	1
17	13	7	7	7	3	1	1
11	14	4	3	3	4	—	1
10	14	6	4	4	4	—	1
11	14	6	6	6	3	—	1
13	14	4	5	5	4	—	1
21	12	6	7	4	4	1	1
14	15	6	5	5	3	—	1
9	13	6	5	6	2	1	1
14	12	5	4	5	4	—	—
15	6	4	2	9	8	2	—
17	14	5	6	3	3	—	1
7	13	5	6	5	5	2	4
14	13	5	5	5	4	1	1

Table 25

Question 12

What do you think are the three most important qualities a husband/
wife should have?

	Understanding/consideration	Love/affection/kindness	Good housekeeper/competent in house	Good mother/loves children	Personal qualities – attractive/clean	Sense of humour	Patience/level-headed	Faithfulness	Equanimity/good temper	Generosity
Area										
South-East	41	33	17	18	14	16	14	12	14	11
South-West	36	31	21	21	14	14	10	13	14	11
Midlands	38	35	17	14	16	15	13	11	12	12
North-West	41	30	21	19	15	12	24	15	9	9
North & Yorks	35	34	18	15	19	17	13	11	6	9
Age										
16–20	6	33	15	19	20	10	12	14	13	6
21–24	9	35	16	15	19	12	16	12	13	9
25–34	13	40	19	16	14	16	14	11	10	13
35–45	10	40	20	19	14	16	14	13	12	10
Sex										
Male	24	22	37	34	28	11	13	12	10	2
Female	52	44	1	1	4	18	16	12	13	19
Class										
AB	44	41	8	9	12	24	16	12	10	12
C1	45	34	16	17	15	18	16	14	12	9
C2	39	31	18	19	16	13	14	11	13	12
DE	30	32	26	19	18	11	12	13	9	8
Social class										
Middle	45	34	11	11	13	16	16	12	13	13
Lower Middle	40	37	22	23	13	20	14	16	9	11
Skilled Working	34	31	24	24	23	15	11	13	13	9
Upper Working	31	29	22	18	18	21	25	16	9	6
Working	35	35	21	19	13	13	13	11	12	11
'Blank'	33	26	23	17	25	14	8	11	11	6
All	39	33	18	17	15	15	14	12	12	11

Tolerance	Love of home/co-operation	Moral qualities/sincerity	Good father/loves children	Shares responsibility and interests	Good cook	Fairness/justice	Thoughtfulness	Good worker and ambitious	Economical	Intelligent	Treats spouse as a person	Virility, strength, courage	Don't know
9	9	11	9	9	6	5	6	5	4	5	3	2	5
8	14	8	9	11	8	7	10	10	8	4	4	—	2
8	10	10	6	10	6	6	7	5	3	2	3	1	7
12	12	7	7	6	6	6	4	4	2	5	3	2	4
13	8	6	6	7	9	6	4	6	8	4	3	1	10
3	7	12	6	6	8	5	5	9	5	7	5	1	10
6	9	10	6	8	7	3	5	5	4	3	3	2	9
9	11	11	10	7	6	7	7	6	4	4	2	1	5
13	10	7	6	10	7	6	5	4	4	4	3	1	5
8	6	12	3	8	14	3	1	2	7	6	2	1	7
11	14	7	12	8	—	8	10	8	2	2	4	2	5
12	7	10	7	10	3	7	7	6	1	6	3	2	5
15	8	10	6	8	3	4	5	5	2	7	3	2	4
8	12	8	8	8	8	6	7	5	6	3	3	1	6
6	12	11	9	8	10	5	3	7	5	2	2	1	8
13	9	9	9	10	4	6	6	6	3	5	2	1	5
10	11	8	8	9	5	3	3	5	4	5	1	2	3
10	11	10	3	8	9	4	4	5	4	4	2	—	7
11	4	12	7	4	5	7	6	3	2	6	4	2	5
6	12	9	8	7	10	6	6	5	5	2	3	1	7
9	8	6	8	10	6	4	5	2	11	7	5	5	8
10	10	9	8	8	7	6	6	5	4	4	3	1	6

Table 26

Question 14

What do you think tends to wreck a marriage?

	Neglect/bad communication	Infidelity/jealousy	Selfishness/intolerance	Poverty/extravagances money problems/working wives	Incompatibility/conflicting personalities
Area					
South-East	30	26	26	22	14
South-West	36	37	18	19	15
Midlands	28	24	23	14	10
North-West	31	22	34	9	10
North & Yorks	26	22	21	17	11
Age					
16–20	28	28	23	8	18
21–24	32	27	20	17	14
25–34	32	23	23	19	13
35–45	26	26	29	18	11
Sex					
Male	26	29	25	15	13
Female	33	22	25	19	12
Class					
AB	27	20	35	18	14
C1	26	25	30	18	15
C2	32	25	23	17	12
DE	29	29	20	17	10
Social class					
Middle	31	22	30	18	13
Lower Middle	28	25	24	18	15
Skilled Working	28	28	22	16	11
Upper Working	26	25	28	14	17
Working	30	29	20	19	11
'Blank'	27	26	20	17	13
All	30	25	25	17	12

Quarrelling	Sexual and fertility problems	Lack of affection	Drunkenness/gambling	Lack of trust/untruthfulness	No house of one's own, bad management	In-laws	Don't know
12	14	9	6	6	2	1	1
10	11	6	11	6	3	5	2
10	6	7	7	8	3	2	2
6	4	3	8	9	2	3	—
8	9	7	8	5	1	3	3
15	5	9	5	7	1	3	5
10	10	7	5	8	2	2	3
11	10	8	8	6	2	2	1
8	11	7	7	7	2	3	1
11	11	7	7	6	2	3	2
9	9	8	7	7	2	2	1
5	13	9	4	6	2	2	2
8	10	10	5	6	3	2	1
11	9	7	8	6	1	2	1
12	8	6	10	7	2	4	3
8	10	8	6	7	1	2	1
10	13	7	7	10	3	3	1
9	10	9	6	8	1	—	1
10	8	8	8	10	4	4	—
12	8	6	9	7	2	3	2
15	13	8	5	3	2	2	5
10	10	7	7	6	2	2	2

Table 27

Questions 9 and 10

Ask husbands

(9) What do you do about housekeeping for your wife?
- (a) Give her the whole pay-packet (and get some back)
- (b) Give her a housekeeping allowance
- (c) Let her cash cheques on a joint account
- (d) Other

	Question 9				Question 10			
	(a)	*(b)*	*(c)*	*(d)*	*(a)*	*(b)*	*(c)*	*(d)*
Area								
South-East	4	21	4	3	2	33	9	4
South-West	5	17	6	2	8	40	2	1
Midlands	6	22	5	1	6	28	9	3
North-West	11	26	5	1	12	19	3	2
North & Yorks	10	21	6	—	10	26	9	2
Age								
16–20	1	1	—	—	2	4	1	1
21–24	6	12	3	—	7	24	7	2
25–34	5	22	5	2	8	34	10	3
35–45	9	29	7	2	4	32	8	4
Sex								
Male	13	45	10	3	—	—	—	—
Female	—	—	—	—	11	55	15	5
Class								
AB	1	14	12	3	1	28	19	7
C1	3	22	9	2	3	23	14	3
C2	7	23	3	2	8	34	5	2
DE	10	21	2	1	8	26	1	3

Ask wives

(10) How do you get housekeeping money?
    (a) Get whole pay-packet from husband (and give him some back)
    (b) Husband gives me housekeeping money
    (c) Cash cheques on joint account
    (d) Other

	Question 9				*Question 10*			
	(a)	*(b)*	*(c)*	*(d)*	*(a)*	*(b)*	*(c)*	*(d)*
Social class								
Middle	3	18	5	2	4	36	13	4
Lower Middle	7	20	7	3	5	25	12	3
Skilled Working	8	33	4	2	7	21	4	3
Upper Working	5	28	4	—	8	23	6	—
Working	8	22	3	1	8	31	3	2
'Blank'	13	22	8	2	6	17	4	6
Age at which education finished								
14 or under	11	31	4	2	5	32	5	4
15	7	20	3	1	9	33	5	3
16	4	18	7	1	3	26	11	3
17	2	16	7	5	4	28	12	4
18	—	14	10	4	—	24	24	2
All	6	22	4	2	6	29	8	3

Table 28

Question 13(b)

What are the three chief faults husbands tend to have?

	Selfish, inconsiderate	Drinking, gambling, etc.	Goes out on his own	Takes wife for granted	Lazy, sleepy	Mean with money	Domineering, bossy	Bad temper, moody	Bad parent	Untidy
Area										
South-East	42	21	23	24	16	17	13	9	10	8
South-West	33	35	29	20	21	17	10	11	13	11
Midlands	34	28	28	16	18	12	12	10	6	5
North-West	50	33	23	19	17	17	16	5	6	10
North & Yorks	34	25	22	18	12	11	8	6	7	4
Age										
16–20	37	26	23	26	14	14	14	7	7	2
21–24	37	27	27	20	15	12	13	7	5	8
25–34	38	24	26	20	19	14	11	8	10	7
35–45	41	26	23	20	15	17	13	10	9	8
Sex										
Male	38	34	27	23	15	11	12	6	8	4
Female	41	19	22	19	17	19	12	10	9	10
Class										
AB	51	12	19	22	12	14	15	8	9	6
C1	47	19	24	29	14	16	17	7	10	8
C2	37	29	23	19	18	15	10	9	8	9
DE	29	35	31	14	17	14	10	9	7	6
Social class										
Middle	42	19	24	25	15	16	14	8	8	8
Lower Middle	46	22	22	20	18	16	14	7	10	6
Skilled Working	35	31	25	20	16	16	13	7	10	10
Upper Working	40	23	31	26	23	10	16	5	15	5
Working	35	34	26	17	17	15	10	9	7	7
'Blank'	35	36	16	15	11	11	8	9	8	4
All	39	26	24	21	16	15	12	8	8	7

Moral faults	Nagging, scolding	Jealousy, lack of trust	Complacent, conceited	Lack of intelligence	Extravagance	Helpless	Letting self go	Gossip/natter	Over-anxious	Bad housekeeper	Frigid, etc.	Too houseproud	Don't know/No answer
6	7	4	3	4	5	2	2	1	1	—	1	—	13
11	7	8	7	3	5	5	—	—	1	2	2	—	8
5	4	5	3	3	4	3	2	1	—	1	1	—	13
3	5	5	5	4	5	2	11	1	—	2	—	1	3
4	5	4	3	3	4	3	2	1	1	1	—	—	18
6	4	8	7	5	4	5	1	—	1	—	1	1	15
5	5	4	3	4	4	2	2	1	—	1	1	—	15
8	6	4	3	4	5	3	4	1	1	1	1	—	10
4	6	4	4	3	4	3	3	1	1	1	1	—	12
5	4	3	4	3	5	2	4	1	1	1	1	—	12
6	7	6	3	4	4	4	2	1	1	1	1	—	12
5	6	4	6	5	5	3	4	—	2	1	1	—	12
6	4	5	5	4	3	4	2	1	1	1	1	—	10
5	6	5	3	4	5	2	4	1	—	1	1	1	12
7	6	4	3	2	5	3	1	1	1	1	—	—	14
7	5	5	5	5	3	3	4	1	1	1	1	—	11
6	7	7	4	4	3	5	1	2	—	1	1	1	9
5	6	3	3	4	4	2	3	2	—	—	—	—	11
5	6	6	3	3	9	5	4	—	1	2	2	—	11
5	6	3	3	3	6	2	2	1	1	1	1	—	13
5	3	8	1	2	5	3	4	—	—	—	—	—	14
6	6	5	4	4	4	3	3	1	1	1	1	—	12

Table 29

Question 13(a)

What are the three chief faults wives tend to have?

	Nagging, scolding	Extravagance/keeping up with the Jones's	Domineering, bossy	Selfish	Bad housekeeper	Letting herself go	Gossip/natter	Bad temper, moody	Jealousy, lack of trust	Goes out on own
Area										
South-East	47	26	16	14	12	12	7	6	6	5
South-West	49	36	11	10	11	10	11	11	12	13
Midlands	38	24	20	16	9	8	6	11	6	8
North-West	31	20	24	29	18	19	5	10	9	7
North & Yorks	37	25	16	14	6	6	14	8	6	4
Age										
16–20	35	20	26	13	5	10	9	7	11	3
21–24	45	20	18	14	8	14	8	9	9	7
25–34	44	28	17	14	11	10	7	7	5	7
35–45	39	26	17	19	14	10	9	9	6	7
Sex										
Male	28	25	18	16	14	13	10	6	7	6
Female	54	26	18	16	8	9	7	10	7	7
Class										
AB	40	24	22	21	8	9	5	9	8	3
C1	41	24	19	19	11	12	9	6	7	5
C2	42	26	17	17	13	11	7	9	6	7
DE	42	28	15	10	10	9	11	8	9	9
Social class										
Middle	44	25	21	18	11	10	9	7	7	6
Lower Middle	43	25	24	18	11	11	9	9	10	3
Skilled Working	40	22	16	15	12	15	7	7	6	9
Upper Working	36	24	14	18	22	17	5	11	3	4
Working	41	30	15	13	10	9	9	9	7	9
'Blank'	36	19	11	10	8	8	7	7	5	6
All	41	25	18	16	11	11	8	8	7	7

Bad parent	Takes husband for granted	Lazy, sleepy	Frigid, etc.	Too houseproud/over-tidy	Over-anxious	Drinking, etc.	Childishness	Untidyness, etc.	Lack of intelligence	Moral faults	Complacent	Mean with money	Don't know/No answer
7	7	4	7	5	5	3	6	4	6	4	3	2	18
8	5	8	4	5	6	6	6	4	2	5	3	1	11
9	10	6	4	5	3	7	4	3	3	4	2	1	17
10	5	10	2	2	9	5	4	7	4	6	1	2	9
4	5	2	3	4	4	3	5	2	5	4	2	2	26
7	16	2	4	7	7	2	3	3	3	1	1	1	25
5	7	5	3	4	4	4	5	4	2	3	2	1	19
6	5	5	5	5	4	4	7	5	4	4	3	3	17
9	7	5	5	4	6	5	5	4	4	5	2	1	16
9	5	5	3	2	6	7	8	3	5	5	3	1	21
6	9	5	7	6	5	3	3	5	3	4	1	3	14
6	6	3	8	3	6	1	10	2	8	4	1	3	17
5	8	3	7	6	8	4	7	3	7	4	4	1	14
9	7	6	4	5	3	5	4	5	2	4	2	2	17
8	6	6	3	4	5	6	4	4	3	5	2	2	21
6	8	5	6	7	6	3	5	3	6	4	2	2	13
6	11	6	5	3	6	6	5	1	8	3	2	1	15
8	6	5	4	4	5	4	3	7	8	3	3	2	19
11	6	6	5	5	6	3	7	4	4	5	2	1	16
8	6	5	4	3	4	7	6	5	2	5	1	2	20
6	5	3	4	3	5	2	5	2	3	5	2	3	27
7	7	5	5	5	5	5	5	4	4	4	2	2	17

Table 30

Question 29(b)

About how often do you have intercourse?

	Daily or more often	6× a week	5–6× a week	5× a week	4–5× a week	4× a week	3–4× a week
Age							
16–20	2	—	—	1	—	1	5
21–24	2	1	1	1	2	3	7
25–34	1	1	—	1	2	3	6
35–45	1	—	—	1	1	1	3
Sex							
Male	1	1	1	1	1	3	4
Female	2	1	—	—	2	2	5
Social class							
Middle	1	—	—	—	1	1	5
Lower Middle	1	2	—	1	2	1	3
Skilled Working	1	1	—	1	2	6	5
Upper Working	1	—	1	1	4	2	6
Working	2	—	—	1	2	2	4
'Blank'	2	2	2	—	1	2	3
Age at which education finished							
14 or under	1	—	—	1	1	1	3
15	2	1	—	1	2	3	6
16	2	—	—	1	1	3	3
17	2	—	1	1	3	2	7
18	—	2	4	—	2	2	2
All	1	1	—	1	2	2	5

3× a week	2–3× a week	2× a week	1–2× a week	1× a week	2 or 3× a month	Less often	Not consistent	Never	Refused
1	1	4	3	4	2	9	7	25	6
11	9	10	4	10	2	4	7	7	5
10	11	20	6	14	4	4	4	5	4
5	5	17	8	22	9	12	5	4	5
8	6	16	5	15	6	8	5	8	5
7	8	16	8	16	5	7	5	5	4
7	10	16	6	17	6	7	5	7	4
6	7	17	9	16	6	10	6	6	3
9	6	16	6	18	5	8	4	4	3
10	7	20	2	18	1	3	5	8	2
8	5	17	7	16	7	9	5	7	4
8	7	17	5	11	3	6	8	5	13
4	4	17	8	23	9	12	4	5	5
10	8	17	6	16	5	7	5	5	4
7	9	15	6	15	4	4	6	11	3
12	7	15	6	7	6	6	7	5	9
10	12	14	18	4	2	6	4	—	6
8	7	16	6	16	6	8	5	6	5

Table 31

Question 29(c)

Do you think this is about average for people like yourself?

	Average	Less than average	More than average
Age			
16–20	22	15	4
21–24	59	12	4
25–34	67	18	4
35–45	63	22	3
Sex			
Male	59	20	3
Female	62	18	4
Social class			
Middle	61	19	3
Lower Middle	58	21	5
Skilled Working	64	17	5
Upper Working	58	14	6
Working	61	20	3
'Blank'	58	16	6
Age at which education finished			
14 or under	63	23	3
15	64	18	4
16	57	16	3
17	55	19	4
18	61	8	8
All	60	19	4

Table 32

Question 22

At what age did you become physically a woman?
At what age did you become sexually a man?

	Under 11	11–12	12–13	13–14	14–15	15–16	16–17	17–18	18–19	Over 19	Don't know	Refused
Age												
16–20	1	8	12	15	25	17	12	1	3	—	5	—
21–24	2	8	15	17	21	14	6	4	4	6	2	1
25–34	2	7	12	19	20	13	11	4	3	5	3	1
35–45	—	6	7	16	20	13	9	4	8	10	3	1
Sex												
Male	1	1	4	11	23	16	14	6	8	9	5	2
Female	2	13	17	23	19	11	6	2	3	5	1	—
Social class												
Middle	2	7	12	19	19	13	8	3	6	7	2	1
Lower Middle	1	7	16	14	26	11	7	4	2	7	3	1
Skilled Working	1	7	10	16	21	13	11	5	6	6	2	—
Upper Working	1	9	8	22	14	11	15	4	1	10	5	1
Working	1	6	8	13	23	16	10	4	6	7	3	1
'Blank'	2	5	10	22	17	11	13	4	5	2	5	3
All	1	7	11	17	21	14	10	4	5	7	3	1

Table 33

Question 28

How important do you think sexual love is in marriage?

		Very	Fairly	Not very	Not at all
Age	16–20	59	34	4	1
	21–24	72	25	2	1
	25–34	65	32	3	—
	35–45	65	30	3	1
Sex	Male	65	32	2	1
	Female	67	28	4	—
Social class	Middle	66	30	3	—
	Lower Middle	67	28	5	—
	Skilled Working	69	28	3	—
	Upper Working	66	31	1	2
	Working	64	31	4	1
	'Blank'	64	29	3	1
	All	66	30	3	1

Table 34

Question 23 Weighted

Which *one* of these statements do you most (a) agree with?
(b) disagree with?
(a) Most women don't care much about the physical side of sex.
(b) Most women don't have such an animal nature as men.
(c) Most women enjoy the physical side of sex as much as men.
(d) Most women enjoy sex more than men.

	Most agree with				Most disagree with			
	(a)	*(b)*	*(c)*	*(d)*	*(a)*	*(b)*	*(c)*	*(d)*
Age								
16–20	8	25	57	7	50	17	11	26
21–24	7	26	59	8	50	16	4	30
25–34	14	24	58	5	40	16	5	41
35–45	16	31	51	3	36	16	7	43
Sex								
Male	7	25	56	7	50	14	4	27
Female	18	29	54	4	34	18	7	48
Social class								
Middle	13	24	58	5	44	16	5	35
Lower Middle	20	32	50	3	37	16	4	45
Skilled Working	10	25	57	5	41	19	3	32
Upper Working	7	32	57	3	52	8	4	36
Working	13	30	50	7	38	15	6	41
'Blank'	10	23	59	5	42	19	5	33
All	13	27	55	5	42	16	5	37

Table 35

Question 24 Weighted (all categories)

When a man and a woman are making love do you think that
women have a real physical climax to the act of lovemaking in
the same way as men?

If yes: Would you say: (a) All women
                     (b) Most women
                     (c) Some women

	Yes	*No*	*D/K*	*All*	*Most*	*Some*
Area						
South-East	70	20	9	8	36	26
South-West	75	16	9	8	45	21
Midlands	62	18	20	6	34	23
North-West	65	20	13	4	45	15
North & Yorks	68	19	11	11	39	19
Age						
16–20	58	9	31	9	37	12
21–24	68	16	16	8	40	20
25–34	71	23	5	8	38	25
35–45	70	22	7	6	37	26
Sex						
Male	77	11	11	13	45	18
Female	59	26	14	2	31	27
Class						
AB	68	18	13	8	36	22
C1	71	16	12	9	38	24
C2	69	19	11	8	38	23
DE	62	22	14	7	37	20
Social class						
Middle	66	23	10	5	38	22
Lower Middle	72	16	11	7	34	30
Skilled Working	72	17	10	10	38	23
Upper Working	68	15	16	7	39	23
Working	67	19	13	7	39	22
'Blank'	70	15	14	14	36	20
All	68	19	12	8	38	22

Table 35a

Question 24 Unweighted

When a man and woman are making love do you think that
women have a real physical climax to the act of lovemaking in
the same way as men?

If yes: Would you say: (a) All women
(b) Most women
(c) Some women

	Yes	*No*	*D/K*	*All*	*Most*	*Some*
Area						
South-East	70	20	9	8	36	26
South-West	75	16	9	8	45	21
Midlands	62	18	20	6	34	23
North-West	65	20	13	4	45	15
North & Yorks	68	19	11	11	39	19
Age						
16–20	59	9	31	9	38	11
21–24	69	17	14	7	40	21
25–34	71	23	5	8	38	25
35–45	70	22	7	6	37	26
Sex						
Male	79	12	8	13	46	20
Female	60	28	10	2	31	28
Class						
AB	68	18	13	8	36	22
C1	71	16	12	9	38	24
C2	69	19	11	8	38	23
DE	62	22	14	7	37	20
Social class						
Middle	67	24	7	5	38	24
Lower Middle	73	17	9	7	34	32
Skilled Working	74	18	8	10	38	25
Upper Working	72	18	11	7	41	25
Working	67	21	11	7	38	23
'Blank'	70	15	14	14	36	20
All	69	21	9	7	38	24

Table 36

Questions 37(a) and (b) Weighted

(a) Do you regularly use any birth control methods?
(b) Which? (sheath, diaphragm, pill, etc.)

	Yes	*No*	*Sheath*	*Pill*	*Withdrawal*	*Diaphragm/cap*	*Coil/loop*	*Spouse sterile*	*Safe period*	*Self-sterilized/sterile*	*Refused*	*No answer/not asked*
Area												
South-East	57	30	32	18	2	5	3	1	1	1	1	6
South-West	46	40	29	11	7	4	2	1	—	1	2	7
Midlands	44	40	23	11	9	5	2	—	1	1	—	11
North-West	36	50	18	11	4	3	1	—	1	—	1	11
North & Yorks	50	36	25	20	6	5	1	—	1	—	—	12
Age												
16–20	16	26	11	5	1	—	1	—	—	—	1	15
21–24	45	31	24	15	5	1	1	—	1	—	1	9
25–34	57	34	25	22	4	6	4	1	1	1	1	8
35–45	48	43	31	10	6	5	1	1	1	—	—	9
Sex												
Male	43	35	26	12	4	3	1	1	—	—	1	13
Female	47	35	23	15	4	4	2	1	1	1	—	6
Class												
AB	54	31	26	18	4	10	3	1	1	1	1	9
C1	53	31	30	16	3	5	3	1	1	—	—	10
C2	51	37	28	16	5	4	2	1	1	1	1	8
DE	38	46	20	13	5	1	1	—	—	—	—	11
Social class												
Middle	49	31	27	15	4	4	3	1	1	1	—	11
Lower Middle	49	32	31	14	5	5	2	—	—	1	1	7
Skilled Working	49	33	32	12	4	2	2	—	1	—	1	7
Upper Working	40	24	20	8	7	4	3	—	—	—	1	6
Working	39	41	20	14	4	3	1	1	—	—	—	9
'Blank'	48	42	23	15	2	6	1	—	1	1	2	15
All	45	35	25	14	4	4	2	1	1	—	1	10

Weighted figures used for Age, Sex, Social Class and Totals.

Table 37

Question 35

On balance do you think that the invention of the pill for birth control is a good or a bad thing?

	Good thing	Good for family planning, over-population	Good for poor parents	Good for women's peace of mind	Qualified approval
Area					
South-East	57	15	1	10	3
South-West	64	9	1	4	4
Midlands	58	7	—	5	4
North-West	60	9	—	1	1
North East & North	60	10	—	1	2
Age					
16–20	59	16	1	5	3
21–24	60	11	—	6	2
25–34	61	10	—	7	4
35–45	56	12	—	5	3
Sex					
Male	62	12	—	4	2
Female	55	11	1	7	4
Class					
AB	62	10	1	8	4
C1	62	12	—	7	3
C2	55	12	—	6	4
DE	59	9	—	2	2
Social class					
Middle	58	11	—	7	4
Lower Middle	62	15	—	5	5
Skilled Working	63	9	—	3	3
Upper Working	61	12	1	5	3
Working	57	13	—	5	3
'Blank'	57	5	2	5	2
All	59	11	—	6	3

Still too early to judge	Specific mention of danger of thrombosis	Vague mention of medical side-effects	Bad from religious point of view	Bad because un-natural, encourages promiscuity	Bad thing	No answer/refused
6	2	16	1	3	14	1
5	1	12	1	2	14	4
6	1	8	1	3	14	5
6	2	7	1	2	19	2
2	2	5	—	2	17	4
4	1	7	1	1	12	5
6	2	12	1	2	13	3
4	1	12	—	3	14	3
5	3	11	1	3	17	3
4	1	10	1	3	12	4
6	2	12	1	3	18	2
5	2	11	—	2	9	4
5	1	10	—	2	13	2
6	2	12	1	3	15	3
2	2	10	1	3	19	4
6	1	12	1	3	15	2
5	2	10	1	1	11	2
3	2	8	—	4	13	4
7	1	7	1	1	15	4
3	2	12	1	3	16	4
6	3	12	1	4	17	3
5	2	11	1	3	15	3

Table 38

Question 36

Now that the pill provides absolute safety, do you think faithfulness is or is not as important as ever in a marriage?

	Yes	Yes emphatically	Yes qualified	Not so important	Pill encourages promiscuity	Refused	No answer
Area							
South-East	81	11	—	5	1	—	1
South-West	79	10	2	7	2	—	1
Midlands	81	7	1	5	1	—	3
North-West	85	7	—	6	2	1	—
North & Yorks	87	7	—	3	1	—	1
Age							
16–20	80	10	1	3	1	—	5
21–24	83	9	1	5	1	—	1
25–34	83	9	—	6	1	—	—
35–45	84	8	1	4	1	—	2
Sex							
Male	84	7	—	5	1	—	2
Female	82	10	1	5	1	—	1
Class							
AB	85	6	1	5	—	—	1
C1	81	12	1	3	2	—	1
C2	83	9	1	5	1	—	1
DE	82	7	—	7	1	—	3
Social class							
Middle	83	10	—	4	1	—	1
Lower Middle	83	9	—	5	—	1	1
Skilled Working	84	6	—	5	1	—	2
Upper Working	77	13	—	7	2	—	2
Working	84	7	1	5	1	—	2
'Blank'	79	13	1	4	—	1	3
Marital status							
Single	80	8	1	5	1	—	4
Married	84	9	1	5	1	—	1
Divorced	88	6	—	6	—	—	—
Separated	71	13	—	4	4	—	8
Widowed	92	8	—	—	—	—	—
All	83	9	1	5	1	—	2

Table 39

Question 16(a) and (b)

(a) Do you think that when you get married a husband should be faithful for the rest of his married life?

(b) Do you think a wife should be faithful for the rest of her married life?

	Yes	A *No*	*D/K*	*Yes*	B *No*	*D/K*
Age						
16–20	87	7	6	92	4	4
21–24	88	8	4	92	5	3
25–34	88	8	4	92	5	3
35–45	92	5	3	94	3	3
Sex						
Male	89	7	4	93	5	2
Female	90	7	3	94	4	2
Social class						
Middle	89	7	4	92	5	3
Lower Middle	89	7	4	92	5	3
Skilled Working	90	7	3	93	3	4
Upper Working	90	8	2	94	5	1
Working	91	5	4	95	3	2
'Blank'	86	11	3	91	7	2
All	89	7	4	93	4	3

Table 40

Question 20

How do you feel about a married man man who has an affair with a woman he does not really love?

	Strong moral disapproval	Disapproval of character	Disapproval of intelligence	Oversexed, lustful	Bad for marriage
Age					
16–20	22	21	8	9	3
21–24	23	20	6	12	5
25–34	21	20	5	14	4
35–45	23	20	7	16	4
Sex					
Male	17	16	8	12	6
Female	27	24	4	16	3
Social class					
Middle	23	22	6	15	5
Lower Middle	18	16	5	18	3
Skilled Working	22	19	6	11	4
Upper Working	22	21	13	8	4
Working	22	20	6	15	4
'Blank'	23	14	4	10	5
All	22	20	6	14	4

Shows something lacking in marriage	Justified if wife cold	Pity – sorry for him	Won't judge	No attitude unless it affects me	It's natural	No answer
16	1	2	9	5	3	7
13	—	2	11	6	3	4
14	2	1	12	5	3	4
16	1	1	8	4	3	3
15	1	1	15	7	4	5
15	1	1	6	3	2	3
14	1	1	10	4	3	3
15	2	2	11	5	4	3
14	1	1	10	4	3	6
23	1	1	11	6	3	2
14	1	2	10	5	2	4
14	1	2	13	8	5	7
15	1	1	10	5	3	4

Table 41

Question 21

How do you feel about a married woman who has an affair with a man she does not really love?

	Strong moral disapproval	Disapproval of character	Disapproval of intelligence	Oversexed, lustful	Bad for marriage	Shows something lacking in marriage
Age						
16–20	22	20	10	9	5	16
21–24	23	16	8	8	6	19
25–34	22	18	5	10	4	19
35–45	23	19	7	12	5	20
Sex						
Male	18	16	8	10	5	17
Female	27	20	6	12	5	20
Social class						
Middle	22	20	6	11	5	18
Lower Middle	22	12	5	13	3	25
Skilled Working	24	16	9	11	6	15
Upper Working	22	22	15	6	6	24
Working	24	19	7	12	5	18
'Blank'	22	11	5	6	7	19
All	23	18	7	11	5	19

Justified for revenge	*Pity – sorry for her*	*Won't judge*	*No attitude unless it affects me*	*It's natural*	*Worse than for men*	*Not so bad as for men*	*Same as for men*	*No answer*
1	2	9	5	1	3	1	16	5
1	1	9	7	1	2	1	11	3
1	1	11	6	—	2	2	10	2
1	2	6	5	1	1	1	12	1
1	1	13	8	1	1	1	19	3
1	2	4	4	—	2	2	4	1
1	1	9	5	1	2	2	12	2
2	3	7	7	1	1	1	13	—
—	2	9	3	1	2	1	13	4
1	—	11	6	1	1	—	18	—
1	1	7	7	—	2	2	9	2
2	2	14	8	1	2	2	11	4
1	1	8	6	1	2	2	11	2

Table 42

Question 30

Apart from kissing people in greeting or in fun (such as under the mistletoe) have you kissed anybody except your husband/wife since marriage?

Question 32

Have you ever had a love relationship with anybody since marriage without actually going all the way?

	30 *Yes*	*No*	*Don't know/* *can't remember*	*32* *Yes*	*No*
Age					
16–20	1	9	—	1	15
21–24	13	47	1	2	56
25–34	21	66	1	4	76
35–45	21	71	1	3	84
Sex					
Male	20	50	1	4	64
Female	16	72	1	3	78
Social class					
Middle	19	63	1	4	72
Lower Middle	21	59	1	4	73
Skilled Working	22	57	1	5	71
Upper Working	15	58	1	—	67
Working	15	63	—	3	71
'Blank'	19	60	—	2	73
Age at which *education finished*					
14 or under	20	72	—		
15	18	62	1		
16	18	52	1		
17	16	61	2		
18	27	47	—		
All	18	61	1	3	71

Table 43

Question 31(a), (b) and (c)

(a) Have you made love to anybody except your husband/wife since marriage?

If Yes

(b) Did you go the whole way in making love?

If Yes

(c) How many partners, one, two, three or more?

	A		B				C	
	Yes	*No*	*Yes*	*No*	*One*	*Two*	*Three*	*More than three*
Age								
16–20	—	11	—	1	—	—	—	—
21–24	2	58	2	1	1	1	—	—
25–34	7	78	5	3	3	1	1	1
35–45	6	84	5	4	3	1	1	—
Sex								
Male	7	62	6	4	2	2	2	1
Female	3	82	3	2	3	—	—	—
Social class								
Middle	5	75	4	2	2	1	1	—
Lower Middle	5	74	3	3	3	1	1	1
Skilled Working	8	69	5	5	3	2	—	1
Upper Working	2	70	2	3	—	2	—	—
Working	5	71	4	3	2	1	1	—
'Blank'	6	70	5	5	2	1	2	2
Age at which education finished								
14 or under	6	83	5	4	2	1	1	—
15	5	73	4	2	2	1	1	—
16	6	63	5	3	4	—	1	—
17	5	72	2	3	1	2	1	1
18	4	69	4	—	2	2	—	—
All	5	72	4	3	2	1	1	—

x

Table 44

Question 17(a) and (b)

If a (a) husband or (b) wife finds (a) his wife or (b) her husband having an affair with another (a) woman or (b) man, what should he/she do?

	Talk it over	Analyse situation	Try to reconcile	Separation	Examine self	Divorce	Divorce as last resort	Physical violence on *erring* spouse	Give one more chance	Separation as last resort
Area										
South-East	31	23	21	13	8	7	7	5	6	6
South-West	21	23	28	14	9	8	6	8	6	8
Midlands	26	23	17	16	7	9	5	4	3	4
North-West	31	32	13	17	3	5	2	5	6	3
North & Yorks	24	23	18	15	8	6	3	7	4	3
Age										
16–20	37	21	23	11	5	13	10	2	3	7
21–24	28	25	20	13	7	8	7	5	5	6
25–34	29	24	19	14	9	6	5	5	5	5
35–45	25	24	18	17	7	6	4	6	5	4
Sex										
Male	24	25	19	17	5	10	8	6	4	4
Female	31	24	19	13	10	4	3	4	6	5
Class										
AB	37	31	18	6	10	2	2	2	4	1
C1	30	25	20	8	11	5	7	5	5	5
C2	27	23	20	18	6	8	5	6	5	5
DE	23	22	17	22	5	10	6	7	5	6
Social class										
Middle	33	28	21	11	10	5	5	3	4	5
Lower Middle	27	25	21	12	11	5	5	3	5	3
Skilled Working	26	25	21	18	7	9	7	4	3	2
Upper Working	25	22	25	10	9	15	5	6	5	7
Working	23	21	16	19	5	8	5	7	5	5
'Blank'	27	19	17	17	5	7	5	8	8	6
All	28	24	19	15	7	7	5	5	5	5

Depends on circumstances	Consider children	Consult marriage guidance bureau	Physical violence on intervener	Verbal reproaches to erring spouse	Verbal reproaches to intervener	Preserve marriage	Make self more attractive	Ignore passing fancy	Do likewise	Do nothing	Have innocent good time	Don't know
7	5	3	2	2	3	3	1	1	1	1	—	3
3	5	2	7	3	2	4	1	1	2	—	—	2
4	3	5	1	2	3	2	—	1	—	1	—	8
2	3	3	2	2	1	2	—	—	—	1	—	3
4	3	2	3	1	2	1	1	1	1	—	—	3
4	1	3	2	1	4	3	—	—	3	1	—	5
4	2	4	3	2	2	2	—	1	1	—	—	4
5	4	3	3	2	2	3	1	1	1	—	—	4
4	5	3	2	2	3	2	1	1	—	1	—	4
4	4	3	4	2	3	2	—	1	1	1	—	4
5	4	3	1	1	2	3	1	1	—	—	—	4
6	3	4	1	3	1	4	—	—	—	1	—	7
7	3	4	2	1	3	3	2	2	—	—	—	3
4	4	3	3	2	2	2	—	1	1	—	—	4
3	4	2	3	2	2	1	—	1	1	1	—	3
6	3	3	2	2	4	2	1	1	1	—	—	3
7	6	5	2	1	1	3	1	1	1	1	—	5
3	3	5	2	1	1	2	—	1	—	—	—	3
5	5	3	2	—	—	2	—	—	2	—	—	7
4	4	2	4	2	3	2	—	1	1	1	—	5
2	5	2	2	2	1	2	1	2	1	1	1	5
5	4	3	2	2	2	2	1	1	1	1	—	4

Table 45

Question 34(a)

How do you feel about people who fall in love with members of their own sex?

	Revulsion, disgust	Pity, Sorry for them	Not understandable/odd	Tolerance	Mentally ill	Dislike	Can't help it/need help	Moral disapproval	Ridiculous	Need psychiatric/medical help	Shouldn't mock them	No decided views or no answer
Area												
South-East	23	28	13	15	10	8	9	3	2	2	—	4
South-West	26	26	12	11	8	8	11	7	4	2	—	5
Midlands	28	16	16	12	10	9	4	4	3	2	—	6
North-West	29	15	10	4	20	6	5	4	5	3	—	6
North & Yorks	18	20	14	10	12	8	7	4	5	3	—	5
Age												
16–20	19	15	14	15	12	5	7	3	4	3	1	8
21–24	23	27	12	13	11	6	7	5	4	3	—	4
25–34	21	24	13	15	11	8	9	4	2	2	—	5
35–45	28	19	14	9	12	10	6	5	3	2	—	4
Sex												
Male	23	16	14	16	10	10	5	5	4	3	—	5
Female	25	28	12	8	13	6	9	4	2	2	—	5
Class												
AB	18	33	16	13	7	6	6	4	—	2	—	5
CI	20	28	13	15	11	8	10	2	3	3	—	4
C2	27	19	14	12	12	9	6	4	4	3	—	5
DE	26	15	11	8	12	8	7	7	5	2	—	6
Social class												
Middle	23	26	13	13	11	7	7	4	2	2	—	4
Lower Middle	24	24	16	19	12	7	6	5	3	4	—	4
Skilled Working	25	19	17	11	13	9	3	3	4	3	—	4
Upper Working	25	28	8	14	13	4	11	1	5	2	—	6
Working	26	15	12	12	11	10	8	5	4	2	—	6
'Blank'	14	23	12	16	14	8	7	5	6	2	—	5
All	24	22	13	12	11	8	7	4	3	2	—	5

Table 46

Question 27

Do you think that a man and a woman can have a real friend-ship without sex playing any part?

	Yes	*No*	*D/K*
Age			
16–20	75	17	7
21–24	71	23	4
25–34	66	28	4
35–45	63	32	4
Sex			
Male	67	29	3
Female	66	27	5
Social class			
Middle	71	25	3
Lower Middle	64	30	5
Skilled Working	63	31	4
Upper Working	75	19	5
Working	63	32	4
'Blank'	61	27	8
All	66	28	4

Table 47

Question 38(a) and (b) Weighted

Ask all single people only.
Do you expect to get married some day?
If Yes, have you any idea when this will be?

	Yes	*No*	*D/K*	*Yes*	*No*
Area					
South-East	17	1	1	6	11
South-West	15	2	1	4	11
Midlands	18	2	3	5	13
North-West	18	—	2	6	13
North & Yorks	13	1	1	3	11
Age					
16–20	85	—	4	27	58
21–24	44	2	2	15	29
25–34	10	1	1	3	7
35–45	4	2	1	1	3
Sex					
Male	36	1	3	11	26
Female	17	1	1	6	11
Class					
AB	15	1	2	5	10
C1	18	2	1	7	12
C2	14	1	1	4	10
DE	21	1	4	5	16
Social class					
Middle	25	1	1	8	16
Lower Middle	26	1	1	15	11
Skilled Working	23	—	2	6	17
Upper Working	39	—	2	15	25
Working	27	2	3	6	21
'Blank'	17	1	4	5	12
All	26	1	2	8	18

Table 48

Question 39(a) Weighted

Have you any special girl/boy-friend at present?

	Yes	No	
Area			
South-East	9	9	
South-West	5	11	
Midlands	8	13	
North-West	9	9	
North & Yorks	6	9	
Age			
16–20	42	44	
21–24	23	22	
25–34	4	7	
35–45	1	5	
Sex			
Male	16	22	
Female	10	8	
Class			
AB	8	8	
C1	10	10	
C2	7	8	
DE	9	16	
Social class			
Middle	12	13	
Lower Middle	15	12	
Skilled Working	9	16	
Upper Working	24	15	
Working	12	17	
'Blank'	8	11	
All	13	15	

Table 48a

Question 39(b)

Where did you meet your boy/girl friend?

	Dance	Social gathering	At work	School or college	Mutual friends/relations	Public house	Pick-up	Friends/neighbours since childhood	Church/chapel meeting/outing	On holiday/leave	Public amusement place	Other
Age												
16–20	6	10	5	4	3	1	3	3	1	1	1	1
21–24	6	3	5	2	1	2	1	1	1	—	—	—
25–34	1	1	1	—	1	1	—	—	—	—	—	—
35–45	1	—	—	—	—	—	—	—	—	—	—	—
Sex												
Male	3	3	2	1	1	1	1	1	1	—	—	—
Female	2	2	2	1	1	—	—	—	—	—	—	—
Social class												
Middle	3	2	1	1	1	—	1	1	—	—	1	—
Lower Middle	1	6	4	—	3	—	—	—	—	1	—	1
Skilled Working	1	1	—	1	—	1	—	1	—	—	—	—
Upper Working	9	—	1	5	2	—	—	—	3	1	—	—
Working	2	2	3	1	1	1	2	—	1	—	—	—
'Blank'	2	1	2	1	2	1	—	—	—	—	—	—
All	3	3	2	1	1	1	1	1	—	—	—	—

Table 49

Question 39(c) and (d) Weighted

(c) Are you on terms of real physical intimacy with him/her?
If Yes
(d) With how many other people have you been on terms of physical intimacy?

	Yes	*No*	*None*	*One*	*Two*	*Three*	*More than Three*
Area							
South-East	6	4	2	1	1	1	3
South-West	2	4	2	1	1	—	—
Midlands	5	4	1	1	1	1	2
North-West	3	7	2	—	—	—	3
North & Yorks	2	4	1	1	—	—	1
Age							
16–20	23	22	10	4	4	3	5
21–24	11	13	3	3	2	1	6
25–34	3	2	1	—	—	—	2
35–45	1	1	—	—	—	—	1
Sex							
Male	11	7	2	2	2	2	5
Female	4	7	3	1	—	—	—
Class							
AB	5	5	1	—	—	1	1
C1	6	5	3	—	1	—	3
C2	4	3	1	1	—	1	2
DE	4	6	1	1	—	—	2
Social class							
Middle	8	5	3	1	1	2	3
Lower Middle	8	9	3	1	1	1	3
Skilled Working	6	4	2	1	1	—	3
Upper Working	4	20	1	—	—	1	2
Working	7	7	3	1	1	—	2
'Blank'	3	7	1	2	2	—	—
All	7	7	3	1	1	1	3

Table 50

Questions 40, 41 and 42

Q. 40 Do you feel you should be absolutely faithful to your present special girl/boy-friend?

Q. 41 Are you faithful?

Q. 42 Do you think that he/she should be physically absolutely faithful to you?

| | Q. 40 | | | Q. 41 | | | Q. 42 | | |
	Yes	*No*	*D/K*	*Yes*	*No*		*Yes*	*No*	*D/K*
Age									
16–20	37	8	—	39	5		37	7	1
21–24	16	5	1	19	3		18	3	1
25–34	3	1	—	4	1		4	1	—
35–45	1	1	—	1	1		1	1	—
Sex									
Male	13	4	—	13	3		14	2	—
Female	8	2	—	10	1		8	2	1
Social class									
Middle	9	4	—	10	3		10	3	1
Lower Middle	11	5	—	13	3		12	4	—
Skilled Working	8	1	—	8	1		9	—	—
Upper Working	17	6	—	20	3		21	2	—
Working	12	1	—	12	1		11	1	—
'Blank'	7	2	1	9	1		6	3	1
All	10	3	—	11	2		11	2	—

Appendix four

Bibliography

Cartwright, Ann (1970): *Parents and Family Planning Services.*

Glass, D. V. (1968): *Fertility Trends in Europe since the Second World War.* (Population Studies No. 1.)

— (1969): *Report of Population Investigation Committee:* Preliminary Results. (Family Planning.)

Goldthorpe, Lockwood, Bechhofer and Platt (1969): *The Affluent Worker in the Class Structure.*

Gorer, Geoffrey (1939): *Himalayan Village.*
— (1955): *Exploring English Character.*

Kinsey, Pomeroy and Martin (1948): *Sexual Behavior in the Human Male.*

Kinsey, Pomeroy, Martin and Gebhard (1953): *Sexual Behavior in the Human Female.*

Mead, Margaret (1930): *Growing Up in New Guinea.*
— (1949): *Male and Female.*
— (1956): *New Lives For Old.*

Peel, John and Potts, Malcolm (1969): *Text Book of Contraceptive Practice.*

Schofield, Michael (1968): *Sexual Behaviour of Young People.*

Tanner, J. M. (1961): *Education and Physical Growth.*
— (1962): *Growth and Adolescence.*

Wrong, Dennis H. (1960): *Fertility Differentials in England and Wales.* (Millbank Memorial Fund Quarterly, Vol. 38.)